counterpleasures

THE SUNY SERIES IN
POSTMODERN CULTURE

Joseph Natoli, *Editor*

counterpleasures

Karmen
MacKendrick

State University of New York Press

Cover:
Saint Sebastian (detail)
Master of the Greenville Tondo, Italian, Umbrian, active 1500–1510
Printed by permission of The Art Museum, Princeton University.
Gift of the Samuel H. Kress Foundation to the New Jersey State Museum;
transferred to The Art Museum, Princeton University.
Photo credit: Bruce M. White

Published by

State University of New York Press, Albany

© 1999 State University of New York

For information, address State University of New York Press,
State University Plaza, Albany, NY 12246

Production by Laurie Searl
Marketing by Fran Keneston

Library of Congress Cataloging-in-Publication Data

MacKendrick, Karmen, 1962–
    Counterpleasures / Karmen MacKendrick.
        p.   cm. — (SUNY series in postmodern culture)
    Includes bibliographical references and index.
    ISBN 0–7914–4147–4 (hc. : alk. paper). — ISBN 0–7914–4148–2
(pbk. : alk. paper)
    1. Pleasure. 2. Sadomasochism. 3. Asceticism. I. Title.
II. Series
BJ1481.M33   1999
306.4′81—dc21   98-26067
                                                                  CIP

10 9 8 7 6 5 4 3 2 1

To the memory of Bob Flanagan,
with gratitude and affection.

The quick of life would be the burn of a wound—a hurt so lively, a flame so avid that it is not content to live and be present, but consumes all that is present till presence is precisely what is exempt from the present.

—Maurice Blanchot, *The Writing of the Disaster*

contents

acknowledgments

Though this work with all its flaws is certainly my own doing (or as certainly as these things get in this postauthorial age), what is good in it has gotten that way with a great deal of help. Among the many who have given that help, I would particularly note the following:

The members of my dissertation committee—Ed Casey, David Allison, Peter Manchester, Richard Boothby, and Louise Vasvari—read, claimed to enjoy, and actually gave me the doctorate for a work that included early versions of the chapters on Sade, Masoch, and saintly asceticism. I am indebted to them for their support and even, in some cases, enthusiasm.

To Brooke Myers, who read the dissertation in a less official capacity, I am deeply grateful, not only for her insightful discussion but for her continuing support of my work and thought.

From the many supportive friends who were among my fellow graduate students at SUNY Stony Brook, I owe particular thanks to a few. James DiGiovanna, Malek Moazzam-Doulat, and Bruce Milem have not only read and endlessly, patiently discussed my own work with me, but they have been generous in allowing me to read theirs, always to my great benefit. Ellen Feder has provided not only great support and intelligent commentary but a great many textual resources and references that I might never have found on my own.

Terry Hoople of Concordia University has provided me with a continuous and valuable exchange of writing and ideas since we met at a presentation of his work, which reminded me very much of what I was trying to do myself.

Many of these ideas were reworked after I was able to present some of them at the New Museum for Contemporary Art, in conjunction with the Bob Flanagan and Sheree Rose exhibit "Visiting Hours." I owe Bob and Sheree for their friendship and encouragement; the exhibit's curator, Laura Trippi, for the same and for inviting me to participate in that presentation; and Ron Scapp, another Stony Brook friend, for arranging my meeting with Laura in the first place, based on his own reading of my work.

Joseph Natoli, the series editor, provided insightful feedback on an earlier draft. My efforts to incorporate his ideas have greatly improved the present work, as have my efforts to incorporate the thoughtful and helpful suggestions of outside reviewers Carol Siegel and Lynda Hart. James Peltz, my editor at SUNY, and production editor Laurie Searl have been models of competence and helpfulness. Undoubtedly there are limits to their patience, but I have not been able to discover them.

I am grateful to my parents, who somehow neglected to teach me to behave myself.

Finally, and importantly, my thanks to Ramin Ashraf, for first showing me both *The Book of Pleasures* and the Perugino St. Sebastian, for unwavering and stubborn faith, and for making me cappuccino every morning, without which I would never write much of anything at all.

introduction

"a pleasure must be incredibly intense"

I wish to fight for more fun, not for less pain.
　　　　　　　　　—Raoul Vaneigem, *The Book of Pleasures*

situating displacement

Foucault's "homosexual ascesis" calls not for less pleasure
but for vastly more pleasure.
　　　　　　　　　—David Halperin, *Saint Foucault*

I am going to open this discussion of odd-seeming pleasures in a
fashion that will appear equally strange—with an appeal to Georges
Bataille's *Theory of Religion*. Bataille begins this work by discussing
the place of the work itself, in a prefatory note titled "Where This
Book is Situated:"

> The foundation of one's thought is the thought of another;
> thought is like a brick cemented into a wall. . . . The work
> of the mason, who assembles, is the work that matters.
> Thus the adjoining bricks, in a book, should not be less
> visible than the new brick, which is the book. What is of-
> fered the reader, in fact, cannot be an element, but must be
> the ensemble in which it is inserted: it is the whole human
> assemblage and edifice.[1]

Bataille's aim, however, is not simply to take his place within the
tradition, but to suggest that every work displaces the tradition:

> In a sense the unlimited assemblage is the impossible. . . .
> This powerlessness defines an apex of possibility, or at
> least, awareness of the impossibility opens consciousness
> to all that is possible for it to think. In this gathering place,

> where violence is rife, at the boundary of that which es-
> capes cohesion, he who reflects within cohesion realizes
> that there is no longer any room for him.[2]

This impossibility implies that to situate oneself theoretically is at the same time to hide from oneself the fact that this situating irrevocably alters the situation. And yet one can only situate oneself, to show where the changes are taking place, or to show what is or was around the displacement.

The work that follows here is in every sense less than Bataille's, but I both recognize the importance of situating it and hope that this situation will disrupt the discussion and understanding, the theory and discourse, and perhaps even the practices, of pleasure. In its way, it is a discussion *of* disruption. I shall have to situate the counterpleasures both within and against various traditions of pleasure, but there is something about these pleasures—pleasures that run contrary to our expectations of pleasure in so many ways—which is, like religion on Bataille's understanding (it will soon become clear that his text was not chosen accidentally or randomly as my opening), inherently disruptive. It is within the tradition of disruption, then, or the situation of displacement (a nicely perverse starting point, I think) that I begin.

More precisely, with Bataille's injunction and understanding in mind, I would situate this work into a trio of contexts: the tradition of theoretical (and often practical) disruption-by-pleasure, by which I would trace its sources and influences; the tradition of opposition to precisely these disruptions, by which I would enter it into the predominant discourse; and the context of various historical periods, by which I would suggest something of the modes of disruption-by-pleasure.

The first of these traces the most direct line of descent. In 1979, Raoul Vaneigem, a former member of the socio-politico-aesthetic-cultural group calling itself the Situationist International,[3] wrote a manifesto under the title *The Book of Pleasures*.[4] This work is self-consciously subversive, left-anarchical in politics, hedonistic in prescription. Vaneigem believes in the power of pleasure to subvert oppressive cultural norms, but he also recognizes the power of those norms to subvert or resubsume the workings of pleasure (in this pairing of ideas he is interestingly close to Foucault).

Vaneigem notes that the socially acceptable forms of pleasure, especially erotic pleasure, have been limited to what is at least potentially re/productive. Arguing that we should, by pleasure, by multiplying and rendering polymorphous our own range of pleasures, free ourselves from the tyranny of the (capitalist) economic (which has made even erotic pleasure a matter of exchange, of implicitly artifactual and quantifiable orgasms, and ideally of re/production), Vaneigem offers a parallel to Foucault's liberatory (or, at any rate, resistant) multiplication of nonproductive pleasures. Because pleasure is not inherently productive (however readily it may be reappropriated by production, or by consumption—that is, by modes of exchange), it has the power, in its polymorphous multiplications, to disrupt a society based on production and consumption, the creation and commodification of the artifact and the construction of the productive and consuming subject. In fact, pleasures can disrupt all manner of cultures and our very understanding of pleasure itself. Such are those gathered here.

More precisely, this, like Vaneigem's manifesto, is a book of pleasures, encompassing the literary pleasures of Sade and Masoch, the religious pleasures of asceticism, and the erotic pleasures of sadomasochism; ending with the conception of counterpleasure as occurring in the context of a strange sort of love. While I recognize that these are pleasures that are not devoid of simulation (after all, simulation is itself a source or sort of pleasure), I have tried not to dissimulate about them. (This is more tempting than it might sound; one does sometimes wish to appear normal, after all.)

All of these pleasures can come under the problematic heading of "transgression." By now we might anticipate their difficult situation: such pleasures prove doubly problematic in the effort to describe and place them, because they are never quite where we think to find them. To transgress is to cross boundaries, but it is boundaries after all that mark places. This is as true epistemologically and ontologically as it is corporeally and topographically.

The theory I shall use to approach the counterpleasures is largely "new," at least post-Nietzsche, -Freud, and -Marx. Thus I shall give the counterpleasures, even where they are modern or premodern, post-modern readings. In fact, I would argue that these are pleasures that *demand* such readings, because our usual modern understanding of pleasure (which I shall detail below) simply does not do them justice, and premodern understandings are not generally available to us. Some sense of the range of influences brought to bear here may make the discussion more readily comprehensible.

Nietzsche understood such pleasures, even where he was wary of them, as he always was of saintly asceticism. A few have followed him in this, which suggests that if these are not the pleasures of every day, they nonetheless have their place in the tradition—but it is, as one would expect, a place of disruption, displacing our sense of the tradition itself. It is difficult, paradoxical, and absurd to find the place of transgression, to set its boundaries. We must see it not in its place but as aporetic, indicated but never locatable at the various sites of rupture, in the work of the philosophers of disruption, of power, and of pleasure. It is to them that the present discussion owes its greatest intellectual debts.

Perhaps foremost among these is, again, Bataille, whose preparation for the pleasures of excess was nearly ideal: from Jesuit seminarian to pornographer to scholar of both Nietzsche and (through Alexandre Kojève) Hegel. Bataille understood both the craving for systematic order and the drive to explode that order. Better than nearly anyone, therefore, he understood both Nietzsche and Sade, working within their displacing traditions without assimilating his work to either of theirs. It is Bataille who breaks language apart to show us why the erotic and the sacred are the same at base, wildly sacrificial and incomprehensibly joyous.

And after Bataille, of equal if different importance, Michel Foucault, who certainly loved systems as well, enough to be labeled a structuralist over his own protests. His love of transgression is subtler, perhaps, but no less present: the possibilities of resistance that fascinated him, those points of rupture in the structures of power, are nothing else. As for pleasure, Foucault is closer to Bataille than his relatively calm surface ever suggested:

> I think I have real difficulty in experiencing pleasure. . . .
> It's not as simple as that to enjoy oneself. . . . Because I
> think that the kind of pleasure I would consider as *the* real
> pleasure would be so deep, so intense, so overwhelming I
> couldn't survive it. . . . A pleasure must be incredibly in-
> tense. But I think I am not the only one like that. I am not
> able to give myself and others those middle range plea-
> sures that make up everyday life. Such pleasures are noth-
> ing for me.[5]

It is on the assumption that, indeed, Foucault "is not the only one like that" that I have written here.

A number of contemporary French thinkers, influenced by the Nietzschean play with structure, have in turn been influential on this work: Bataille's friend Maurice Blanchot, who takes friendship seriously; who, like Foucault, understands the seductiveness of death; like Nietzsche, the power of return; like Bataille, the dizzying bursting spiral of bringing the two together. And after Blanchot, and sometimes responding to him, Jean-Luc Nancy, who has somehow emerged from the study of Heidegger with an entirely and gracefully Nietzschean sense of what it would mean to turn love to loss itself, which re-turns us to the Bataillean ecstasy of the sacrificial. In seeming opposition to Foucault, but in fact at times intriguingly supplementary to him, Jean Baudrillard, who understands the seduction of that which undermines from within. Finally, Gilles Deleuze, who has understood Freud enough to see Nietzsche in him, who has loved desire as a force and not a lack, and who has, not incidentally, given us the only decent philosophical work on Masoch. It is by writing not *on* any of these figures but by trying to write *with* them and *from* them that I have attempted to work on Sade, Masoch, the ascetic saints, and those whose erotic lives embrace disruption in its joyous forms.

Though I shall not situate this work primarily within or after Situationism, I do wish to make note of Vaneigem's work as part of this context of displacement, an instance of the explicit connection of pleasure to political subversion. He gives us an important sense of the overt politicization of the pleasures of transgression. Still earlier, Bataille had emphasized the transgressive potency of un(re)productive pleasures, linking the erotic to the sacred and both to the economy of sacrifice, of extravagant Nietzschean excess—another way out of the economy of production and consumption.[6] Bataille does not advocate the turning of pleasure against any particular political constraint,[7] but his sense of pleasure, especially pleasure at its most intense (he added religious extravagance and aesthetic delight to eroticism in his understanding of intense pleasure, on which I pick up here, incorporating literature, asceticism, and the erotic), as culturally and intellectually subversive is undeniable.

Michel Foucault picks up both the Nietzschean strain also present in Bataille's thought, and the explicit politicism of Vaneigem to argue for the subversive potential of unproductive pleasures.[8] Foucault argues, as does Roland Barthes,[9] that pleasure has been marginalized in academic discourse, which has spoken of desire as if it were irrelevant to delight: "We are always being told," Barthes writes, "about Desire, never about Pleasure; Desire has an epistemic dignity, Pleasure does not."[10] The dissociation of pleasure and desire is extraordinarily curious, but not incomprehensible. The austerity that has made desire philosophically acceptable is conspicuously absent from pleasure; pleasure is harder to disembody, it is insistently sensuous even when it arises in the relative disincarnation of text (see the chapters on Sade and Masoch following). Desire alone, if we *could* dissociate it from pleasure, wouldn't necessarily be disruptive; factor in pleasure—and, still more, suggest that pleasure may inhere in desire itself—and the world is less tidy (and noticeably more entertaining). It is this multiplicity of disruptions that draws us here; this work is intended to explore both the spaces of delight and the concomitant effects of opening those spaces.

Pleasure is destabilizing and threatening not only to the political and cultural orders but to all manner of orders—sacred and profane, as Bataille notes; body and text, as Barthes points out;[11] theory itself, as both Foucault and Bataille imply—and as one of our most important, and culturally influential, theories of pleasure makes clear, quite against its own apparent agenda.

This theory, in which the problem unfolds itself, is Freud's. Freud, too, provides (albeit despite himself) a way into the understanding of subversive pleasures. It is because of the self-inverting element of Freud's theory that he seems to me to belong here, rather than in the context of opposition to counterpleasure. Freudian pleasure theory is worth a fairly lengthy exploration, since it is here that our everyday understanding of pleasure is, I think, grounded—whether or not we are familiar with its theoretical underpinnings.

Freud is wrong about pleasure, as it happens, or more precisely and more importantly he is wrong and right in intriguing admixture, and too intellectually honest to hide those lines of thought and inquiry that subvert his own conclusions. Freud is a would-be perfect modernist, creating rationality out of primitive chaos, adhering to his own imperative, *Wo es war, soll ich werden* [Where id was, there ego shall be.][12] (In Foucauldean terms, we might note that the psychoanalytic process of bringing what is hidden to consciousness is neatly analogous to the projects not only of confession but of discipline, with its panoptic gaze and its orderly embodiment.) But Freud is postmodern despite himself, as if the paradoxicality,[13] carnality,[14] and seductive irrationality[15] of the unconscious to which he devotes his work have infiltrated the conscious and scientific rationality to which he devotes his desire.

Pleasure for Freud, in the theory that he wants to put forth, is mechanistic, dynamic, hydraulic: it is the release of *tension*, which is identical with excitation, stimulation, and perhaps even sensation. Freud's honesty first compels him to acknowledge that we seek (desire) and take pleasure in excitation, most conspicuously in erotic tension, but this he can subsume within his paradigm. He argues that the intensity of pleasure is proportional to the quantity of tension released, so we seek excitation in order to maximize this quantity. Any pleasure we feel in excitement is anticipatory—in his *Three Essays on the Theory of Sexuality* (1905) he labels it "forepleasure," a matter of looking forward to a real pleasure.

It is here that we start to see the theory turn upon itself (and here that we begin to glimpse the emergent possibilities of counterpleasure). The paradox of the erotic begins in the problem of forepleasure, which will also turn out to be the problem of the inherent perversity of the "normal." Forepleasures are precisely those which are essential as preliminaries to "normal" sexual pleasure but which, if lingered over, become "perverse." In brief, the perverse pleasures are either unduly sustained or overinvested in excitation, or they exaggerate some *Partialtriebe*, a piece of the ordinary libido, such as the desire to see or be seen by the loved object.[16] Thus they represent the inherence of the perverse within the normal: a slight shift in emphasis, and the latter becomes the former.

The problem here is the pleasure inherent *in* the preliminary or partial aims, which may be so strong that instead of being promptly and properly rushed through,[17] these preliminaries become themselves the "aim" of sexual activity. In this confrontation with paradox, Freud displays what Deleuze calls the characteristic of (nonparadoxical) good sense, which "is always distributive: On the one hand and on the other (*d'un part et d'autre part*) is its formula."[18] Thus Freud writes: "On the one hand these activities are themselves accompanied by pleasure, and on the other hand they intensify the excitation."[19]

If we had merely to deal with a tension that is a necessary preliminary for later pleasure without in itself being pleasurable, or even with an activity that includes separate elements of both pleasure and unpleasure (as Freud's statements suggest), we could perhaps resolve the problem. But such a simple solution eludes us. In some connections, in fact, "the concepts of 'sexual excitation' and 'satisfaction' can to a great extent be used without distinction."[20] Yet the urgency of excitation, of sexual tension, is, Freud says, "wholly alien to the nature of pleasure."[21] Tension is *necessarily unpleasurable*; this is the very heart of the pleasure principle.

To understand this, we should clarify that principle a bit. The pleasure principle is given various formulations throughout Freud's work, but shows some constancy in meaning. An early version occurs in the *Project for a Scientific Psychology* of 1895. "Since we have certain knowledge of a trend in psychical life towards avoiding unpleasure, we . . . identify that trend with the primary trend towards inertia. . . . Unpleasure would have to be regarded as coinciding with . . . an increasing quantitative pressure. Pleasure would be the sensation of discharge." [22] Numerous other formulations follow; that there are so many and that they are so similar—pleasure is always the discharge of tension or the maintenance of minimal tension—shows us the importance of this principle throughout the development of Freud's thought.[23]

If there is a pleasure-in-tension (even to the point of pain), then Freud's entire definition of pleasure, as grounded in the pleasure principle, is undermined. Either pleasure is not at all the release of tension (which seems improbable) or pleasure may be *both* tension's release and its increase; it may even be paradoxical. It is true that Freud in his later work sees a second principle, the compulsion to repeat, as equally fundamental, or perhaps even more basic than the pleasure principle. But this compulsion turns out to be of no help. In fact, it complements the pleasure principle in two ways. First, unpleasurable situations may be repeated until one has mastered them, thus relieving the tension associated with these situations and one's memories of them. Second, the ultimate desire to repeat takes us back past the origin of life itself; it is a phylogenetic repetition-compulsion that becomes the desire to repeat the unliving (preorganic) state—a state of utter tranquillity, free of the innumerable small and large disturbances of the living body.[24]

We may also wish to repeat pleasures. But this wish turns out to be itself uncomfortable: "The state of being in need of a repetition of the satisfaction reveals itself in two ways: by a peculiar feeling of tension, possessing, rather, the character of unpleasure, and by a sensation of stimulation projected into the peripheral erotogenic zone."[25] Once more we are confronted with the realization that excitation (notably, but as Freud points out later, not exclusively sexual excitation) is itself pleasurable.[26] (So much so that one could claim, as Bataille does, that "an absence of need is more unfortunate than an absence of satisfaction."[27]) Any physical sensation, in fact, can be pleasurably erotic—even pain.[28] In keeping with Freud's underlying biologism one might claim that a certain amount of tension must be built up for the possibly of release to exist, and an organism would be more likely to seek out such tension if this were itself pleasurable, and without the quest for sexual release a species that reproduces sexually would quickly die out. But this doesn't help us much in attempting to understand the nature of pleasure or of its connection to desire.

Matters become still more complex (and more obviously paradoxical) as Freud's initial dualism of the instincts (in which the sexual instincts work for the preservation of the species and the ego instincts for that of the individual) develops into a theory that encompasses both ego and sexual instincts in the life instinct (Eros) and opposes both to the newly posited *Todestrieb*—the death drive, Thanatos. The life instincts work to preserve life, the death instinct to destroy it (sometimes violently, by breaking into pieces the bonds—from intracellular to civilizational—that Eros has formed), seeking thereby to attain to a primal quiescence (life, after all, is noisy). The problem is this: the death drive, which within the organism relaxes cellular tension to a primal unliving condition and which, externalized, destroys the interpersonal unities that Eros seeks to build, fits the original pleasure principle much better than Eros does. It is the death drive, not the erotic impulse, that releases tension (the ultimate relaxation is death). How then can pleasure fit into this newly complicated theory? Is Eros disconnected from pleasure? It cannot be, of course, but Freud's attempts to retain the pleasure principle cause him to come very close to saying this.

It is not insignificant that Freud's orderly divisions complicate themselves beyond any possible resimplification in his discussion of one of the most improbable and inexplicable pleasures, that of masochism, which presents for him a unique "economic problem." Here Freud attempts to grasp the relation between pleasure (the release of tension) and pain (the increase of tension). The opposition simply will not hold still. Not only may tension-building be pleasurable, it is also the case that tension's release is not always pleasant,[29] and even constancy, in the sense of the maintenance of a (low) level of tension, becomes unpleasurable: this is the meaning of boredom. Masochism most significantly entangles pleasure and desire, excitation and delight—in its appearance of extreme aggression against the self it nonetheless exemplifies the triumph of the erotic over the relaxation of death. In fact, Leo Bersani, one of Freud's most interesting interpreters, sees masochism as possibly coextensive with sexuality itself, arguing that "sexuality is ontologically grounded in maso-chism" or is "a tautology for masochism."[30]

Freud, who cannot resolve this conceptual tension, does not take pleasure in its sustaining—his is a reasonable, rational, nonmaso-chistic desire. He does his best to ignore the tensions that this and other perversity create within his theory.[31]

What is important about the role of all manner of perversity in Freud's theory isn't anything so simple as the destruction of Freudian theory (which would in any case not be terribly interesting, as simple refutations seldom are, though they are sometimes useful). It is rather that theory's fragmentation and complication, the expo-sure of its paradoxicality, and the ironic, playful return of Freud's own repressed. This repressed is the occasional, perverse identity of pleasure and pain; the displaced delight of voluptuousness, going beyond its proper place as forepleasure; the undermining of the prin-ciple of pleasure by the very instincts in which it is grounded. The sole aim of perverse sexuality is pleasure: pleasure in the service of nothing whatsoever, not even the release of tension. But if the in-crease in tension is perversity, all sexuality is more or less perverse. What we see here is a pleasure that attaches to tension, a pleasure in intensity, bearing with it a drive to increase intensity, to further ten-sion. The introduction of the death drive only tells us that an inten-sity of destructiveness solves none of our puzzles.

The problem comes down to this: Eros is the instinct to take plea-sure in both the intensification and the release of tension; Thanatos drives us to enjoy both violent fragmentation and absolute stillness. The pleasure principle seems in each case to account only for the lat-ter half of each pair, and so it is here that Freud's emphasis falls. The former members of each—intense, fragmented, fragmenting, and perverse—cut across the psychoanalysis of pleasure at every point to open impossible spaces. Freud's theory of pleasure has not been sur-passed by other modern theories; in much of this text I hope to show just how deeply implicit it remains in the dominant (and often in the radical) conceptualizations of pleasure. It tells us that pleasure is op-posed to pain and that intense sensation is to be avoided, yet pain and intensity emerge from within the theory itself. It tells us that only gratification is pleasurable, yet we find ungratified desire within numerous forms of delight, and at times as a delight in itself.

I have dwelt at such length on Freud because his is not just the quintessential modern theory of pleasure but the quintessential the-ory of modern pleasure—an enlightened, rational, ego-syntonic pleasure; a sense that pleasure has an orderly, delimited economy, and desire is to be directed to the ends of reason. Perversity is the explosive twist at the heart of the modern theory of desire, that which must eventually render it postmodern. Freudian theory vividly and paradigmatically exemplifies the destabilizing power of perverse pleasures—for pleasure itself, for theories of pleasure, and for pleased subjects. Indeed, the perverse subject in Freud shows a weirdly familiar set of traits in its pleasures: they are fragmented, indirect, multiple, and nonsensically multidirectional.[32] They are perverse pleasures for perverse subjects, for those whose subjectivity fragments into the postmodern play with positions of identity.

the problem of pleasure in subversion

> celebration: the time of transgressing the taboos.
>
> —Georges Bataille, *Erotism*

But we mustn't leap to the assumption that we are therefore radical and subversive and unspeakably cool whenever we take pleasure, even perverse pleasure. Judith Williamson was surely right to comment on "left-wing academics . . . busy picking out strands of 'subversion' in every piece of pop culture from Street Style to Soap Opera."[33] There are important criticisms of postmodern theory precisely upon this point. The postmodern emphasis on *pleasure* (so avidly sought by Barthes and Foucault) too readily falls into a happy, even celebratory acceptance of the easiest pleasures, in our culture's case a consumerism that plays a bit too nicely into the power structures dominant in late capitalism.[34] I would certainly argue with this as an exhaustive definition of the complex theoretical and stylistic modes grouped under the heading of the postmodern. And as I shall argue below, in a manner already implicit in my appropriation of Vaneigem, the counterpleasures are conspicuously resistant to absorption by exchange value. At the same time, it is just as certainly the case that some decontextualized elements become consumer objects—from the monastic fashions briefly popular in the early 1990s to the fad for sadomasochistic gear that shows few signs of abating. (In the introduction to the discussion of sadomasochism itself, I shall note some of the criticisms along these lines.) But context, as any good masochist knows, is everything; each of the counterpleasures makes its particular kind of sense in its own social and historical setting.

Thinkers from Nietzsche to Foucault have noted, in varying terms, the ready incorporation of pleasure by the dominant powers: Nietzsche's "crude, musty, brown pleasure as it is understood by those who like pleasure, our 'educated' people, our rich people, and our rulers!",[35] Vaneigem's bourgeois re/productive eroticism, Foucault's realization that power is only powerful when it makes us want and enjoy the very construction it offers—all of these recognize pleasures that function *against* the possibility of subversion. Yet neither is it the case that the counterpleasures are simply a snobbish refusal of other, nonsubversive pleasures—they are, rather, pleasures that tend away from all sorts of teleologies. Even the "aim" of subject-shattering can be approached only indirectly, and will destroy the pleasures if it takes them over. All one can do is to give oneself over to pleasure, and it will take one beyond oneself, or not. In this giving over, the distinctions between "normal" and "perverse" pleasure begin as differences of degree, or more clearly of *intensity*, and this intensification at some level becomes indistinguishable from a difference in kind. This insight, which is properly owed to Bataille,[36] is one that can only be developed by its exploration in all the chapters that follow.

We should also avoid being too impressed with our own transgressivity because, in a sense, "we" do not matter so much. We-subjects are also threatened and destabilized by perversity. The criticism that "postmodernism . . . often delivers in the end a subject more sovereign than any white male ruler, able to perform itself quite freely and without constraint"[37] may be best met here, in modes of delight that explode or transform the very possibility of subjectivity. These criticisms of the postmodern, met I believe by these counterpleasures (which postmodern theory best allows us to understand, though the pleasures cut across a range of historical periods) are linked. Subjectivity is deconstructed by the nonteleological (the refusal of artifactuality as teleology). When pleasures refuse teleology and the artifactuality of gratification, they cut across the boundaries of this subjectivity at multiple points, in pleasure as the defiance of pleasure. It is only the multiplying of pleasure's possibilities and the defiance of its unfragmented norms that lend to pleasure the value of subversion, transgression, or resistance.

Finally, especially in dealing with contemporary counterpleasures, we must be careful about the ways in which a notion of using pleasure to subvert or resist the rigidifying danger of the modern order plays into that order itself: pleasure is not subversive if we make of it something useful, even if that use is to subvert. This does not forbid us to recognize the transgressive possibilities of perverse delights, nor does it mean that we cannot incorporate the pleasure of knowing this transgressivity into the pleasures of perversity.[38] There is an explosive quality to these pleasures that goes beyond the possible aims of a subject. Their political potency does not lie, then, in strengthening or even in reaffirming the rights and personhood of the oppressed; it is far subtler and shiftier. Nor, if they are really to be effective, can this effectiveness be their sole or primary aim: itself a fine little perverse knot, hard to unbind.

Thus, beginning in a love of pleasure, I shall not always, and seldom stridently, insist upon the political in what follows. The displacement of theory and subject is at least as powerful as more overtly political modes of transgression. Theoretical discourse and subject-construction are as basic and as important as explicit politics. Where some pleasures become more apparently politicized than others (specifically, both asceticism and sadomasochism, as practices of the body, seem to give more direct offense than the textual pleasures of Sade or Masoch) it is because these pleasures are the most visible and so most disturbing—and so most readily condemned, most subject to external prohibition. Their politicization comes from without as well as within, as a reaction to what opposes them as well as through their own quest for intensification. There is thus an ambivalence built into the celebration of these delights in political terms: not only does the political, with its tendency to righteousness and project, threaten to *overwhelm* the delight, but the delight we take in the political can all too readily become purely reactive. That is, it becomes a pleasure in seeking out evil in order to destroy it, rather than delighting in itself and taking on opposition only as an extension of that delight.[39]

the context of opposition

> We don't use the word "originality.". . . we apply the term "abnormality."
>
> —Maria Marcus, *A Taste for Pain*

The context of our discussion of pleasure began in Freud, though by noting Freud's own textual inversion. The context of our connection of pleasure and power begins in Nietzsche, whose embrace of the paradoxical is far more overt; and continues as these notions are used by a number of more contemporary thinkers. In each specific case we must also situate the discussion in the context of an opposition to counterpleasure, which in general has surprisingly Freudian roots (ignoring the self-inversion of the Freudian texts), as well as in the context of other counterpleasures. The specifics of these modes of opposition appear in the introductions to each of the specific pleasures, but a general introduction to them will orient us.

I have emphasized the importance of avoiding reactivity, an importance on which I place both practical and conceptual value. But I have also noted that one cannot blindly ignore the context of opposition, even if one intends not a direct reaction but a more radical reconception. With that in mind, we might note that there are also linkages among the oppositions to the counterpleasures that may in fact help us to see some connections across the pleasures themselves.

The counterarguments to the counterpleasures place them firmly within a set of institutions long (and not *altogether* incorrectly) characterized as oppressive, specifically as patriarchal, or oppressive to women: pornography, Christianity, and erotic domination (conceived as an extreme mode of heterosexuality). But the counterpleasures take up a highly disruptive place within, at the margins of, and explosively beyond each of these institutions. That is, Sade and Masoch do not give us pornography in any usual sense; they make use of pornographic techniques to problematize pleasure and unfold startling possibilities of language and narrative structure. The ascetics intensify both the Christian turn against the body and the incarnate and corporeal aspects of that "same" tradition, revealing in their practice the seductive, defiant elements of religious practice that radically problematize its disembodiment, its hierarchicality, even its misogyny. Sadomasochistic eroticism intensifies relations of control and subordination by fundamentally (that is, at the very beginning or foundation) altering their meaning, removing power from its orderly binarism of oppression to create a transgressive, postsubjective and highly Bataillean erotic.

I shall later note in more detail that however they appear initially, all of the counterpleasures discussed here are in fact modes of asceticism. That is, all defy pleasure as we have come to understand it; all are *strategies* of pleasure against the simple gratification of desire. Sade and Masoch defy our need for narrative closure, sadism and masochism our opposition of pleasure to pain and tension. And the saints whom we have always called ascetic turn out to be engaged in practices of remarkably subversive delight.

This brings up another side of situating these pleasures. Though much of their discursive context is oppositional, there is a double danger in addressing a discussion of counterpleasure to those who would oppose it. First, if we are resisting reactivity, which so opposes the real possibilities of affirmation, we will certainly not do best by reacting, though this is sometimes an important step:

> You see, if there were no resistance, there would be no power relations. Because it would simply be a matter of obedience. You have to use power relations to refer to the situation where you're not doing what you want. So resistance comes first, and resistance remains superior to the forces of the process; power relations are obliged to change with the resistance. . . . To say no is the minimum form of resistance. But of course, at times that is very important.[40]

A celebratory discourse must look quite different from one which is defensive; it must say more than *no*.

Second, we run a real risk of getting caught up in a discourse that can only define negatively that which resists or perverts it. Here I would point to the example of Eve Sedgwick's discussion of homophobia, as David Halperin presents it:

> The great virtue of Sedgwick's analysis is that it delivers lesbians and gay men from the temptation to play what is ultimately a mug's game of refuting the routine slanders and fantasies produced by the discourse of homophobia. The reason it is pointless to refute the lies of homophobia is not that they are difficult or impossible to refute—on the contrary, taken one at a time they are easily falsifiable . . . —but that refuting them does nothing to impair the strategic functioning of discourses.[41]

I think that we must start from the pleasures and see whether the objections fit. That is, I think that an internal analysis of such pleasures (insofar as an analysis of border-breaking could be called "internal"), rather than an external and suspicious critique, will provide us with greater intellectual pleasure, greater political power, and not incidentally more fun.

I shall nonetheless take note as we go along of objections and re-jections, of resistance to and against these pleasures—because such resistance, even where I take it to be wrong-headed, is by no means stupid, and so merits address. Again, to write is to work in context, and the wall into which I would dis/place this brick of a book is largely composed of hostile critiques. Just as I have used contempo-rary theory to analyze this range of practices (because I think it is rel-atively recently that theory has become adequate to this kind of boundary-play), so too I have looked at contemporary objections to them.

A particularly troubling element in this discussion has been the fact that the common context of the opposition seems to be certain strains of feminism. While these strains, primarily cultural feminism with a belief in the unique identity and characteristics of women, have begun to seem a bit old-fashioned, they have not altogether lost their force or their influence. For the most part the counterpleasures fit much more comfortably within the context of a "bad girl" femi-nism or of a postmodern feminism or postfeminism, which is consid-erably less secure about the identity of "woman." This fit is improved considerably when we move into the feminist-influenced realm of queer theory, though here too some of the discussion, especially of as-ceticism, will be at least unexpected. All of these pleasures are edgy and strange, and this is a part of their common attraction. If they were to find a place within any feminist tradition, it might be within the space opened by writers such as Carol Queen, who remarks that, as a bisexual gender-bending s/m switch, "I never *could* resist crossing lines. Once you've done it a few times, I guess, you get a taste for it."[42]

The counterpleasures, as I shall repeatedly note, display exactly this taste. I have tried to avoid giving into the temptation to cover over the violence inherent in these pleasures, and this too is out of line with the good-woman modes of thought. But I think that Lesley Stein is right to remark in "The Body as Evidence," "It may well turn out . . . that the intertwining of sex and death and violence are not uniquely male properties."[43]

In light of both the sometimes hostile context and the epistemo-logical tendency toward displacement I've written with one eye to misrecognition—not of this work, which would be a bit presumptu-ous, but of these pleasures. It isn't that these are such rarefied or eso-teric pleasures; it is only that we cannot be certain of recognizing that which is never where we expect to find it. What's more, I think we've become unconscionably comfortable in believing that we have located and understood the transgressive. This is the risk of a positive discourse that remains, I believe, caught up in reactivity. This is a danger that needs to be addressed.

It is here that the tendency of these pleasures to dis-locate our thinking is important. We seek easy classification; a pleasure, even a counterpleasure, is normal or it is pathological. To pathologize is to dismiss from serious consideration. But to normalize any of these pleasures is equally dismissive. To normalize, which is part of what it means to take any marginal element into the mainstream, is to render safe and harmless, and *that* is to render these pleasures null, because they are pleasures *dependent upon* transgression. The assimilation of the marginal by the mainstream is not evil, except perhaps in the most purely aesthetic terms. But where the "marginal" is, as it must be here, the transgressive (and certainly "transgression" has become trendy enough that its mainstreaming seems a very real possibility) assimilation can only be the same as denial. What transgresses is precisely what cannot be contained, what bursts the boundaries, rendering the center (the safe, harmless, assimilationist center) nowhere at all.[44]

relations among the counterpleasures

> Intensity: the attractiveness in this name lies not only in its generally escaping conceptualization, but also in its way of coming apart in a plurality of names, denominations which dismiss the power that can be exerted as well as the intentionality that orients.
>
> —Maurice Blanchot, *The Writing of the Disaster*

Aside from noting the risks and the objections, we can situate the discussion by trying to see something of what these pleasures *are*. I have already suggested that we will not be able to grasp these pleasures by simple relations of opposition or assimilation. In fact their relations are complex, involving neither historical linearity nor ontological dependence, but sets of similarities and distinctions. In common they share a love of boundary-play. This does not mean, as it is often understood, that these are pleasures arising from a loathing of limits, or from a somewhat adolescent desire to shock the bourgeoisie. They delight in the existence of boundaries, that they may be broken and overleapt; in the establishment of limits, that they may be surpassed. I would argue with Terry Lovell's characterization of postmodernism as "a theory which declares that there *are* no boundaries."[45] There are indeed boundaries, but these too can be objects for play. Sade is most conspicuous in this, as we shall see,[46] and contemporary sadomasochists perhaps most articulate and forthright.[47]

Such playful delight fits at least one conception of queer pleasure—pleasure that is not quite identical with any pleasure that happens not to fit established norms. It is, rather, a pleasure *in* the lack of fit, a delight in resistance itself, but not in reactivity; a delight in the mobility of the structures of power, the rupturing of boundaries.[48] Jacques Derrida has linked the boundary to the opening of the aporetic, the unthinkable space that makes displacement not only possible but at once as necessary and as impossible as Bataille's situating of the work.[49] This reminds us that the epistemological space of the transgressive is always edgy, at the edge, at the cut across the boundaries of the possible, at the space opened—for language, for body, for culture. In more than one sense, then, these are limit-pleasures, forms of edge-play.

Another important common strain, on which I have already briefly remarked, is the idea that all of these are variants on asceticism. Foucault remarked on the need for new pleasures, and on the power of pleasure to disrupt the dominant structures of power: "What we must work on, it seems to me, is not so much to liberate our desire but to make ourselves infinitely more susceptible to pleasure."[50] But he simultaneously called for a new asceticism: "Can that be our problem today? We've rid ourselves of asceticism."[51] One might dismiss the oddness of this pairing, suggesting that perhaps Foucault spoke rather sloppily in what was presumably an unrehearsed interview. But ascesis is, as he carefully notes in his work on the history of sexuality, not the denial of pleasure but a strategic structuring of pleasure, a mode of caring for oneself, surpassing or transcending oneself (or, in the Nietzschean mode, self-overcoming). A new ascesis is a new strategizing of pleasure, a new disruption in the relations of power. All of the counterpleasures both refuse some more customary conception of pleasure and strategically construct a new pleasure in self-surpassing.

There are common elements in these pleasures' disruptive movement, which may explain why they seem incomprehensible to so many. The pleasures collected here are pleasures that queer our notion of pleasure, consisting in or coming through pain, frustration, refusal. They are pleasures of exceptional intensity, refusing to make *sense* while still demanding a philosophical unfolding. This unfolding takes odd forms; that of an infinite self-reflexion[52] or a rupture of language in the very act of description.[53]

They are pleasures so absurdly difficult in attainment that we must sometimes suspect that the pleasure comes in the intensity of the challenge itself. They are pleasures we forbid ourselves because they would cease to be pleasures if we who forbade were not identical with we who enjoy. They are pleasures that refuse the sturdy subjective center, defying one's own survival, promising the death not of the body but, for an impossible moment, of the subject—as Bataille, perhaps, has best shown us.[54] They are pleasures that twist our conception of subjectivity, defying and even denying the subject who is, we have always supposed, required for pleasure—someone, we have always thought, must be pleased.

So we have always thought, though for a long time we have known better: if Heraclitus didn't tell us, Nietzsche certainly did. The subject unsettled in its intentionality, its boundaries, and its stability is subject to pleasures that don't come within the economy of gratification, the gratifying economy of work and production (thus we return to Vaneigem's insight). Nietzsche told us: for him the subject was a grammatical fiction, and pleasure was identical with an increase in power[55]—but power increases only in its outlay, and not as a return upon investment. In our own time Judith Butler, like Nietzsche, argues that the body may exceed the signification "subject," urging "the critical release of alternative imaginary schemes for constituting sites of . . . . pleasure."[56]

At the same time, each counterpleasure is particularly suited to its cultural context; each engages some element of subjectivity that is particularly significant for its time and place. In this suitability, each participates in the relation Butler describes as performativity, "this relation of being implicated in that which one opposes, this turning of power against itself to produce alternative modalities of power, to establish a kind of political contestation that is not a 'pure' opposition, a 'transcendence' of contemporary relations of power."[57]

Thus Sade, in the context of Enlightenment rationality and the coming of the democratic equality it implies, pushes the possibilities of reason to their irrational limits. Masoch, writing in the nineteenth-century context of European Romanticism, uses the imagistic and emotive (the faculties of imagination and affect) as the essence of the subject[58]—and as the impossible in his texts. The medieval saints grounded their already problematic sense of self in the duality of embodiment and soul (*both* immortal), a tension they exploited to trans-

gress the boundary between carnal and divine. In our time, with subjectivity constructed by the orderly divisions and controlling gaze
that strive to make us both more efficient and more knowable—the
subjectivity of individuating discipline in the market demographics
of late capitalism—sadomasochistic pleasure plays with the control,
movement, sensations, and possibilities of the body to turn carnality
to its full, postsubjective power. Disrupted subjectivity has always
been at once attractive and disturbing, and the disruption of subjectivity is significant in each of these pleasures.

   This work is intended not to re-claim (no one can own or claim
the transgressive) but to re-mind us that transgression isn't normal. I
would remind us as well that the pathological is not, though we
often forget this, the only option to the normal. To accept a nameless
third term (neither normal nor pathological) which remains nonsyn-
thetic means transgression of the boundaries of pleasure itself. This
third term carries elements of the transgressive, the subversive, the
seductive. Pleasure, even counterpleasure, does not exhaust the
transgressive, but it remains an important aspect of our exploration
of that term, particularly if we accept the Nietzschean link between
pleasure and power.

   Because we have come to so value "experience" in theory, I
would be pleased to say that these are my pleasures too, but of
course they are not (though nowhere do I speak solely from abstraction). It is important to me not to have spoken altogether exter-
nally—and in fact I can only write from a rather impassioned
engagement—nor to have undertaken to pronounce upon cultures in
which I do not share even historically. There are utterly fascinating
traditions of counterpleasures in non-Western cultures and litera-
tures; we can think immediately of the elegantly stylized violence of
certain Japanese prose, or certainly the ascetic traditions of more than
one of the Indian religions. My intent here is not at all to insist upon
the primacy of the West but to write what I more honestly can.
Though I cannot call these "my" pleasures, certainly I have been
theirs, as captivated reader, entranced ascetic (though fleetingly, and,
despite a Catholic upbringing, without the appropriate context), ex-
ploded subject, but they elude ownership.

   Finally, honesty, in admiring if inadequate emulation of Freud,
compels me to confess here what can only be the trait of a confirmed
theory-addict, or unreformable philosopher: I have been drawn to an
abstract element of these pleasures, the ways in which they twist and
break our efforts to theorize them. I am delighted both by the plea-

sures and by their elusiveness, their sustaining of an intellectual tension. I would bring to these pleasures the power of thought. It is my
hope that this work, entering the discourse on pleasure and desire,
will enlarge the space for that of which it speaks—a space still, all
fashionable trends to the contrary, surprisingly cramped and narrow;
a space that, if I have done my work well, will show itself best in defying our efforts to locate it definitively.

PART ONE

THE CLASSIC COUNTERPLEASURES

Before you it does the work

—Paul Celan, "Confidence"

the literary eroticization of the death drive

Sadism and Masochism as narrative structures

> Sex has become, strictly speaking, the actualization of desire in pleasure—all else is literatures.
>
> —Jean Baudrillard, *Seduction*

> But my notes have a curious tendency, as I realize at last, to annihilate all they purport to record.
>
> —Samuel Beckett, *Malone Dies*

As promised, I shall begin this first discussion with a look at the context of opposition, which in the case of Sade and Masoch has generally meant the opposition to pornography. (It is possible to confuse these two authors' work with sadistic or masochistic practice and object to it on that ground. However, this is to shift the focus away from the works of literature with which they in fact present us.) I am not going to defend pornography, though I certainly believe that could be done, but rather intend to show that both Sade and Masoch in their work undermine the very project of the pornographic, and to show why the specific objections against pornography fail to address their work.

The objections to pornography come from both radical feminists and the religious right. The former center upon the idea that pornography, in its overt sexualization of the body (especially the female body), devalues and even denies the personhood and subjectivity of those portrayed, leading to misogynistic attitudes, casual violence against women, and (an argument made by the more sex-positive among these groups) bad sex, since good sex depends upon caring intersubjectivity. The latter tend simply to oppose the titillating possibilities of the graphic portrayal of sex. (Some Christian objections are more nearly allied to those of radical feminism. These see as immoral much of what pornography, in their eyes, glorifies—violence, nonmonogamy, and the lack of a context of interpersonal commitment—which the feminist critiques see as antiwoman.)[1] Because the Christian and even the more generally right-wing political arguments are more often founded upon an unshakable belief system, I shall chiefly consider the more thoughtful feminist arguments.[2] While I believe that the arguments for this position are largely bad, the real issue with Sade and Masoch, whose work I evaluate here, is otherwise. In fact I would argue that their work is *subversive* of the pornographic genre as these theorists see it. In their subversiveness of this more widespread pleasure, these works take their place in the context of counterpleasure.

The aim of pornography, according to these antipornographic arguments (and in most propornographic arguments, as well), is neatly Freudian: sexual stimulation (by visual imagery or, more rarely, textual description) followed by sexual release (autoerotic or, in the arguments of the more extreme antipornography activists, nonconsensually partnered) via the corporeal mimicry of the acts or at least the attitudes depicted. It is claimed that this mimicry treats women as objects only; for some theorists, it is enough that those depicted are "used" for erotic stimulation (that is, women are already objectified if their images are put to erotic purposes).[3] For those who object to pornography, this aim and function are importantly understood as almost exclusively male; Susan Gubar in "Representing Pornography" writes of "the long history of pornography, a gender-specific genre produced primarily by and for men, but focused obsessively on the female figure."[4]

Catharine MacKinnon goes so far as to insist, "pornography is masturbation material. It is used as sex. It therefore is sex. Men know this."[5] She insists as well that the stimulating effects of pornography on men are irresistible: "Sooner or later, in one way or another, the consumers want to live out the pornography further in three dimensions. Sooner or later, in one way or another, they do."[6] Evidence linking the reading or viewing of pornography to sexual violence, or even to an overbearing insistence upon consent obtained by persistent nagging, is at best ambiguous.[7] Nor does evidence suggest that pornography has, as its opponents most often insist, a purely male-oriented appeal:

> Considering the impact of pornographic material on sexual arousal and behaviour, the studies of the 1970s reported that a large proportion of adult males and females did find sexually explicit material arousing; men tended to display more arousal in response to films and photographs, women to written material.[8]

This finding, if true, has some relevance to MacKinnon's influential position. MacKinnon elides not only image and act (a man who sees a pornographic image will find a woman to treat as a sexual object) but also image and *word*. Her famous antipornographic text may bear the title *Only Words*, but her focus is on images, particularly photographs and films (those forms of pornography that statistically appeal to more men, and can give her the strongest case regarding the "use" of women in the making of pornography). This has been true of much of the argument that pornography harms women. (One important exception to this neglect of literature is, surprisingly enough, Andrea Dworkin, who like MacKinnon sees words as indistinguishable from actions, but who does work on literary analysis in such texts as *Pornography* and *Intercourse*.)

Sade and Masoch, however, are conspicuously literary, and translate rather poorly to other media.[9] Of course, both created before film or photograph, still less cheap video, was easily possible; but what is important here is not what else they might have done but what they did, the works we in fact have. (After all, neither of them chose to work in the visual arts, which more nearly approach the effects of film or photography.) MacKinnon's analysis simply does not translate across media boundaries so easily or at least so obviously as she supposes.

It would already be problematic to try to evaluate these written works by theory designed to deal with the pornographic image. In fact, though, neither Sade nor Masoch fits within the tradition or the aims even of *written* pornography. But this claim cannot be made casually, because some opponents of pornography have seen them as the paradigmatic examples of the practice. Others see "sadism" as central to pornography, understanding by the term a set of practices derived from the acts described in Sade's work (not the practices of those who consider themselves sadists in consensual contexts). Andrea Dworkin devotes an entire chapter of *Pornography: Men Op-*

pressing Women to Sade—the only author accorded this dubious privilege. Though her work is hugely problematic (notably for its failure to consider the relevance of language and style—works are only plots—or the distinction between physical act and text; and for its sometimes startling leaps to the assumption of causal connection), it is hardly insignificant that for a woman who is one of *the* leaders in the movement against pornography, Sade is *the* pornographer.

Similarly, the collection *Take Back the Night* includes an article by Susan Griffin from her book *Pornography and Silence*,[10] under the title "Sadism and Catharsis: The Treatment is the Disease." Her argument here is that pornography, far from providing a cathartic outlet for a harmless release of male sadistic tendencies, in fact stimulates these destructive desires, which are presumably too much like those of the Marquis. Susan Gubar, in her article already cited, makes Sade's *Philosophy in the Bedroom* an important part of the history of pornography. George Steiner ominously suggests "there may be deeper affinities than we as yet understand between the 'total freedom' of the uncensored erotic imagination [presumably responsible for pornography] and the total freedom of the sadist."[11] Kathleen Barry brings this range of criticisms together, as Gubar also notes, referring to "Kathleen Barry's point that pornographic texts and pictures which stimulate male masturbation accompanied by conscious fantasies of 'cultural sadism,' function as 'handbooks or blueprints for sadistic violence, mutilation, and even gynocide.' "[12] These are not the only voices in the antipornography movement, even on its feminist side, but they are among its loudest, and their arguments are heard.

The reasons for the association of Sade, and to a lesser degree Masoch,[13] with pornography are fairly clear. If one reads casually and with a singularity of purpose that is willing to disregard the lengthy and spectacularly boring lectures on philosophy and politics, which form a considerable part of these works, and to ignore the elaborate framing devices that both authors employ, and to refuse to confront the unsettlingly deliberate failure of erotic resolution within the overtly sexual passages of text, then Sade (especially) exemplifies what these theorists consider pornography: violence in a sexual context, sexual explicitness with a focus on body parts and disregard for relationality, the degradation of women (and men, but this doesn't seem to perturb such theorists). Masoch, again, tends to portray the degradation of *men* (but of course, one might argue, as degraded they are necessarily feminized), but in other respects his work also fits this list of traits. Ergo, the works are pornographic. But this list of things we must ignore, to which we can add the odd use of language and the strangeness of narrative structure, are a lot to disregard. And it is in fact in these disregarded elements that Sade and Masoch's work fails as pornography and becomes something of different, perhaps greater, philosophical interest.

It is not accidental, that is, that as pornography their work is a series of failures. Their language is wrong; it is in Sade's case too clinical, in Masoch's too florid; it is too overloaded with details that contribute nothing to any discernible sexualization of a scene (Masoch is obsessed with hats and interior decorating, Sade with machines and philosophy lectures). Their structure is wrong, failing to lead to climax: Sade's narrative climaxes are immediately irrelevant (it is only the next that matters) while Masoch's never quite manage to appear. The philosophical reflections that intersperse both sets of work, though Sade's more often, would make for *very* slow one-handed reading. The pornographic tropes of explicit, repeated, poorly contextualized sexuality greatly change meaning here; they become not merely subverted but self-subverting, losing their stimulating or prescriptive "value" (which might lead to masturbation or intercourse) in their bizarre overuse. As I shall suggest, they are violent beyond any pornographic possibility; they are in love with the manifestations of death as it invades the very possibilities of language.

Without this oppositional context, these analyses of Sade and Masoch might at first seem altogether aesthetic, entirely apolitical. Thus, one would think, the pleasures here discussed must not be particularly powerful forms of subversion (even if subverting the aims of pornography ought to count). But even aside from the intrinsic interest of the literary, the classical or literary forms of Sadism and Masochism—that is, to be narrowly specific, the texts of Sade and Masoch—give us two *subversive* forms of literary pleasure. That is, they subvert our customary pleasures not only in the pornographic but also in the novelistic. They reveal to us unexpected pleasurable possibilities inherent in textuality even as they subvert our sense of narrative structure and time. Our culture's demand upon language, as Foucault has pointed out, is that of confessional speech—tell everything. The demand for utter, explicit exposure is especially pronounced in pornography (for some, this differentiates the pornographic and the erotic). But when *everything* is told, as Sade shows us, no trace of language remains. The subversion is nearly perfect:

the confessional demand is defeated by being too perfectly met. Similarly, everything, in a disciplinary culture and a disciplinary discourse, must be *articulated*—yet in these strange narratives we encounter language in the face of the inarticulable—the force of silence within language. What both writers give us is language, nonetheless; it remains language, but a language in its very detail and precision become strangely inarticulate.

This approach does not create literature that is, in any customary sense, a pleasure to read. One could quite legitimately call both Sade and Masoch very bad writers. Sade's grammar-book clarity is placed alternately in the service of grotesque anatomical detail and of numbing political rhetoric. Masoch's famous "pornography" has an unmistakable air of the worst type of romance novel, full of heaving bosoms and sartorial detail. Thus it seems reasonable to suppose that it is linguistic transgression, and not the usual reader's (or, for lack of a more polite term, wanker's) pleasure, that draws philosophers and literary theorists to both Sade and, less frequently, Masoch.

I have not, of course, analyzed every conceivable aspect of the considerable bodies of work that Sade and Masoch have left us. Rather, I have concerned myself with the ways in which these works construct *pleasure*. Because the objects of analysis are works of literature, the analyses focus on textual pleasures, particularly on their temporal structures, their forms of repetition and their peculiar rhythms.

We need to understand these pleasures, literary pleasures that language cannot survive, not only for what they can tell us about language and the possibilities of literature but also to see how different they are from the pleasures discussed in the later essays here, those of actual sadomasochistic practice beyond literature. I have attempted to keep this distinction clear by using capitalized terms (Sadism and Masochism) where referring to the literary pleasures, reserving lower-case for extratextual practices. I have not, however, "corrected" others' use of the terms.

More precisely, we need to see that the continuity of these works with the other counterpleasures is not that of simple succession or precedence. They do not redescribe the sufferings of the saints, though Masoch hints toward this. Nor are most of the acts they describe noticeably popular with practicing sadists or masochists. However, their disruptive refusal of the usual meanings of pleasure (stimulation leading to gratification), and the corresponding perversity of their subjective senses of temporality, do indeed carry over to embodied practices. The relation of language to body is never simple, and certainly the relation of counterpleasurable literature to counterpleasurable act is not one of imitative depiction in either direction (from act to literature or vice versa). This may perhaps teach us to be careful in assuming that any practicing "sadist" acts like the Marquis de Sade of either life or text, or that Masoch himself or in the person of his protagonist Severin is a prototypical "masochist." The discussion of Sade and Masoch's texts is *not* a history of s/m, and if we are to understand any of these pleasures, then understanding *why* they differ will be important—if only to counter the claims we shall later note that these men are virtually responsible for, or at any rate identifiable with, all sadomasochistic practice.

This discontinuity of act and description, then, is important not only to an understanding of contemporary practices, but for our understanding of Sade and Masoch. We discredit both if we see them as script writers. Their works are important not because of the acts or scenes they depict, but, once more, because of their use of language (Sade's precision, at once crystalline and clinical; Masoch's feverishly imagistic detail) and their narrative structures (making, as I shall show, remarkable and divergent uses of the pleasures of repetition). They are important, if not really "good," works of literature, and literature is important, because language and art are important, and all the more so if they refuse to be reduced to the useful.

Another point follows from the fact that this discussion is not a history of sadomasochistic practice, nor an outgrowth of the more perverse strains of Christianity (though this last is not as strange a claim as it might seem. Susan Griffin insists that "every theme, every attitude, every shade of pornographic feeling has its origins in the church."[14] Here too the discontinuity is not complete). The distinction between representation in description and enactment in the flesh means that a literary interest is not a practical endorsement. Periodically these figures, particularly Sade, reemerge into intellectual fashion as models of transgressive daring. But if one could somehow embody Sade's pleasures in a nonliterary context (and I am not at all convinced of this possibility; Sade's I believe is a pleasure *dependent upon* textuality)[15], it is hard to see how they could be defensible— Sadean pleasure depends in considerable part upon the necessary unwillingness of at least one of the parties involved in the scenes described. The relations of body and text in Sade's writing are complex and interesting, but what is most fascinating about the text—its repetition and acceleration, its grammatical purity in the face of ethical defilement—is lost in the attempt to translate from the page to the flesh.

Much work done on sadism and masochism in recent theory has in fact come out of literary interests. The theorists themselves may be quite clear about this, as is Carol Siegel in *Male Masochism*, in which she argues that "masochism has meaning only in reference to language, [so] I will focus my investigation of it on its textual inscriptions and on some of the literary events attending its birth into history."[16] Kaja Silverman bases her analysis of Sadism and sadomasochism, terms she rightly distinguishes,[17] on literature and film, though not all of her theoretical sources (Theodor Reik chief among them) seem to be aware of the importance of examining the practices of the flesh as well. (In fact, Reik seems to base his analysis of his patients on their fantasies rather than their practices, and Silverman is not always careful to draw this distinction.)

Unlikely as either is, it would be less politically problematic to render Masoch's pleasure extratextual than it would be to do the same for Sade. In fact, Masoch's fetish for contractual alliance and explicit mutual agreement is really very politically correct, and some masochists actually like *Venus in Furs*, despite occasional reservations about its style. But the more extreme form of this contractual fetishism, an immobility that denies the completion of any movement, a sensuality aimed at its own destruction, is finally foreign to the flesh and, like Sadistic acceleration, has its proper place on the page. This, of course, problematizes the Dworkin-MacKinnon style argument that would draw a straight causal line from pornography to violent behavior, or even to relatively mild behavioral displays such as masturbation.

Both Sadism and Masochism, in these classical forms, are fascinating literary structures, and their peculiar rhythms of acceleration and suspension show up in much literature that we wouldn't generally regard as sadomasochistic, or even pornographic[18] or erotic. Literary investigation, however, is limited in what it can tell us about extraliterary practice. Here we find only a narrative counterpleasure, but counterpleasurable structures will already be seen to be in—and, intriguingly, slipping out of—place. Whatever the place of pornography, oppressive or liberating, it aims at arousal and the possibility of gratification, which these texts repeatedly and determinedly defy.

Here we begin in a vein at once structured and structural. It is *form* that fascinates—but, like Sade, we find ourselves most profoundly drawn by the moment of form's self-inversion or -destruction, by its autotransgressive aspects. Anarchy, seductive though it can be, has nothing on the fascinating spectacle of self-immolating form. This self-immolation of the texts' narrative pleasure provides their link to the other counterpleasures: not only are these, like those, paradoxical; they are unsurvivable, even by the relatively disembodied, wholly discursive subject. Though I have emphasized my belief that we must avoid the terminological temptation of seeing the practices that go by the names of sadism and masochism as fully continuous with these texts, I must note again that there is a commonality of disruption, a disruption through the intensification of ordinary possibilities to the extreme at which those possibilities invert in meaning. What remains fascinating is that these texts, finally, are as pornographic as not, using the conventions of pornography (that is, its habit of presenting repeated sexual descriptions with little concern for caring, relationality, or the more personal or subjective traits of the bodies depicted) against its aims (sexual arousal and gratification). In their narrativity they must be distinguished from more bodily pleasures, but at a more abstract level, in their tendency to displace by intensification, they share a great deal. This is a level of theoretical subtlety (though it is not really very subtle) that more overtly politicized thought might wish to reject, but theory is never so rarefied as it seems. Thought, as Foucault reminds us, is always a little bit dangerous.

2

Sadism

Whilst in many places the effect . . . on the reader undoubtedly is somewhat emetic, nowhere does it tend to be
an aphrodisiac.

—John M. Woolsey[1]

Though the topics of Sadean and Masochistic pleasure have a certain prurient appeal, it may still not be immediately apparent why they should matter to us philosophically, what might be theoretically intriguing about them. What makes the perversity of classical Sadism or Masochism (that is, these literary works, as opposed to contemporary practices) philosophically interesting (and ultimately transgressive), I would suggest, is the *paradoxicality* of their pleasures.

I have already used the term "paradoxicality" in connection with the self-inversion of Freudian theory, and it has a particular fit for perversity. To say of something that it is paradoxical is not to say that it is either untrue or illusory, but that its truth is unstill, that its sense is multiple and mobile. Our word "sense" has among its original meanings that of directionality (though this meaning today is stronger in the Romance than in the Germanic languages).[2] Directionality is not unrelated to the understanding of "sense" as meaning: what Deleuze in *The Logic of Sense* calls "good sense" is sense that moves only in one direction, pointing us to one final truth. Paradox moves meaning in double directions at once; it is polysensuous, or, to be Freudian, polymorphously sensuous. In fact, in its refusal to follow a single straight path paradox partakes of the turning-away which is both perverse (from the Latin *perversus*, turned the wrong way) and seductive (from the Latin *seducere*, to lead aside or away).[3] Paradox as polymorphously sensuous leads us (astray, seducing us) straight into the perverse. The paradox that is Sadism moves between reason and the infinite. Here we shall see three forms or aspects of this notion, touching on three senses of reason: as discursive, as free, and as objectively disinterested, each with its infinite countermovement.

The work of Donatien Alphonse François, Marquis de Sade, has had a philosophical importance altogether disproportionate to its apparent literary value—though in its way Sade's use of literary language is extraordinary, and those philosophers who have taken his work most seriously have been theorists of the literary as well as of the philosophical, and often among those responsible for the blurring of the distinction between the two. In fact, it is in the literary oddities of Sade's texts that their philosophical value resides, more than in the rather trite philosophical diatribes with which he punctuates them (of which Bataille accurately remarks, "the philosophical dissertations which interrupt de Sade's narrative at the least excuse make them exhausting reading").[4] The oddities and the philosophizing are not, of course, altogether separable, but Sade exemplifies better than he explains.

Many interpreters have pointed out the double impossibility of Sade's project: it is at once incommunicable (unwriteable) and unreadable. Bataille remarks that "since language is by definition the expression of civilized man, violence is silent."[5] It is their very violence, their Sadistic essence, that these texts *cannot* communicate except, to use Bataille's formulation, in the language of the victim. Violence itself, he argues, is contrary to language and to linguistic expression.[6] In Bataille's claim that violence is essentially *silent* we find an echo of Freud: the death drive, too, is silent—and this drive is, of course, destructive, fragmenting and fragmented, violent.[7] Antipornography activists argue that the (masculine) violence of pornography has the effect of silencing others (women)[8]—but if violence itself is silent, then the sense of destruction must take quite a different turn.

To understand the paradoxical expression of inexpressible violence we turn to the paradoxical movement of the Sadistic pleasure attained in that violence. The most readily and superficially apparent characteristic of Sadistic pleasure as it appears in Sade's work is that it arises through the act of inflicting pain on another person (more rarely, and so far as I know in Sade's case not at all, on animals, for reasons that will come up later). As such, it seems less puzzling, though often much more violent, than the apparently self-destruc-

tive pleasures of *receiving* pain in action or in description, the pleasures described in Masoch, or the ascetic pleasure of self-deprivation
and mutilation. As it turns out, it is every bit as odd.

That the infliction of pain is violent is not a claim likely to encounter much opposition, at least when the victim is unwilling and
the pain is a major motive for the act. (In fact, if we are willing to distinguish between different senses of violence, it may be violent to inflict pain even under other conditions, but this less restrictive claim
would require argument that seems unnecessary here—Sade's depicted violence certainly meets the stated conditions.) More strangely,
it may be violent to inflict *pleasure* as well, as also happens to the
characters in Sade's texts. Here the violence arises in the forcible elic-
iting of undesired sensation. Still, it is not altogether clear just what
(and more, just where) this violence is. What, if violence is silent,
finds its way to expression in "the violently impure, monstrously . . .
unwieldy Sadean text"?[9] If violence is silent, who or what speaks
(and writes) through the Marquis de Sade? It is, as Bataille suggests,
on and through the victim that Sadistic violence is communicated
and written, on whom the violence of Sadistic pleasure leaves its
mark, its trace, its disfigurement. Often in Sade we find stories first
spoken, then corporeally inscribed, to make them real, to make them
last—and then, through Sade, written, to make them last longer
still—and we might note here that for at least one of Sade's interpreters, Maurice Blanchot, the real violence is in the writing. What,
then, is the violence that we find inscribed—or, as we shall note, failing to be inscribed—on the bodies of those victims?

It is, to be Cartesian, a violence against "mind" as well as "body"
(though the failure of this disjunction will be evident). The former
will become important when we look at reason as freedom. It is in the
latter, the violence against the body, that Sadism is most immediately
evident. Here it becomes clear that, despite superficial similarities, the
works of Sade and Masoch do not depict reciprocal perversions in
which the role of the torturer and tortured are merely exchanged.
Even Freud, who apparently never considered the more radical differences between Sadism and Masochism in literature or practice, recognizes this disparity, remarking in 1924 that "masochistic tortures
seldom convey an impression of such seriousness as the brutalities—
phantasied or actual—of sadists."[10] Sadean violence aims to produce
pain as intense and various as possible—that is, correspondingly,
pleasure as intense and prolonged as possible. To this end Sade
equips his libertines with elaborate devices of torture as well as with

wildly improbable personal proportions, the better to leave their marks on the necessarily unwilling bodies of their victims.

A closer look at the nature of this marking, via Blanchot's analysis of writing, will open up a first reading of the Sadean paradox.

marking and effacing

> Effaced before being written. If the word trace can be admitted, it is as the mark that would indicate as erased what was, however, never traced. All our writing . . . would be this: the anxious search for what was never written in the present, but in a past to come.
>
> —Maurice Blanchot, *The Step Not Beyond*

In Sade's texts only that which can be *told*, can be made public in words, can thus be made sense of, may be (described as being) done. If I were to say that Sade's characters can only do what can be said and then written, I should at least approach tautology; the characters have, after all, a purely textual existence. It is more interesting that Sade deliberately draws attention to the telling of stories. Many of his texts are constructed *as* the telling of stories by characters urged or forced to serve this function by other characters.

The most spectacular example of this, the *120 Days of Sodom*, is presented as a series of courtesans' stories, which are then echoed by the actions of the libertine audience. In his notes to himself at the end of the mercifully unfinished manuscript, Sade writes "above all, never have the four friends do anything until it has first been recounted. You have not been sufficiently scrupulous in that connection."[11] In accord with this attention to the narrative character of the novel, Sade provides an oddly postmodern commentary to the reader, for example: "and I am absolutely convinced the reader has already had occasion to be grateful for the discretion we have employed in his regard; the further he reads on, the more secure shall be our claim to his sincerest praise upon this head, why, yes, we feel we may almost assure him of it even at this early stage."[12] or: "A little patience, friend reader, and we shall soon hide nothing from your inquisitive gaze."[13] and again: "'Tis for the reader to invent the combinations and scenes he'd like best, and kindly consent to be conveyed, if 'twould please him to accompany us, directly to the throne room, where Duclos is about to resume her narrative."[14] Not only the reader but the writer himself is incorporated into the text: "Everyone knows the story of the brave Marquis de S*** who, when informed of the magistrates' decision to burn him in effigy, pulled his prick from his breeches [et cetera]."[15]

In Sade's elaborate narrative layering we are given a hint toward one of the paradoxes, one of the necessary impossibilities, which drive the violence of Sadistic rage. It is a violence driven by rage at its own limits, the limits of textual repetition. There is a multiple repetition at work in which spoken words which recount events once enacted (the courtesans' stories of *120 Days*, the successive narrations demanded of Justine), are then rerepeated by those acts' inscriptions on the flesh of the Sadists' victims—exactly the sort of inscription that, upon the body of the courtesan or of Justine, preceded the speaking. Already suggested, and emphasized by Sade's incorporation of both reader and writer into the text, is a repetition with neither origin nor end, words before and after acts, yet another repetition of the "same"—the text as written. The written text precedes the action that it can only follow, action that took place and that can only take place in the text. Thus the writing exists in Blanchot's "past to come."

The insistence of repetition is itself a form of violence, and Sade has plenty of it. The peculiarity of repetition in inscription plays itself out as reason is of and in discourse, written as well as spoken. In Sade's work the effort to inscribe—to mark the page and the flesh— has two kinds of outcome. The first and most odd is exemplified in the person of Justine, the embodiment of structuralist linguistics. Written language, says Roland Barthes, is paradoxical: "immutably structured and yet infinitely renewable" (Justine too has this renewability), "unless," Barthes adds, "for some perverts the sentence is a *body*."[16] For some perverts like Sade—and, of course, like Barthes. Justine like language reappears new, pure—at times even reborn as virginal—for each retelling, for each new use. No one can inscribe her surface permanently; even the brand on her shoulder is finally removed, while her soul, of course, is eternally unsullied. She returns insistently, astonishingly, as an uninscribed surface—until inscription has its final revenge, and she is burned through and, according to the text, thoroughly disfigured, by lightning. (We shall see the contrast with Masoch, who throughout his work is preoccupied with the creation of lasting impressions.) Justine may be objectified, but she is no ordinary object.

In this lightning stroke, the second outcome of inscription appears: inscription may last only to have the surface itself disappear.

Many of Sade's libertines are thoroughly scarred in more or less disgusting ways. Many of the victims of the cloisters, convents, or castles that enclose the movements of Sade's texts retain their scars—the amputated digits and limbs of the children of *120 Days*, for example, do not grow back. But at the height of inscription—when the body has been mutilated in every conceivable fashion, or when it no longer exists as an inscribable surface, being covered over and not infrequently torn open with marks—it disappears from the text. A body that has reached a maximum of inscription is declared dead and is strikingly absent thereafter (there is surprisingly little necrophilia in Sade). When she is burned straight through, left dead and disfigured, Justine likewise vanishes; there is no more room to write on her. A fully inscribed, thus uninscribable body/page no longer exists. To inscribe every surface is to destroy both the meaning and the possibility of inscription, to write without white spaces. Inscription no longer exists: it can only be present as yet to come. Or, as Blanchot says, "writing marks, but does not leave marks."[17] Repetition is the mark of impermanence.

Writing's time as repetition guarantees inscription's permanent impermanence. Sade's heroes want infinite repetition, crimes of infinite reverberation, effects that will go on forever (keep repeating pain's infliction). But infinite repetition also means the impossibility of permanent inscription—it means that the blown-apart universe recoheres, that Justine resurfaces virginal and trusting, that a fresh body replaces the vanished corpse. It is not merely as act, self-evidently violent and enraged, that Sadistic pleasure is impossible; it is impossible because it is a textual pleasure that carries within it a desperate drive to exceed the text. (That is: it is a drive to the infinitely repeatable which exceeds the discourse that is its only place.) To write is to seek permanent inscription; since Plato, we have seen the writer's act as a quest for immortality. Thus when Sade responds to the loss of his manuscript of *120 Days of Sodom* by "weeping tears of blood," as he claimed to do, he expresses the rage of impermanence as much as any perverse sociality desirous of sharing his work. Yet writing, as the quest for infinity, comes somehow both first and last without ever lasting: to write is already to mark the absence of what is written, the silence of the speaking voice, the empty space left by the once moving body.

First expression of the paradox: the impossible drive to the infinite as writing, the desire for the mark that lasts, already effaced and disappearing in its own completion.

thought and the unthinkable

One day I counted them. Three hundred and fifteen farts
in nineteen hours, or an average of over sixteen farts an
hour. . . . Four farts every fifteen minutes. It's nothing. Not
even one fart every four minutes. It's unbelievable. Damn
it, I hardly fart at all, I should never have mentioned it.

—Samuel Beckett, *Molloy*

The second expression is hinted at in the necessary unwillingness of
Sade's victims. The importance of dread and fear in his characters'
victims, the importance of some *understanding* of their own plight, is
one reason that animals seldom appear in Sade's texts: presumably
animals lack this rational capacity.[18] In the Sadean text violence is always preceded by threats of violence; even if a particular act may
seem unpremeditated, the victim has already been made aware of his
or (more often) her potential role as victim. The victims in Sade's
texts are forbidden the psychological comforts of friendship, prayer,
the possibility of escape. It is imperative that the victims recognize
their entrapment, the impossibility of escape, their unfreedom—the
violence against their existence as free. This would put them neatly
into line with the meanings of pornography, but for a pair of problems. The less significant is the number of women among the libertines (Juliette is the most spectacular, but she is not alone)—a
relatively insignificant point as women too may objectify women.
More important is the violence of the libertines, regardless of gender,
against themselves, not just in what they do but in the satisfaction
and satiation they forbid themselves.

Unwillingness is essential to Sadistic pleasure because, says one
of Sade's heroes, it provides the necessary contrast by which pleasure is heightened: "It is the pleasure of comparison, a pleasure
which can only be born at the sight of wretched persons. It is from
the sight of him who does not in the least enjoy what I enjoy, and
who suffers, that comes the charm of being able to say to oneself: 'I
am therefore happier than he.' "[19] But what is more interesting than
mere comparison, what lends Sade's discourse its paradoxicality, is
the relation of its violence to reason. With the violence of the Sadistic
text, and more with its constant acceleration of violence, pain, and
cruelty, we edge toward the second formulation of the Sadistic paradox: Sadistic pleasure moves between reason and the infinite not
only as reason is discourse, but as reason is thought and freedom—
as reason is Kantian.[20]

Sade's works are, as more than one commentator has pointed out, exceedingly rational, and not merely because "pornography has reason on its side."[21] In fact, the Sadistic text often takes on the character of a mathematics textbook. This is particularly evident in *120 Days of Sodom*. Here great care is taken with the scheduling of events, with the listings of characters, their measurements, their convoluted relations to other characters.[22] In places this becomes rather comic, for example: "He employs eight women to frig him; each of the eight must be situated in a different posture. (This had better be illustrated by a drawing.)"[23] or: "In connection with that evening's entertainments, we must fully explain the character of the Saturday punishments—how they are meted out and how many lashes are distributed. You might draw up a list itemizing the crimes and, to the right, the appropriate number of lashes."[24] This absurd precision gives the text an odd air of Beckett, his obsessed characters counting away—or of Kant, tidying up the categories of pure reason.[25]

Sade presents his pursuit of pleasure as ultimately rational, in oddly Epicurean terms: "The idea of oblivion has never frightened me."[26] "The torch of reason is now dispersing the shadows into which superstition has plunged you."[27] Yet Sade's discursive rationality is self-inverting; as Pierre Klossowski points out, "Sade immediately puts universal reason into question; he makes it contradict itself by being applied."[28]

Some commentators, including Deleuze, see Sade's despair as reflecting the limitations of action compared with the reach of reason. This seems a legitimate reading. But it may also be that the violent activity of Sadism *is* that of reason—that reason really is every bit as violent as Sadism suggests, that Sade is perhaps more like Kant than we have supposed. The raging frustration of the Sadist would be the frustration of Kantian reason: the inability to burst *all* bounds, to transgress all limits, to conquer the infinite. Deleuze's claim that Sade is enraged by the inability of his actual or enacted crimes to match reason's scope seems to separate reason and violence. My own reading is closer to that of Bataille, who claims that "discursive thought is evinced by an individual engaged in action,"[29] linking rather than unjoining the two. Elsewhere he notes that "de Sade's doctrine is nothing more or less than the logical consequence of these moments that deny reason. By definition, excess stands outside reason."[30] This implies the paradoxical movement of Sadistic action toward the infinite: reason, as both discourse and violence, undone from within by the very force of its own movement.

Reason destroys itself by pushing toward the excess that stands outside it, following reasonably, as a matter of logical consequence,
what turns out to defy it.

Kant links reason to freedom: it is through reason that we are
free. We are free rational beings, and to be either free or rational entails both. When one recognizes the nature of one's own freedom,
one is forced by that very recognition to grant freedom to all rational
beings.[31] Reason as freedom therefore limits freedom: because of the
way in which we are free (that is, as rational), we may not act as we
please.

Within the Kantian system, reason is a regulative faculty with regard to cognition—to thought—as well as action.[32] It makes systems
in which every thing is to be included, in its proper place; what falls
outside the system has no place.

Our great rationalists and systematizers of reason, from
Descartes to Kant and Hegel, would have been appalled, or even in-
furiated, by the notion of there being anything left over, any excess.
Reason is never excessive; it is always precisely enough. Things left
over imply bad mathematics. Sade, yet another great (though entirely perverse) rationalist, is perturbed by bad mathematics. Notes
at the ends of the second and third sections of the *120 Days* finish the
series of stories with a calculation of their number and the editorial
remark "find out why there is one too many."[33] Yet where Descartes
curbs his will to maximize his reason (setting reason's limits at what
is clearly and distinctly revealed by the natural light),[34] Sade urges
will's full force, delighting precisely in breaking every limit he can
find. Where Kant uses reason to set limits to exhort philosophers to
remain within them,[35] Sade sets limits solely to have the pleasure of
going beyond them; he is only sorry that he cannot conceive of a
crime still greater than the annihilation of the universe and its God.
Where Hegel carefully uses reason to gather seeming contradiction
into a greater synthesis, which finally omits nothing,[36] Sade uses reason to push beyond reason, to rip his world apart as his characters
dismember their victims.

Good systems of reason are constructed to include all possible
knowledge. Sade must strive for impossible knowledge, for what exceeds all boundaries and defies all possible inclusion. He must push
beyond what the most tolerant citizen of the most liberal republic
could accept; to be accepted or tolerated is to be contained within.
His characters strive for the unacceptable—not merely that which
would perturb society matrons or textbook committees, but that

which cannot come within the compass of any acceptance, the crime that would blow apart the universe. The Sadistic hero is enraged by the limit that appears as soon as reason, which should promise the infinite, emerges. The infinite opposes reason from within reason: it threatens to use reason to destroy reason.

Reason by its very nature requires and sets limits; it may be self-limiting (limited by no other force) but it is never unlimited. Sadism is driven by a passion for the unlimited, which comes out of reason itself but can only use reason to move toward the infinite: hence the counterrational demand that the victims of reason be free rational beings. All rational men, and not a few women, are frightened by infinity.[37] The infinite suggests that there are no limits—but reason is the process of setting limits, of placing concepts into their proper niches.

Sade's characters, to say it again, wish for crimes of infinite reverberation. They demand pleasures of infinite (unexperiencable) intensity—as we shall see, for the sake of intensity they will take pleasure through the detour of apathy and ultimately disregard "pleasure" itself. Reason says, "This is enough. Resist the temptation to go beyond it." The infinite poses precisely this temptation; Sade's imperative is to resist the urge to remain within limits. He systematically sets about exceeding any possible system, any conceivable order, any stretch of comprehension. Sade must demand the infinite, that which goes beyond conception, that which defies the limits that unlimited reason so unfairly places. While ordinary pornographers may enjoy the sense of freedom that so worried George Steiner, the freedom of the Sadean hero is far from total; it is by its own rationality self-inverting.

apathy and intensity

Detached from everything, including detachment.
—Maurice Blanchot, *The Writing of the Disaster*

It is not altogether clear, if it is evident at all, how this movement between reason and infinity is a movement constitutive of a particular sort of *pleasure*. A third description of the paradox, implicit in what has already been said, may be more persuasive. This is a movement more clearly of pleasure, that between apathy and intensity. This formulation, too, should clarify the paradoxical *self*-destructiveness of reason.

Sade himself is explicit about the value of apathy, even of insensibility, and his interpreters have made much of the point. Bataille sees apathy as the very source of libertine ferocity:

> All the great libertines who live only for pleasure are great only because they have destroyed in themselves all their capacity for pleasure. . . . They have made themselves insensitive; they intend to exploit their insensitivity, that sensitiveness they have denied and destroyed and they become ferocious. Cruelty is nothing but a denial of oneself carried so far that it becomes a destructive explosion; insensibility sets the whole being aquiver, says de Sade.[38]

Note the interesting, and at first glance odd, claim linking Sadism and self-denial. Klossowski, whose interpretation of Sade is much influenced by Bataille,[39] interprets Sade's "You shall have acquired the habit of doing evil" as "the purpose of the deliberate apathetic reiteration"[40]—thus Sade becomes a sort of inverted Aristotle. Simone de Beauvoir links this apathy to Stoic and Epicurean indifference, thus emphasizing the relationship of apathy to reason: "hedonism ends in ataraxia, which confirms the paradoxical relation between sadism and stoicism."[41] Both pleasure *and reason* deny themselves—Sade's is a surprisingly thorough negation. It is in its deliberate and explicit valuation of apathy that the Sadean text moves most clearly beyond both teleology and the pornographic. Apathy refuses gratification: its aim is the resistance of aim, vital to the desire to be thrown outside time into infinite reiteration. Yet only a sufficient intensification can generate an adequately violent explosion.

It seems improbable that Sade's characters should be apathetic. After all, Sade makes a point of the frequency of their sexual activity. They are continually seeking, it seems, to inflame their own desire, and are enraged by the occasional failure of their objects to excite them. The constantly increasing intensity of the violence inflicted in the *120 Days* suggests that the four friends who are its heroes are at pains to keep from becoming jaded, to keep their lives interesting. In tandem with them, the text accelerates both rhythmically and descriptively: the stories shorten, the frames become more elaborate, the acts are intended to be more shocking.

However, it is precisely the numbing effect of this intensity at which the Sadistic libertine, with his author, aims—or more accurately, this effect which is at once numbing and inflammatory. Sade

writes of one such hero that "he was just as much an atheist, an icon-
oclast, a criminal after having shed his fuck as when, before, he had
been in a lubricious ferment, and that precisely is how all wise, level-
headed people should be."[42] "Sensitivity proves weakness," says
Sade.[43] Other passages in Sade suggest the accuracy of Bataille's observation, linking apathy to the source of Sadistic desire: "His presence of mind once restored, his frenzy was immediately replaced by
the most complete indifference to the infamies wherewith he had just
indulged himself, and of this indifference, of this kind of apathy, further sparks of lechery would be born almost at once."[44]

We might be willing, perhaps, to concede that intensity leads,
or can lead, to apathy. We have all been to some extent benumbed,
if not by Sade's texts, then by television footage of war, by newspa-
per accounts of child abuse, by all the reasonable discourse on violence. The secret of Sadistic apathy is that it also engenders
intensity, that it is of indifference that its violent lechery is born,
and likewise its still more violent pleasure: "The soul," says Blanchot, "passes on to a kind of apathy that is metamorphosed into
pleasures a thousand times more wonderful than those that their
weaknesses procured them."[45] Juliette prescribes apathy after being
chastised for her lack of it; her first crimes are too passionate.
Deleuze notes of another character that "enthusiasm is precisely
what [Sade] dislikes in Rétif, and he could rightly say (as he always
did when justifying himself publicly) that he at least had not depicted vice as pleasant or gay but apathetic. This apathy does of
course produce intense pleasure, but ultimately it is . . . the pleasure
of negating . . . the ego itself. It is in short the pleasure of demonstrative reason."[46] (That is, it is the pleasure of reason in negating
the individual, personal, subjective, and passionate. Once more we
note a divergence from the traditionally active, engaged, and
pleased subject—the man who triumphs over women-as-objects—
of stereotypical pornography.)

On the other side of apathy, moving in the opposite direction, we
find intensity. Indeed, Jane Gallop suggests that, on Bataille's interpretation of Sade, pleasure is deliberately transformed into pure intensity: "the intense pleasure must be so violently extreme that it is
no longer pleasure but simply pure intensity."[47] The *120 Days*, most
clearly of all Sade's works, is an effort to build to an infinite intensity
of violence, an effort that finally ascends into absurdity, beyond the
possibilities even of Sade's bizarrely creative use of language. Thus
one of the last scenes of *120 Days*:

Then her nerves are laid bare in four adjacent places, the nerve ends are tied to a short stick which, like a tourniquet, is twisted thus drawing forth the aforesaid nerves, which are very delicate parts of the human anatomy and which, when mistreated, cause the patient to suffer much. Augustine's agonies are unheard-of.[48]

After this Sade's descriptive powers come down to: "the most refined tortures are put to use . . . they are all much more painful, more severe than the others employed upon Augustine."[49] The intensity of Sadistic violence is responsible, nearly as much as the philosophical interludes, for the unreadability of Sade's texts. But, as I have suggested, violence can only go so far. Sade is perhaps as much disheartened as he is philosophically excited by the possibility of actually enumerating all the possible permutations of erotic violence. Certainly his characters are not merely disheartened but enraged at the limitations they see on their own abilities, lamenting the fact that "there are . . . but two or three crimes to perform in this world, and they, once done, there's no more to be said; all the rest is inferior, you cease any longer to feel. Ah, how many times, by God, have I not longed to be able to assail the sun, snatch it out of the universe, make a general darkness, or use that star to burn the world! oh, that would be a crime, oh yes, and not a little misdemeanor such as are all the ones we perform."[50] Similarly, one character urges the others on to "whatever infamy you wish to propose, even if it were to dismember Nature and unhinge the universe."[51] (That not everything repeated is physical violence suggests that Deleuze is right in his claim that Sade is attempting to create violence by sheer force of repetition, a violence as much against the sensibilities as against the corporeal subject.[52])

It is here that Sade's precise language becomes so important. The precision of detail and clarity of structure both reinforce the repetition—the exactness of similarity, the minute detail that pushes each perversion further—and highlight the violence, all the more shocking in that it is never *out of control*—it never burns the world nor unhinges the universe.

Sade's violence is not admirable—"To admire Sade is to diminish the force of his ideas,"[53] as Bataille writes, or, as Blanchot says, "To say, I like Sade, is to have no relation at all to Sade. Sade cannot be liked, no one can stand him."[54] To like Sade is to defy the demand for apathy as well as to ignore the deliberate outrage Sade perpetrates on every civilized sensibility that he can recall. His unadmirable violence is, however, impressive. It is also repetitive; its intensity builds in its repetition, and yet it is only by repetition that the necessary apathy can be cultivated.

Some of Sade's repetition is simply repetitiveness. Inventive though he is, and insistent upon fine distinctions, in the course of his work much is repeated, and at certain points even the most patient (or perverse) reader is likely to be moved to great weariness at the notion of yet another detailed portrayal of yet another vigorous "embuggering" by yet another oversized male member. Repetition is essential to the oddly intense and demonstratively rational pleasure of apathy; "it is through the intermediary of description and the accelerating and condensing effect of repetition that the demonstrative function achieves its strongest impact."[55] Repetition's effect is crucial both to reason—everything must be iterated, however like what came before, however redundant it may seem—and to infinity, again and again, more and more, without limit. (Though much pornography seems repetitious, seldom is the effect so clearly relevant to the movement of the text.) Apathy displays reason's objective disinterest. Intensity demands infinite sensation and builds from within apathy to render both impossible even as both are attained in repetition.

Pierre Klossowski sees Sade's *time*, the repetitive time in which the text occurs, as that of the dream, space of infinite repetition. Sade brings, as Bataille has pointed out, violence (the essentially silent force of the unconscious death drive) to consciousness.[56] In Sade, Klossowski argues, consciousness deliberately makes itself an accomplice to its own invasion by "dark" forces; it casts itself "suicidally" into the time of infinite reiteration.[57] Sade never gets to the object of his reverie, of his waking dream or masturbatory fantasy; he suffers, Klossowski writes, from constantly being-in-potency.[58]

Finally this is the most notable trait of Sadistic violence: it is *never enough*, however-too-much it may be for the reader. Never enough, an impossible demand for the infinite, for the near immortality that repetition gives to the Sadistic gesture. Deleuze remarks: "The sadistic hero appears to have set himself the task of thinking out the Death Instinct (pure negation) in a demonstrative form, and is only able to achieve this by multiplying and condensing the activities of component negative or destructive instincts."[59] But of course the Death Instinct proper is inaccessible to the light, to reason—thus to reason to death is to destroy reason itself. Sadistic pleasure depends upon an extreme eroticization of the death drive, and is as paradoxical as either instinct within it. "The fact is," writes Bataille, "that what de Sade was trying to bring to the surface of the conscious mind was precisely the thing that revolted that mind . . . From the very first he set before the consciousness things which it could not tolerate."[60] Kaja Silverman, in her analysis of Fassbinder's *Berlin Alexanderplatz*, writes that "Sadistic ecstasy . . . hinges upon a 'swelling' of the self."[61] One need only add that the self is swollen to explosion.

The final Sadean violence is not against the other, the body of the victim, but against consciousness itself, using its own methods—its own iterative, discursive, and free rationality—to bring into it the potent force of destruction, the infinite intensity of repetition. When everything has been said again, all sense is shattered. Sade is the absurd culmination of Enlightenment rationalism; in his texts reason is pushed to the limit at which it negates its ostensibly pleasurable and liberatory character.

3

Masochism

François Jacob writes that the pleasure center has been located, somewhere in the brain or in the spinal cord. A mir-
acle: it is immediately juxtaposed with the center of
displeasure. . . . What marvelous naiveté. And where
would one locate masochism, in pleasure or displeasure?

—Jean Baudrillard, *The Ecstasy of Communication*

There is considerable psychological, particularly clinical, work available on masochism. As a clinical phenomenon, it seems to attract
rather more sympathy (if hardly more comprehension) than sadism.
But aside from psychoanalytic work, including Freud's, which cannot help edging from psychology into philosophy, there has been little philosophical work on the perverse literature of Leopold von
Sacher-Masoch—startlingly little, in fact, compared to the philosophical interest and literature generated by Sade's work. In fact,
even the *psychological* work on masochism applies poorly to Masoch;
it tends to focus on self-infliction of pain. (Even Freud classifies such
acts as masochistic, but his work lacks a separate category of ascetic
pleasure—sublimation covers only a part of it.)

Like Sade's version of Sadism, Masochism in its classical or literary form is only incidentally about pain. Practices of nonliterary
masochism may well involve a greater degree of pain than is described in Masoch's texts (the reverse is true of Sade and sadism),
and this may not be accidental. I shall argue later that pain has an
explosive effect, a *shattering* effect, which is incompatible with
Masoch's desire to create and freeze an eternal image. Here too,
while the acts described appear pornographic, the nature of the description works quite against this reading. Masoch is at least as

poor a pornographer as Sade, for nearly the opposite reason: where Sade's universe pushes toward an impossibly violent explosion, Masoch, with equal but more subtle violence, brings the universe to a halt, squeezing the life out of each instant until finally it holds still.

Freudian classifications

> In his treatment of perversions Freud seems to admit of a polymorphous system with possibilities of evolution and direct transformation, which he regards as unacceptable in the field of neurotic and cultural formations.
>
> —Gilles Deleuze, *Masochism: Coldness and Cruelty*

In *Coldness and Cruelty*, one of the few genuinely philosophical works on Masochism, Deleuze argues against the popular and psychoanalytic tendency to fuse sadism and masochism into the single entity, "sadomasochism." Sadism and masochism, he points out, differ in technique (both literary and practical), in their concerns, in their intentions, and in the philosophical problems they raise and address.[1] Nonetheless, the inquiry into Masochism often opens or develops out of the inquiry into Sadism, as his does and as mine does here, and one can make useful distinctions where parallels cannot be drawn. Of course, I must continue to emphasize the important distinction between these literary and more embodied versions of such practices. Sade to a very limited extent and Masoch to a greater extent may provide ideas or phantasy structures, but they lend themselves poorly to enactment.

Sadism and Masochism are converses only if we limit the notions of Sadism and Masochism to taking pleasure in inflicting and receiving pain, respectively; otherwise, the structural differences are considerable. Deleuze has pointed out that "even though the sadist may definitely enjoy being hurt, it does not follow that he enjoys it in the same way as the masochist; likewise the masochist's pleasure in inflicting pain is not necessarily the same as the sadist's."[2] He notes as well that "there are even limiting cases of masochism without algolagnia and even algolagnia without masochism."[3] Carol Siegel rightly points out in *Male Masochism* that Deleuze's reading in "Coldness and Cruelty" is not contrary to Freud's account (unlike his antipsychoanalytic argument, made with Felix Guattari, in *1,000*

Plateaus).[4] Thus it does not seem illicit to bring the two figures together here. In "A Child Is Being Beaten," Freud finds in a common masochistic phantasy (that of watching a child being beaten by a vaguely paternal figure) a lingering, though repressed, phantasy of paternal love; regressed to the sadistic-anal stage and then forced to revert upon the subject by guilt and, oddly enough, the love-impulse, which refuses to allow outwardly directed aggression. In "Instincts and their Vicissitudes" (1915) he considers masochism, again, only the passive introjection of primary active sadism. He, too, assumes an identity of literary and practical forms.

In the general introduction, we saw how problematic masochism is for Freudian pleasure theory. This problematic character holds for literary Masochism as well. It is only in 1924, with the brief but remarkable essay "The Economic Problem in Masochism," that Freud recognizes the possibility of primary masochism—that is, a masochism that isn't merely derived from sadism. His analysis works well for literary Masochism—rather better, in fact, than it does for the practices called masochistic. This inquiry, he says, "has led me to assign a peculiar position, based upon the origin of the instincts, to the pair of opposites constituted by sadism and masochism and to place them outside the class of the remaining 'perversions.' "[5]

In this piece Freud analyzes three forms of masochism: feminine, moral, and erotogenic, the last of which is at the root of the other two, which are properly variants upon it.[6] In defining primary (erotogenic) masochism, he returns to a notion from 1905's *Three Essays on the Theory of Sexuality*, to suggest that the polymorphously perverse character of infantile sexuality, within which any intense stimulus may be erotically stimulating, is the foundation of erotogenic masochism.[7] This explanation strikes him, however, as insufficient, and the work of *Beyond the Pleasure Principle* (1920) allows him to add the concept of instinctual fusion, critical to his later understanding of both sadism and masochism (briefly, instinctual fusion is the merging of erotic and death-oriented instincts into a single instinctual expression; lustful aggression is the most frequently used example). Just how this fusion occurs remains unclear; "We are entirely without any understanding of the physiological ways and means by which this subjugation of the death-instinct by the libido can be achieved."[8] (Note, though, that masochism *subjugates* the death drive: it is thus, however idiosyncratically, life-affirming. More precisely, it affirms life in refusing to oppose it to death, a very Bataillean move: "Humanity pursues two goals: one, the negative, is to preserve life [to avoid death], and the other, the

positive, is to increase the intensity of life. These two goals are not contradictory, but their intensity has never increased without danger."[9])

Freud hypothesizes that the original (*ursprünglichen*) erotogenic
masochism expresses the force of the death drive remaining bound
within the organism.[10] Here the death drive (in its pure unextrojected
form, as the organism's drive toward its own destruction) has become fused or infused with the erotic—necessary for any *expression*
of the death impulses, since by itself this drive is, as Freud points out
(and we have already seen) silent. That is, it never comes to expression unless it is already mixed with the erotic; its pure form is internal and destroys the organism itself. In moral masochism, in which
morality has become resexualized and the unconscious feeling of
guilt powerful,[11] this fusion may take an extreme form, such that
even suicide may become eroticized.[12]

Sade, as we have seen, attempts through a particular form of repetition the expression of these fused instincts. The accomplishment of
this expression in Masoch's work is altogether different, centering
not upon reason and infinity but upon act and image. The fusion of
the instincts permeates language as much as act, and here too we
must endeavor to take account of the sheer force of silence—a silence
not imposed from without, but already and violently active within,
now emphasizing not the subject's rationality but his (or just perhaps, her) affectivity and, especially, imagination.

suspension and repetition

> Don't be in too much of a hurry to conclude when it's a
> matter of pleasure.
>
> —Jacques Derrida, "Parergon"

The stifling boredom and numbness created by Sade's texts arise
from their repetitive and enumerative quality. Too much happens too
often, breeding not contempt but exhaustion. The boredom generated by Masoch's work, on the other hand, results from the fact that
practically nothing ever happens at all, leaving the reader in a constant and finally wearying state of suspense. We have already seen
that Sadistic apathy, consequent upon boredom, is essential to Sadistic pleasure. For Masoch, too, boredom has vital consequences (the
encouragement of masturbatory or coercive sexuality not, I must
suggest, among them). As Kaja Silverman notes, for Theodor Reik
this suspense is perhaps the single defining factor of masochism,

suggesting again that Reik's analysis may fit literature better than it does bodies. Silverman writes:

> The last of the qualities associated by Reik with moral masochism—suspense—would seem to be at the center of all forms of masochism, in addition to being one of the conditions out of which conventional subjectivity develops. [Though by which, as Silverman later notes, this subjectivity may also be shattered.] Reik rings some complex changes on this word, which he connects with uncertainty, dilatoriness, pleasurable and unpleasureable anticipation, apparent interminability, and—above all—excitation. Masochism exploits all these themes in one way or another because it always seeks to prolong preparatory detail and ritual at the expense of climax or consummation.[13]

This suspension becomes characteristic as well of a curious repetition. Freud remarks in the "Economic Problem in Masochism" that for the Masochist "the real situations are in fact only a kind of make-believe performance of the phantasies."[14] The phantasy in Masoch is fetishistic—imagistic and frozen. The *tableaux vivants* of Masoch's works, the elaborately described scenes in which so little occurs, are created only so that they may be re-created as still images, remade as still lives (*naturs morts*).

Sade, despite his fascination with well-formed buttocks and large penises, is no fetishist; his images pile on layer after layer of clinical description, but there is no *lingering* over them and no later return. (Indeed, Sadean activity may be designed to make return impossible; the more beautiful and desired the object, the greater the degree of its mutilation and annihilation, the more desperate the effort to mark it permanently.[15]) Sade's heroes merrily trot their large penises from one pair of well-formed buttocks to another; they do not go back. Aside from reminiscences such as those of the story-telling courtesans, designed to prompt future action, there is for Sade only a relentless pursuit of new and novel pleasures. The Sadistic text moves from word and image to repeated acts before its repetition as writing. Masoch's text, on the contrary, moves from act through writing to repeated image. Though it may well be that for Sade there is a fetishistic importance to the *setting* of Sadistic activity, even that, as Beauvoir claims, "the enactment of the erotic scene interested him more than the actual experience,"[16] it is still the en*act*ment of the scene that is critical.

In Masoch's work there occurs a sort of reversal of the Sadean movement from story to enactment. The reversal is not exact; Masoch moves from "actual" scenes (that is, scenes that are presented in the narrative as having occurred) not to further stories but to images. One might suppose that this insistence on images, invoking the gaze, would bring him closer to the analysis of pornography given by MacKinnon *et al.*—but the images turn out to be so insistently frozen that they *cannot* stimulate action without losing their power. This, I suspect, is no small part of their point.

Thus, for example, in *Venus in Furs* the gaze of the hero, Severin, alights on an image of himself and Wanda, the titular Venus, reflected in an ornate mirror: "My eyes alighted by chance on the massive mirror that hung opposite and I let out a cry: our reflections in its golden frame were like a picture of extraordinary beauty. It was so strange and so fantastic that I felt a deep pang of regret that its forms and colors would soon vanish like a cloud."[17] In fact, later in the novel this scene will be painted, fixed as an image, by a German painter helplessly in love with Wanda, who will also take with him a small portrait of Wanda painted in secret, having been, apparently, infected with this same desire to sustain and hold onto images. This sort of scene is common in Masoch's work; Deleuze notes that "the novels of Masoch display the most intense preoccupation with arrested movement; his scenes are frozen, as though photographed, stereotyped or painted."[18] This movement into stillness gives to Masochistic humiliation the same immortality as Sadistic violence—"In [Masoch's] view the plastic arts confer an eternal character on their subject because they suspend gestures and attitudes"[19] —a notion that echoes Nietzsche's view of the Apollonian arts, which include the arts of vision.[20]

In this Masochistic focus on the fixed image and arrested movement, we are given a crucial difference between the Sadean and Masochistic imaginations and forces of desire. Annie LeBrun writes in her commentary on Sade, "Such is Sade's discovery about the paths taken by desire: its persistence in the imagination depends on the extent to which it is rooted in concrete reality."[21] For Masoch this is reversed: concrete reality is insignificant except insofar as it provides images to which the fetishistic memory may return. Real scenes, as Freud suggests, are valued only as prototypes of images, dress rehearsals for phantasies; the persistence of the image itself is practically guaranteed. A Masochistic image, however, does acquire its persistence through its incarnation first as act (and the image in Masoch's texts is almost always described in act first); the relation of desire to the levels "reality" and "phantasy" is complex and clearly does not occur only in one direction or the other—instead it is such as to mix levels, to undermine our secure confidence in their distinction, to render pleasure oddly insubordinate to reality.

Sadism (in the sense of Sadeanism) is the wild repetition of reason, Masochism of imagination, each preoccupied with the death instinct, as fragmentation and as stillness. As the emphasis on images suggests, Masoch is an aesthete, and so too are his protagonists. Moreover, his is a very visual aesthetic. The sequentiality of process and change, the movement of hearing, kinaesthesis, and to some extent touch, the developing and unfolding of words or acts in life or literature, interests him only insofar as it can be stopped. Masoch places the fetishistic elements of his images next to, not after, one another, visually.[22] Like Nietzsche's ideal rhapsodist, at his greatest intensity the Masochistic hero is wholly illusion and delight in illusion, "hence the theatrical impression which is conveyed at the point where the masochist's feelings are at their deepest and his pain and sensation most intensely experienced."[23] This theatricality is an important effect of Masoch's language, heavily and melodramatically adjectival, imagistic rather than active, romantic rather than pornographic.

In Sadism repetition runs wild through discursive reason, annihilating not only others but consciousness itself, thus pleasure itself, though not necessarily its unconscious determinants. In Masochism the running wild of repetition occurs in the realm of the image, which is set, frozen and fetishized, constantly before the gaze of the enraptured Masochist. The libertine in Sade is only interested in phantasies because they provide material for acting out concretely (within the narrative frame); the hero in Masoch is only interested in concrete acts (again within this frame) because they provide scenes that can be frozen in the imagination. At the risk of pounding the point to death (a movement more appropriate to Sade), this reverses not only Sadism but the understanding of pornography as that which provides imaginative "blueprints" for sexual activity. We move not from the image to its enactment but from the act to its infinite suspension.

contractual fixation

> Quick, now, here, now, always.
>
> —T.S. Eliot, "Burnt Norton"

Unlike the Sadist, the Masochist is not interested in the destruction of limits; instead he is, perhaps inversely, fascinated by their destructiveness. Both forms of literary perversity are boundary play, but the ways in which boundaries are put to use are quite distinct. In fact, much of the activity (such as it is) of Masoch's novels, and apparently of his life as well, consists in the preparation and signing of *contracts*, by which everything is put into its place. Once signed, these contracts are not to be broken, whatever their results. In *Venus in Furs* Severin writes that Wanda "has drawn up a contract by which I am to commit myself on my honor to be her slave for as long as she wishes."[24] Similarly, a contract actually signed between Masoch and Fanny von Pistor (part of an affair that was apparently the basis for *Venus in Furs*) states that "on the occurrence of any misdemeanor or negligence or act of lèse majesté, the mistress (Fanny von Pistor) may punish her slave (Leopold von Sacher-Masoch) in whatever manner she pleases."[25] (She may, so to speak, put him in his place.) This contract had a six-month duration.

A similar contract between Masoch and his wife, Wanda (the former Aurore Rümelin, who renamed herself after Masoch's Venus), states that "I shall be allowed to exercise the greatest cruelty;" that "you shall be no more than my slave groveling in the dust;" and "should you ever find my domination unendurable and should your chains ever become too heavy, you will be obliged to kill yourself, for I will never set you free."[26] These contracts might seem to reinforce the view of Masochism as passive—but it is precisely the Masochist who insists upon them; the torturer or slave-owner must be talked into joining, and properly "educated" in her (for Masoch this role is always female) role—an education that may require some time and effort.

Thus it is in fact the Masochist's pleasure that the contract seeks to insure, and at his bidding. Wanda remarks to Severin that "if I now take pleasure in hurting and tormenting you, it is entirely your fault. You have made me what I am."[27] The Masochist secures his pleasure, fixes it in place as part of the scene set, by the contract. The Sadist's pleasure, on the contrary, arises in transgressing all social contracts, even those that are implicit. This pleasure of breaking limits reflects the Sadean pleasure of constant acceleration; Sacher-Masoch's pleasure in fixing the terms of the contract likewise reflects the pleasure of making things still.

The Masochistic, highly visual imagination wants everything fixed, set forward and visible. It has nothing of the urge to break and displace, which is so strong in the contrary impulses of the demonstrative reason of the Sadist. In this imaginative/ rational opposition we have the two movements of the force of the death drive: to make still and to break apart.[28] The movement in Masoch's texts is away from movement; in the fixed terms of the contract as in the fixed vision of the image we find a defiance of even narrative teleology.

frozen images

> . . . you stepped
> out of your clothes and brought your naked body
>   before the mirror, you let yourself inside
> down to your gaze; which stayed in front, immense . . .
> —Rainer Maria Rilke, "Requiem"

Although the phenomenon of instinctual fusion may be at work in the narratives of both Sade and Masoch, the expression and eroticization of the death drive occurs, as I have already indicated, altogether differently in the two cases.

In the Masochistic construction of images, as will be evident by now, we are also given the distinction between Sadean and Masochistic repetition. Deleuze explains the difference by noting that repetition is "a function of acceleration and condensation" for Sade, while for "Masoch it is characterized by the 'frozen' quality and the suspense."[29] This essential frozen quality of Masochism is, as it turns out, more than metaphorical. Masoch's heroes may be cold only in third-class railway cars or unheated hotel rooms, but his heroines are so chilled that they must be wrapped in furs and set before the fire—and even then they are inclined to sneeze.[30]

What is the point of all this freezing, assuming it is not some patriarchal desire to depict the feminine as fragile (and thus rather unsuited to the role of dominatrix)?[31] Part of freezing's role is to function as an eternal, or at least indefinite, postponement of climactic possibilities. It appears that Masoch has taken Freudian forepleasure (the pleasure that *anticipates* the release of tension) to its limit; he is engaged in infinite awaiting. ("Formally speaking," writes Deleuze, "masochism is a state of waiting; the masochist experiences waiting in its pure form.")[32] In this suspension, reality not only takes second place to phantasy, it is disavowed: "pleasure is postponed for as long as possible and is thus disavowed. The masochist is therefore able to deny the reality of pleasure at the very point of experiencing it . . . In Masoch's novels, it is the moments of suspense that are the climactic moments."[33] The suspense itself is the "aim" sought—once more short-circuiting any attempt to put the text to use in extratextual action. Again, we may contrast this to the pleasure of the Sadean libertine. For Sade, the climax, however delayed, is ultimately reached and is too soon over with, and his libertines respond by moving as quickly as possible to the next pleasure. Ultimately, Sadistic apathy negates affect altogether; Beauvoir remarks that Sade knows obsessive desire but not "emotional intoxication."[34] We might also note in a related connection a startling remark made by Linda Williams in her influential work *Hard Core*: "the erotic and the pornographic intersect in hard core. The one emphasizes desire, the other satisfaction."[35] If this is in fact a distinction between erotica and pornography, we shall have to label *Venus in Furs* almost purely erotic.

Like Sade, Masoch attributes coldness to his characters, but this is a different matter than it was for Sade. The coldness characteristic of the Masochistic ideal "is not the negation of feeling but rather the disavowal of sensuality."[36] Deleuze remarks that "sensuality is movement."[37] This plays upon one sense of sense, movement with a sense of direction. It plays as well upon our sense that the sensual is opposed to the frozen (or frigid), which is incapable of the movement that indicates bodily pleasure. Masochism's first direction seems antisensual: the negation of movement allows the fetishized image to be eternally preserved. Severin loves Wanda "as one can only love a woman who responds to one with a petrified smile, ever calm and unchanging. I adore her absolutely."[38] Any process that threatens too much movement must be halted. In fact, it often seems as if in Masoch's texts all processes are halted before they can get anywhere, or at least before they can be over with. Severin admits to this in himself: "Some people begin everything and finish nothing (*alles anfangen und doch nie etwas zu Ende bringen* [literally, never bring anything to an end]): I am one of those people."[39]

One might assume that finality would seem *desirable* from the Masochistic standpoint. After all, finality is the pleasure of death, whether *petit* or *grand*; what's more, it brings movement to a halt. But the Masochist doesn't just want no movement, as we shall see below. The postclimactic image is not fetishistically interesting. On the other hand, too much movement, of course, could undo the frozen suspense that defies climax; such possibilities are blotted out of the text and out of the hero's awareness. Thus, in this passage in which Things threaten to Happen, we do not know if anything does: "I tore off the ermine jacket and the lace and felt her naked bosom heaving against mine. Then I lost consciousness."[40] Hence the frustration and boredom of the reader (even of the reader who is not appalled by the Harlequin Romance prose)—nothing happens precisely because nothing must be allowed to happen, nothing must disturb the image. The desirable is the frozen.

This takes us back, as it happens, to the wide variance in Sadistic and Masochistic levels of violence. Sade attempts to maximize violence in both intensity and iteration, to be infinitely cruel again and again forever. Masoch's apparent violence is much more limited, echoing Freud's observation that even the phantasies of the masochist do not approach those of the sadist for brutality. In *Venus in Furs* we find the hero pricked with pins, whipped, and forced to take a third-class railway car (while his cruel mistress travels first-class). But we do not find violated virgins, roasted newborns, and involuntary amputations (as we do in Sade). Although Severin claims to phantasize about being tortured like the martyrs ("To endure horrible tortures seemed . . . the highest delight . . . Sensuality took on a sacred character.") Wanda is right in her claim that he would not in fact enjoy such things,[41] and because this is Masoch's novel and not Sade's, these phantasies are not described as being enacted.

The point is not merely to avoid climax. Were it so, the aim would be easily accomplished by avoiding, as much as possible, stimulation to either body or imagination, to any form of desire. This is the Stoic approach—do not indulge in unreasonable desires— taken one step further, to the denial or suppression of any desire at all. Masoch's characters, on the contrary, deliberately arouse their desires, and delight in this arousal (as, we recall, did Sade's), by recurring to their beloved images. They enjoy their own frustration—they are, again, at a significant remove from the thoughtless actors supposed by antipornographic theory, who cannot tolerate even the frustration of being told *no*.

This complication indicates that the point of Masoch's text is not merely a still point; its double sense is not *only* stillness but stillness *and* the movement that counters it. The image that is not or has not been real-ized has less power than the image of reality that has been frozen. (But the frozen image already includes the "actor," and is not a simple objectification of the characters imagined.) The already inanimate provides a singularly unexciting object for the death drive.

sensuality and movement

Desire itself is movement
Not in itself desirable;
Love is itself unmoving.

—T.S. Eliot, "Burnt Norton"

We can take this apparent contradiction further. Masochistic pleasure as countersensual, antimovement, might make sense, at least of a sort—it might be intelligible to good sense even if incomprehensible to most tastes. But Masoch has undone the possibility of this with his characters' account of themselves. Not only are they sensualists; they are self-described as "supersensual:" "the martyrs were supersensual beings who found positive pleasure even in pain and who sought horrible tortures, even death, as others seek enjoyment. I too am supersensual . . . ," Severin grandly declares, "just as they were."[42] The arousal that Severin experiences upon reading *The Lives of the Martyrs* appears to mirror an episode in Masoch's own life, recounted in "A Childhood Memory and Some Reflections on the Novel": "I would sit in a dark secluded corner of my great-aunt's house, devouring the legends of the Saints; I was plunged into a state of feverish excitement on reading about the torments suffered by the martyrs."[43]

In this same piece Masoch writes that "much later I isolated the problem that inspired the novel *Venus in Furs*. I became sure first of the mysterious affinity between cruelty and lust, and then of the natural enmity between the sexes which is temporarily overcome by love, only to reappear subsequently with elemental force, turning one of the partners into a hammer and the other into an anvil."[44] Although this realization may have been the germ of the novel, the actual cruelty therein is sufficiently complicated by delays, frozen movements, and by the necessity of oath and contract for it to suggest that far more than this "mysterious affinity" is at work—or at least that this affinity is far *more* mysterious than Masoch supposed.

What, then, is the pleasure-direction of sensuality? I have suggested that sensuality has some identity with movement itself. And indeed the Masochistic novel, which never gets anywhere, is nonetheless full of movement—but it is, invariably, movement that is quickly arrested. *Arrested movement*, though, is movement begun; it is not at all the same as a more lasting stillness. It would do Masoch's heroes no good simply to gaze at paintings and photographs, to kiss the cold feet of statues, or to read the *Lives of the Martyrs*, however much these may fire their imaginations. They must instead set into motion the images of these objects—*so that* they may be *frozen* into images. Literary Masochism is imagination's triumph over the "real," though as I have said the real as act also precedes the imaginary, as when the image of Severin and Wanda, itself echoing and freezing their action, is remade into a painting. The fascination of the *tableau vivant* is the tension between its stillness and its once and possible movement. Like the artist, the narrative Masochist moves between phantasy and reality, between image and act; the pleasure of Masochism needs both. The image that has never moved holds little more fascination than the act that is allowed to finish; the image that was never real represents no *triumph over* nonimaginative reality. It is the moment of *suspension* that is crucial here, meaning that both movement and stillness are essential. What *repeats*, however, is stillness and nonmovement (that is, the eternity of the fixed image), opposing, again, the repetition of Sadean pleasure, in which it is the act born out of the image that repeats.

Sade violently annihilates consciousness (and thus "self") by forcing destruction into the real, rational conscious world, forcing into consciousness what consciousness must find intolerable. Masoch's method is subtler but no less devastating: consciousness is not ripped apart but slowly *stopped*. Put at the service of the still image it is doubly negated: first by stillness (as still as death)[45] and second by its replacement by phantasy.

The Sadist renounces "normal" pleasure for both apathy and intensity. The new pleasure of Sadism follows upon repetition, depends upon it, instead of repetition following a previous pleasure. The Masochist renounces pleasure for waiting and watching, for the new pleasure of suspense and the fetishized image. Here, too, pleasure becomes dependent upon repetition: in this case the repetition of the image, not only as reiteration but as permanence or endurance. Deleuze notes, in pointing out the secondary importance of pain in both Sadism and Masochism, that "there is a kind of mysticism in perversion: the greater the renunciation, the greater and the more secure the gains."[46] This perverse is at an extreme remove from the greed for gratification. In mysticism itself renunciation takes on still stranger forms, as will be apparent in the discussion of asceticism.

In the literary eroticization of the death drive, then, we find the subversive potential of both language and eros, their power to defy the very limits they construct and the very unities they seek. I do not think that the importance of either Sade or Masoch is that of setting precedent for practice. In fact, theirs are not practicable pleasures; they are extraordinary instances of the power of language and the strangeness of narrative, and of the dual workings of violence as it turns within and against the language that struggles to frame it. That pleasure, even literary pleasure, can be more or other than gratification is an important and unsettling realization, and this defiance of gratification is one element that will resurface, though much altered, when we turn to the body. Sade and Masoch defy the powers of the subject, whether determined by rationality or imagination; thus they turn the reader's prurient pornographic pleasure to a self-destructive delight. In turning to the body in the discipline of asceticism, we find a still stranger defiance of both subjectivity and pleasure-as-satisfaction.

4

a s c e t i c i s m

seducing the divine

the lives of the saints

None of my sufferings has been equal to that of not having
suffered enough.

> —Blessed Margaret Mary Alacoque,
> cited in E. M. Cioran, *Tears and Saints*

Boundaries appear to be violated here—boundaries between spiritual and physical, male and female, self and
matter. There is something profoundly alien to modern
sensibilities about the role of the body in medieval piety.

> —Caroline Walker Bynum,
> *Fragmentation and Redemption*

The counterpleasures are pleasures of excess, which is to say pleasures of transgression. In being the pleasures of and in exceeding the
limits of reason or moderation, they are also pleasures that cross
what we thought were genuine boundaries.

Within this grouping of excessive pleasure, asceticism holds a
strange place—and a singular fascination for the philosophers of excess (particularly for Nietzsche and Bataille, both of whom see it as a
remarkably *savage* form of enjoyment). Asceticism would seem to be
the very opposite of excess, a defiance even of the more moderate demands of one's bodily and social selves, certainly a defiance of hedonistic extravagance. Yet it is in this *defiance* that we find not only the

pleasure of asceticism, but its *excessiveness*: it is a denial beyond all moderation.

It is with asceticism that we shall begin the turn toward practices and pleasures of the flesh. The particular fascination of asceticism is in no small part the tension between its ostensibly spiritual demands and its blatant physicality. I should note that I do not consider myself qualified to discuss non-Western asceticism, beyond noting the importance of its existence; the analysis here is largely Western and more specifically Christian. Christianity, however antisomatic its current manifestations, is in its origins a highly corporeal religion, with its foundations in the incarnation and bodily resurrection of its deity. Its early practice, too, is physical and worldly; as Peter Brown notes, "The [early] Christians looked to the earth alone. They claimed power from heaven; but they had made that heaven remote and they kept its power to themselves, to build up new separate institutions among upstart heroes on earth."[1]

Despite Masoch's devotion to tales of martyred saints, and even my remark that asceticism is a form of excess, the inclusion of religious asceticism in this context may be a bit unexpected, and the focus on Christianity still more so. In fact, one might reasonably expect Christian *opposition* to this inclusion—to putting the saints between pornographers and perverts, even if the pornography does fail and the perverts are often religious in their descriptive language. After all, most self-identified Good Christians are strongly opposed to pornography, and would impatiently dismiss any arguments regarding the subversion of pornographic intent in either Sade or Masoch. Such irrational, antisocial intensification; such multiplicity of partners; and most particularly such determined defiance of procreativity scarcely fit the program of contemporary Christianity. (In its construction of the erotic as the handmaiden of the procreative, contemporary Christianity lines up startlingly well with both Freudian biologism and capitalist culture—and even, as we shall see in the next discussion, with the feminist demand for equal time in gratification. Each presumes a measurable outcome and denies the delights of desire.) That a plausible interpretation might see the mannerisms and permutations of narrative structure as at least equal in importance to the events described is unlikely to sway those for whom those events are absolutely beyond the range of the acceptable, even in the realm of imaginative depiction. That perverse eroticism might be a contemporary manifestation of a sense of the sacred will not persuade those for whom the erotic is not to be valued on its own.

I am not going to argue that Christianity as it is usually conceived in the twentieth century is in fact transgressive, nor even that
the Catholicism of the Middle Ages, on which I focus here, was itself
transgressive, though that seems to me more nearly true. I intend instead a discussion of a transgression within the context of early and
more particularly medieval Christianity, which attitudinal shifts
within Christianity have rendered very unlikely today. This Christian asceticism merits discussion here for a number of reasons, which
should be addressed before I turn to the objections to ascetic practice
itself.

First, I've already noted that there is an evident strain of religious feeling, however variably permuted, in the other counterpleasures described. Sade's delighted atheism remains extremely
Catholic in sensibility; his "extremes" of perversion, reserved for the
culmination of the *120 Days*, entail the desecration of the Host, the
altar, in general the trappings of Catholicism—a perversity dependent for its intensity upon a lingering belief, without which it becomes at most an act of wedging bits of bread into noncustomary
orifices or performing sexual acts in unusual locations, neither of
which is particularly shocking. Masoch's devotion to the martyrs is
actually formative; the saints provide his first image of the joys possible in suffering. Contemporary sadomasochistic practice is, as I
shall argue, structurally more similar to religious asceticism than to
literary perversity. (Guy Baldwin, a twentieth-century s/m practi-
tioner, provides a wry commentary on a similarly formative experience: "Christ was reportedly a guy who was a sensitive renegade, set
himself up to be on the receiving end of some very serious suffering,
and taught that submission to a higher authority was the key to salvation. Who could be surprised that I turned out to be a lifelong gay
sadomasochist with Christ as my role model?")[2]

There are frequent elements of religiosity in collections of both
essays and fiction on sadomasochism. In fact, there are works made
up entirely of such religiously oriented texts, such as the fiction and
essay collection *Ritual Sex*[3] or the in-progress, Pat Califia-edited collection *The Crook and the Flail*.[4] These attest to the strength of the alliance between erotic and ascetic, with considerable use of Catholic
imagery[5] of martyrdom, crucifixion, even transubstantiation—and
popular mythology has it that half of any leather gathering will be
lapsed Catholics.[6]

This imagistic, ritualized character of Catholic practice, the precision and rigidity of its hierarchy, and the implicit transgressivity of

transubstantiation (which not only re-materializes the divine but presents God for human consumption) all play into the more explicitly perverse, precisely by giving us boundaries. Contemporary Catholicism, having absorbed much of the sociable reasonableness of Protestantism and avowing the "resurrection of the Spirit" rather than of the flesh, is no longer friendly to the pleasures of asceticism, and indeed as I shall note the Catholic Church was never entirely secure in their disruptive presence.

The movement away from the carnal, an important development in Christianity, is at the same time a strengthening of Christian antifeminism, the ground of much feminist criticism of Christianity, as Morny Joy notes in her response to Margaret Miles's intriguing interpretation of Augustine:

> For it is all too apparent that a social devaluation of the body has accompanied the exclusion or oppression of women. At the root of these discriminatory attitudes is a binary system, endemic to Western philosophy/theology, that has associated men, and things qualified as male, with the superior state of spirituality or rationality. At the heart of this system is what Elizabeth Grosz has termed "a profound somatophobia."[7]

Arthur Mielke, in *Christians, Feminists and the Culture of Pornography*, notes several voices in this tradition: "[Mary Jo] Weaver's assertion that Christian tradition from the Patristic period onward is 'full of scorn for women' (70) is echoed in a *Christian Century* article by scholar of religion Mary Ellen Ross who contended that many Christian thinkers (like pornographers) have 'contempt' for women and for 'human physicality' (1990, 246)."[8] The objections to asceticism, then, are divergent. Contemporary Christianity dismisses it as both pathological and, more implicitly, oversomatic. Feminist thought not necessarily sympathetic to Christianity sees it as one more mode of oppressing the body with which "woman"—often through Christian philosophy and theology—has been identified.

It is tempting to see asceticism, as it was to see literary Sadism and Masochism, as a manifestation of this "somatophobia" and thus as implicitly misogynistic. On the surface, it plays exceptionally well into an antisomatic strain, the turn away from the pleasures of the flesh. Asceticism, tending to weaken the flesh as well as defying its wants, should keep or should have kept good Christians in line. What is it doing among a list of transgressive, defiant delights? Isn't it in fact the extreme of internalized oppression? Isn't it, as Susan Griffin argues, a prior form of obscenity?[9]

An answer requires not only the work I have tried to do in the following analysis of asceticism, but a bit of history as well. History requires sources, of whom Caroline Walker Bynum strikes me as one of the most interesting. In both *Fragmentation and Redemption* and *The Resurrection of the Body*, Bynum notes the prominence of women in the rosters of ascetics. This, of course, might be an internalization of the Church's rather unfortunate official attitudes toward women, a turn against their bodies. And since women were associated with body and nature, men with intellect and spirit, this turn would be more likely in women's case. In fact, though, this practice asserts the presence of the body in the space of the sacred.

Here I should reemphasize that early and medieval Christianity remained resolutely incarnational in focus.[10] The incarnation is, after all, the formative fact or fiction of Christianity, and the resurrection of the flesh its promised salvation. This carnal emphasis remained, to a considerable extent, until the fourteenth century:[11] "No mainstream theologian of the late Middle Ages denied the doctrine of bodily resurrection. None . . . denied that, under normal circumstances, God will reassemble and reanimate at the end of time the same material particles (*eadem in numero*) of which body was composed on earth."[12] The British theologian Rosemary Haughton emphasizes this peculiarity of Christianity: "Christianity is, far more than any other, a physical religion, which is one reason why many spiritually minded people find it gross and fleshly, and try to refine and 'spiritualize' it. But it is inescapably 'fleshly,' being founded in the human flesh of . . . Christ."[13]

It is this emphasis on the fleshness of Christ and the salvation of the body that marks the piety of medieval women: "To [medieval women], humanity was, as Mechtild of Hackeborn said, the 'Word made flesh.' Behind medieval women's concern with physicality lay the doctrine of the Incarnation."[14] Asceticism is to some extent an imitative bond with the suffering of the embodied god; there must be some connection between the physicality of the divine (as incarnation) and of salvation, and the physicality of religious practice in asceticism. But that suffering is to be taken seriously; asceticism is powerful, empowering, and still unquestionably violent.

Again, I see a movement of transgression by intensification: it is the intensification of the element of physicality in practice that undermines the order of the Church and in fact the orders of sacred and profane. But we should explore a bit further the frequently feminine character of asceticism, as again the strongest arguments against it may be feminist: that is, that Christianity itself is patriarchally oppressive and that its antisomatism is an instance of this, exemplified in asceticism. It matters how ascetic women saw themselves, as well as whether we can, from across the centuries, theorize their pleasure as transgressive.

We find early examples of asceticism among men—some quite well known, such as the famous Egyptian hermit Antony, or the incalculably influential North African Augustine. As Bynum notes, theirs is not, despite their condemnation of carnal temptation, a thoroughgoing rejection of the body. The real question that such figures raise is itself transgressive:

> Why . . . did some fierce ascetics, such as Jerome and, in his own way, Augustine, strain to lift every organ and particle into the crystalline hardness of heaven? Why did propaganda for the monastic movement sometimes insist (as Athanasius did in his *Life of Antony*) that "this body" shall rise, or argue (as did John Climacus) that we become incorruptible already in this life if we keep ourselves pure and glorify God? Why bring heaven so close to earth?[15]

Margaret Miles picks up on this transgression in emphasizing the eroticism of Augustinian spirituality:

> And it is difficult . . . to imagine pleasure that is both intense and permanent. The senses fatigue; they cannot sustain a receptive sensitivity to any stimulus for very long. But what Augustine wants is sensual experience that remains—or is continually renewed at optimal excitement.[16]

This is the aim of asceticism as well—the refusal of finitude, exhaustion, and limit—*all through the body*. Which is, of course, impossible.

Despite these early instances, Christian asceticism reaches its high point later (in the mid- to late Middle Ages) and among women. This does not follow or accompany an intensification of women's subordination. Indeed positive images of women, devotion to the Virgin, and the canonization of women saints all increase noticeably around the same time.[17] Importantly for asceticism, the connection between women and body also becomes more pronounced at this time:

> Compared to other periods of Christian history and other
> world religions, medieval spirituality—especially female
> spirituality—was peculiarly bodily; this was so not only
> because medieval assumptions associated female with
> flesh but also because theology and natural philosophy
> saw persons as, in some real sense, body as well as soul.[18]

It would be absurd to deny that women in Christianity were repressed and marginalized in the Middle Ages (as Bynum also
notes).[19] But asceticism, far from playing into this oppression, pulls
against it precisely by appearing to embrace it: "We must not forget
how profoundly asceticism . . . rejected the gender and class inequalities of secular society."[20] Asceticism was a way to take an un-
blameable and yet defiant action. I shall attempt to show the
movement of ascetic delight, the way in which it intensifies bodily
experience to transgress the boundary between physical and spiritual—which echoes, after all, the transgression at the origin of Christianity, the puzzle of the incarnation. This imitation, as we shall see,
poses its own temptations, and their resistance its own peculiar
reward.

I would situate this practice outside those criticisms commonly
made of it, then, because of its historical position and because of the
role it plays in strengthening many who practice it. Once more I must
caution that in this dis- or replacement I do not wish to normalize asceticism. It is indeed violent; it too has its infusion of fascination with
death. It is, as I shall suggest, arrogant and at times peculiarly inhu-
man. We cannot value it *despite* these elements, as they are in fact intrinsic to it. In fact, though, we find fewer criticisms of asceticism
than of other counterpleasures. Asceticism occupies a curious cultural place for us, I think; we still half-incline toward the traditional
respect for its discipline, but increasingly regard its excesses as
pathological. Asceticism seems to have become increasingly pathol-
ogized as our emphasis on *gratification* as morally, politically, psy-
chologically, and even biologically correct has strengthened.
Asceticism, of all the counterpleasures, is most spectacularly ill-
suited to consumer culture.

As I have already hinted, this increasing pathologization is strikingly apparent in the attitudinal progression of Catholicism, a traditional stronghold of ascetic practice. While ascetic extremes have
long created unease in Church officials—not everyone can easily celebrate starving saints, who may also be directly defiant of ecclesias-

tic hierarchies—it is only recently that the Church has turned its official frown to asceticism more generally. Ascetic practices once endorsed by such pillars of the faith as St. Ignatius Loyola (founder of the Jesuit order, who in his famous *Spiritual Exercises* advocates external over internal self-inflicted damage, as it is more readily controlled), are now permitted only by such extremely conservative holdouts as the right-wing group Opus Dei (and there in degrees that would strike the medievals as mild).

Asceticism is too profound to be done justice by either pathologizing or normalizing. If it is a strangely archaic bodily practice, that is more because of its social place and professed goals—the mortification and denial of the flesh, the attainment of heaven on earth (as transgressive or boundary-breaking an aim, incidentally, as one could imagine)—than because of its behavioral conduct. In fact, in some ascetic behaviors, such as flagellation (sometimes in bondage) and the use of fire, we see early signs of practices now given a more erotic spin. This is not to *reduce* either ascetic or sadomasochistic practice to the other. It is, rather, to show a commonality of transgression in the flesh.

ascetic pleasure and popular opinion

> I have not said that everything is bad, but that everything is dangerous, which is not exactly the same thing as bad.
>
> —Michel Foucault

> *Et ne nos inducas in tentationem, sed libera nos a malo.*
>
> —Pater noster

Asceticism is often treated as a subsidiary form of extraliterary masochism—a pleasure taken in the pain of self-denial. Freud seems to have had his doubts about this identity, but places ascetic practices, though tentatively, within the category of moral masochism.

> One is much tempted, in explaining this attitude, to leave the libido out of account and to confine oneself to the assumption that there the instinct of destruction is again turned inward and is now raging against the self; yet there should be some meaning in the usage of speech, which has not ceased to connect this norm of behaviour in life with eroticism and calls these maimers of themselves [*Selbstbeschädiger*] masochists too.[21]

Pronounced asceticism is indeed marked by a *raging* destructive urge, at a level of rage that seems closer to Sade's heroes than to the relatively formal rage of Masoch's contractually obligated dominatrices. Its transgressive aspects, too, seem counter to masochism's fixation on fixity. The search for "divine life," Bataille tells us, "requires that the seeker after it shall die."[22] But the rage at limitation is an affirmation of a world beyond limit, and divine *life* is a mode of life, after all.

The evident pleasure of asceticism is less quickly described than that of the narratives of Sadism or Masochism. It has two distinct (though hardly unrelated) facets, one entailing the forgoing of ordinary pleasures (self-denial), the second entailing the deliberate self-infliction of pain and of bodily damage, which may be considerable (self-injury or self-mutilation). This divergence is more apparent than real; ascetic self-denial often yields damage and considerable pain.

As I've remarked, asceticism's reputation is quite different from that of sadism or masochism, either practical or literary. Unlike those practices, it is explicitly associated with *religious* tradition. The most famous Western ascetics are probably the Catholic saints, and certain Eastern traditions (perhaps most notably Hinduism and Jainism) value ascetic privation as an activity of considerable spiritual worth. A secondary association links the ascetic and the *intellectual*; it is considered at least odd to be both rigorously intellectual and sensuously indulgent. (It is perhaps not irrelevant to remark in this context that one of the symbols of St. Antony is the book.) Freud remarked that intellectual power may be strengthened by sexual abstinence, which may reflect this link. In line with these associations, the ascetic is regarded not as a pervert but as an admirably disciplined individual. In the classical Christian understanding the ascetic aim is perceived not as deviant (*mis*directed) but as sublimated (*re*directed).

The most obvious distinction between asceticism and any understanding of sadism or masochism is simply the fact that while the masochist enjoys being hurt by another and the sadist enjoys hurting others (a vast oversimplification, of course, in both cases), the ascetic's damage is almost always self-inflicted. In this difference many of the transgressive modes of Sade and Masoch are eliminated. No contractual alliance is drawn in asceticism, although there may be a sense of bargaining or trade: the pleasures of the body, say, for the immortality of the soul (actually, again, it is never so simple). Nor does ascetic practice parallel Sadean antisocial transgression, though it may undermine the authority of social institutions—consider the example of the hunger strike, or the remarkable ability of women such as St. Teresa of Avila or St. Catherine of Siena to bend the masculine hierarchy of the Church to their wills.[23]

Though it often produces vivid images—one need only think of St. Teresa, virgin and sculptural inspiration—asceticism is not essentially imagistic in Masoch's frozen sense. That is, it does not set up and recur to scenes by moving from real to phantastic. Though certain ascetic *behaviors* are fetishistically repeated, they are repeated on the same plane, as acts. The ascetic is closer to Sade's proud sovereign, who embraces even his own pain without bending, than to Masoch's submissive protagonist, who demands to be humiliated and delights in flinching before the whip—even though humility is a constant quest for the religious ascetic. As Deleuze points out, the Sadist may enjoy receiving pain and the Masochist may enjoy inflicting pain—but this does not reverse their roles. The two perversions are structurally dissimilar. Sade's efforts are always accelerative, while Masoch works to freeze and suspend. Asceticism is action and not image; ascetic *pride* is key. To receive pleasure from one's own pain is undoubtedly perverse (by which label I would celebrate rather than condemn), but not essentially Masochistic in the sense to which Masoch properly lends his name. Recall as well that Masochism can exist without algolagnia, and that we must be careful about lumping together all practices of pain.

ascetic practice

> Put briefly: perhaps the entire evolution of the spirit is a
> question of the body; it is the history of the development
> of a higher body that emerges into our sensibility. The or-
> ganic is rising to yet higher levels.
>
> —Friedrich Nietzsche, *The Will to Power*

The various forms of bodily mutilation practiced by early Christian and medieval saints indicate much more than self-denial at work. In some cases, ascetic extremes seem to be instances of self-denial carried into the realm of self-injury. This is notably so in ascetic sleep- and food-deprivation; the deprivation that is celibacy strikes us, in general, as less extreme, even when abstinence is taken as far as possible. Athanasius writes in his protohagiographic *Life of St. Antony* that Antony "ate once daily, after sunset, but there were times when he received food every second and even every fourth day. . . . A rush mat was sufficient to him for sleeping, but more regularly he lay on the bare ground."[24] St. Catherine of Siena, who seems to have fasted to death, is also recorded as having slept "as little as 30 minutes every two days."[25] Feats of starvation and sleep-deprivation are common in hagiographic literature, where they illustrate the saints' spiritual strength against worldly pleasure, even pleasure so moderate as that of food or sleep. It is interesting to note that in at least some cases the saintliness of such activity is in doubt. Catherine's family and her confessor both "suspected a diabolic trick" in her self-starvation.[26] Sister Veronica Giuliani, "in her lifetime . . . never had the satisfaction of full acceptance by her worldly brothers and sisters that she was in God's grace and not an agent of Satan."[27] Such stories seem to be common.

Ascetic practice becomes more startling when it goes beyond self-denial—even extreme forms thereof—into self-mutilation. The hair shirt is a popular and relatively mild form of self-damage, worn by ascetic saints from Antony onward.[28] Equally popular, less mild, and more dramatic than the wearing of hair shirts is the practice of flagellation. Unlike masochistic flagellation—also, of course, very common—asceticism generally involves beating *oneself*, often even in secret. The witness whose gaze would fix the image is missing. (There are cases, such as that of Mary Magdalen de' Pazzi, of ascetics who also engage in whipping and being whipped by others. Such instances seem to be relatively rare, however, and may indicate a different kind of admixture of sadistic or masochistic elements within the ascetic practice, another direction taken by the fused instincts.)

Several cases of self-flagellation are quite dramatic; a few examples may serve to give a sense of this. St. Catherine is reputed to have done more than fast and stay awake: "Three times a day she flagellated herself with an iron chain . . . each beating lasted for one and one-half hours and blood ran from her shoulders to her feet."[29] Benvenuta is also reputed to have beaten herself thrice daily, "anchoring the chain around her hips and then whipping her back."[30] Many more, similar, cases are available.[31] The solitude, or at a minimum the isolating self-infliction, of this beating distinguishes it from the occasional scenes of flagellation in Sade. Even the triumphant libertine being beaten, who shares the arrogance of the ascetic, requires an outraged audience and a wielder of the whip. The Masochistic protagonist likewise needs an other, a dominatrix (the lack of the masculine form is revealing) under contract, a sense of humiliation with its triumph in paradox. The triumph of asceticism is every bit as paradoxical, but quite different.

Among female ascetics in particular, there appears a practice of binding the body with cords, ropes, or bands of metal that cut into the skin.[32] Other practices include the overcoming of profound revulsion, as in the kissing of lepers' sores or the famous story of St. Catherine: "While dressing the cancerous breast sores of a woman she was tending, Catherine felt repulsed at the horrid odor of suppuration. Determined to overcome all bodily sensation, she gathered the pus into a ladle and drank it all. That night she envisioned Jesus inviting her to drink the blood flowing from his pierced side."[33]

Two points here suggest a closer affinity to Sade than to Masoch. The first is the overcoming of disgust and its parallel to Sadean copraphagia, common practice in Sade's work among both Sadists and their victims. The second is the frequent need to leave marks on the body, even if no one sees them—to gouge or rip, to scar, to starve, to deform and defy the flesh. (In both cases permanence is desired, permanence and visibility, a history of defiance written on the flesh.) It seems that common language, despite Freud's deferral, is a poor guide here, fooled by the superficial similarity (of pleasure in receiving pain) into referring to self-mutilation and self-denial as forms of masochism. The contractual and imagistic nature of Masochism is not apparent in ascetic practice, even though the ascetic saints have proven a useful image-source for both literary and practicing masochists. (Nor, despite the parallels, would we want to reduce asceticism to some kind of self-directed Sadism.)

In self-mutilation or self-destruction there is a tremendous and irrational *expenditure,* an expenditure of oneself—since, as Bataille writes, "mystical and ecstatic states ([though they] don't entail moral or material ruin) can't do without certain extremes against the self."[34] This sacrifice may constitute the sacred in more than just etymological terms: "From the very first, it appears that sacred things are constituted by an operation of loss."[35] A contemporary (1987) psychiatric account notes that "the claims of some mentally ill self-mutilators that they are gods or godly agents become more understandable in light of the interconnectedness of religious sentiments and the concept of sacrifice and the sacred, violence, and suffering."[36] Such secular practices, too, tend to gouge and mark; burning and slicing the skin are most common, while extremes include ocular enucleation.

Even having seen these instances of asceticism, it is relatively difficult to grasp the movement of ascetic pleasure, because asceticism is explicitly opposed to both pleasure and desire. The first pleasure of asceticism, however, depends upon desire: the ascetic in fact courts temptation.

desire and temptation

Lord, give me chastity and continence, but not just yet.

—Augustine, *Confessions*

"The saint," Bataille writes in *Erotism*, "is not after efficiency. He is prompted by desire and desire alone and in this resembles the erotic man."[37] Geoffrey Galt Harpham suggests that "asceticism does not exclude desire, it complicates it; it proposes gratifications which are represented as both 'anti-desire' and yet (and for this reason) more desirable than desire because they do not insult the conscience."[38] The matter is, I believe, more complicated than that, more complicated even than is indicated by his later remark, "temptation . . . may be 'courted' as a way of burning off impurities, enabling the ascetic to 'take cognizance' of desire without approving it,"[39] although this may get closer to the heart of the matter. Asceticism is a pursuit of pleasure as much as Sadism or Masochism. The ascetic may ask not to be led into temptation, but the ascetic desire for desire, and for tempting objects of desire, is strong. Antony untroubled in the desert would scarcely have inspired Athanasius, let alone Flaubert; Antony is famously *tempted*: "Once again the enemy cast before him the softness of pleasure, but he, angered and saddened . . . pondered the threat of the force of judgment and the worm's work, and setting these in opposition, he passed through these tests unharmed."[40]

Perhaps the most vivid recognition of ascetic paradoxicality appears in Friedrich Nietzsche's ambivalence toward asceticism.[41] Nietzsche recognizes the movement between the desire for desire—the desire to be tempted in order to overcome (here we recognize boundary-play again)—and the desire for peace—freedom from desire—in asceticism, in a number of remarkable passages. The saint, he says, "takes pleasure in the wild uprising of his desires."[42] Her actions are driven in no small part by cruelty: "There is also an abundant, over-abundant enjoyment (*Genuss*) at one's own suffering, at making oneself suffer—and wherever man allows himself to be persuaded to self-denial in the *religious* sense—to self-mutilation, as among Phoenicians and ascetics . . . he is secretly lured and pushed forward by his cruelty, by those dangerous thrills (*gefährlichen Schauder*) of cruelty turned *against oneself.*"[43] Here desire works for and against itself, taking pleasure in its increase—the pleasure we might call, with Freud, voluptuousness (*Wollust*)—and pleasure in its own violent denial—the pleasure one would call cruelty.

Startlingly, we also find in asceticism—pure, chaste asceticism—the paradox of Eros, the movement between desire's furtherance and its cessation, taken to violent extremes, with satisfaction removed from the picture. The ascetic does not merely *resemble* the erotic but takes erotic pleasure to a one-sided extreme. Unlike Freud's "normal" Eros, in which voluptuousness always takes second place to release,[44] asceticism makes explicit its violence against desire *and* satisfaction. This violence extends beyond the *desire* to take in the *desirable* as well. Instances abound. St. Margaret "was dismayed that her hard mortifications were not destroying her natural beauty as rapidly as she wished, and so she went to [her confessor] and said, 'have pity and allow me to redouble my rampage against this odious body.' "[45] (Her confessor, however, denied her request to be allowed to slice her face with a razor.) Eustochia of Messina, to "counter her natural beauty . . . burned her face at the oven and discolored her skin with herbs."[46]

The ascetic courts temptation and raises desire *in order to* do violence against it. Only a very strong temptation is a worthy opponent for the ferocious ascetic will. Thus the ascetic will starve to overcome the will to eat, forgo sleep to overcome the body's demand for rest, indulge in pain to overcome the urge for peace. In Freud's terms, the ascetic saint is a twisted erotic; in Nietzsche's a twisted artist, inspiring a similar respect:

> So far the most powerful human beings have still bowed worshipfully before the saint as the riddle of self-conquest and deliberate self-renunciation. Why did they bow? In him—and as it were behind the question mark of his fragile and miserable appearance—they sensed the superior force that sought to test itself in such a conquest, the strength of the will in which they recognized and honored their own strength and delight in dominion (*herrschaftliche Lust*).[47]

There is quite a peculiar delight in strength among these saints, so many of them characterized as being of the weaker sex.

Whereas Freud sees forepleasure, the pleasure of voluptuous-ness, anticipation, waiting, as anticipatory pleasure at the impending release of tension, in asceticism the role of desire as "forepleasure" is quite changed. Ascetic desire is built up only as a preliminary to, even an excuse for, the pleasure of pain. This may take the form either of a violent refusal of satisfaction or of a self-mutilatory punishment for the desire itself, but it remains the case that desire is sought and deliberately intensified, as the only suitable obstacle for the overcoming ascetic will. The desire is for desire to turn against desire.

In other respects, along other axes, asceticism proves to be equally paradoxical.

humility and arrogance

Perhaps this was everything: thus to kneel . . . :
to kneel: and thereby hold one's own
outward-willing contours tightly reined
                        —Rainer Maria Rilke, "The Donor"

Ostensibly, the saint strives through asceticism to break her will and pride, to engender humility. Once more, we have an appearance of fit with the criticisms of Christianity, which see objectification or subjection of women as an aim. And once again we must note that the complexities of the matter turn our conclusions in quite another direction. Harpham notes that the ascetic "discipline of the essential self is always defined as a quest for a goal that cannot and must not be reached"—worthiness to identify with the suffering Christ.[48] This humility is supposed to follow upon the perception of one's own unworthiness—one's weakness and sinfulness. Thus St. Catherine, for whom the destruction of self-will is essential,[49] relates what Christ has told her: "Those who go the way of great self-contempt are, it is true, more apt to reach perfection than the others. Both will reach it if they exert themselves, but the former will get there sooner."[50]

The soul, as Christ also tells Catherine, must recognize the weakness of the human will: "At no time does the soul know herself so well, if I am within her, as when she is most beleaguered. Why? I will tell you. She knows herself well when she finds herself besieged and can neither free herself nor resist being captured. Yes, she can resist with her will to the point of not giving her consent, but that is all. *Then* she can know that she is nothing."[51] Even where the ascetic will seems to have triumphed over the body, victory and triumph properly belong to God, as in Antony's case: "Working with Antony was the Lord, who bore flesh for us, and gave to the body the victory over the devil, so that each of those who truly struggle can say, It is *not I, but the grace of God which is in me.*"[52] The paradox is evident: it will take great strength of will to make the will into nothing, to deny one's own strength in its very use, to give to the vehicle of temptation victory over temptation itself.

What the recognition of one's own weakness engenders is often contempt, what Nietzsche calls *spernere se sperni* (rendered by Kaufmann as "scorn of one's being scorned").[53] St. Catherine urges "holy hatred" of oneself. St. Dominica vows that "hatred of myself . . . will be my way of fleeing from sin," and prays "Oh God, teach me to hate my body and despise myself. Give me your love, and my hatred."[54] The violence is real—and the love, as I shall argue in my final chapter, is not separable from it.

In fact, as Nietzsche writes of the ascetic philosopher, "he does *not* deny 'existence,' he rather affirms *his* existence and *only* his existence."[55] He adds in *Human, All-Too Human* that "this shattering of oneself, this scorn for one's own nature . . . which religions have made so much out of, is actually a very high degree of vanity . . . Man takes a truly voluptuous pleasure in violating himself by exaggerated demands and then deifying this something in him that is so tyranically taxing."[56] Indeed, the arrogance of asceticism is conspicuous. To drive oneself past all human limits is an odd form of humility; the humble accept limits and move reasonably and moderately within them. Ostensibly the ascetic saint places all faith and power in God, echoing Christ's "Let not my will, but thine, be done," and adding the line addressed to Christ: "Lord, I am not worthy to receive you"—but, the ascetic silently adds, *I shall become so*—shall attain this impossible and forbidden value. The ascetic submission before the divine will is in fact a direct challenge to that will, a merciless seduction that will make it impossible for the divine to absent itself. It is undoubtedly this challenging will, which sets itself an impossible overcoming, that draws Nietzsche's sometimes grudging admiration. In its denial of carnal pleasure and its attraction to the seductiveness of death, asceticism draws his condemnation; as an extraordinary self-overcoming, his regard.

Only a vast immodesty can lead one to undertake the discipline of asceticism, which may even include the desire to atone, Christlike, for *others'* sins (consider the flagellant sects of the plague years). The self-discipline entailed is exceptional: Bataille notes, "I have said that discipline, committing us to the ways of work as it does, moves us away from the experience of extremes. Agreed, at least in a general sense, but this experience has its own discipline."[57] This discipline is not less but *more* rigorous than that of the "ways of work." Only arrogance presumes to lead a life no body can withstand. Bataille remarks upon the ultimate founding sacrifice at Christianity's beginning: "The success of Christianity must be explained by the value of the theme of the Son of God's ignominious crucifixion, which carries human dread to a representation of loss and limitless degradation."[58] The ascetic sacrifice does in fact presume to echo that originary sacrifice, that identity that "cannot and must not be reached."

Ascetic arrogance is not, however, unfounded; ascetic humility is not unreal. The hatred of the weak and sinful self, and especially the body, which one *is*, is real—the measures taken against it are evidence of that. The sense of unworthiness driving these extreme measures is undoubtedly just as real. The arrogance of overcoming that unworthiness is as evident to the ascetic as it is to us—hence the insistent need to drive oneself to further humility. The ascetic goes the Sadean libertine one better by pursuing desperately a goal which is not merely *impossible* but is in fact *forbidden* as a goal, and is thus demanded and prohibited at once.

As I have suggested, one might, in Nietzschean terms, call the ascetic a twisted artist, and the ascetic pleasure is the pleasure of the artist, a pleasure in transformation, an arrogance that expresses a will so absolutely set upon its goal that arrogance no longer seems the right term, a goal so impossible that to pursue it takes arrogance and humility in their extreme forms at once—a goal that it is impossible for the ascetic not to pursue. This notably powerful will seeks out obstacles to humble itself—obstacles that somehow never quite break it. Like the artist who finds utter freedom in submission to capricious rules,[59] the ascetic has the presumptuousness to take the path that she sees as utterly necessary—at once impossible and unavoidable.

power and death

> You're not willing to lose yourself. You will have to come on your own account. From anguish you derived pleasures so great—they shook you from head to toe.
>
> —Georges Bataille, "A Story of Rats"

Not all cruelty, even against oneself, is unequivocal negation. In the same passage in which Nietzsche refers to the "overabundant enjoyment" of asceticism, he remarks that "even the seeker after knowledge forces his spirit to recognize things against the wishes of his heart . . . and thus acts as an artist and transfigurer of cruelty. Indeed, any insistence on profundity and thoroughness is a violation, a drive to hurt the basic will of the spirit which unceasingly strives for the apparent and superficial."[60] (Here we see another possible ground for the ascetic-intellectual pairing.) The discipline of self-overcoming, of which I have already spoken, is carried in asceticism to a perverse extreme, overcoming even life where it stands in the way of the will.

Asceticism might seem to be the most defiant no one could imagine—a no to pleasure as satisfaction, a deliberate defiance of desire even in the pleasure of its increase, a renunciation of society and companionship, of comfort, finally of life. But behind this is the yes that arrogance and defiance suggest: "Assenting to life even in death is a challenge to death, in emotional eroticism as well as physical, a challenge to death through indifference to death."[61]

This is the deepest paradox of asceticism, subsuming those of arrogant humility and voluptuous self-denial. The instinctual fusion occurs at so basic a level that even the term "fusion" seems to lend life and death too much independence.

Nietzsche, almost startlingly in the face of his general antiascetic tirade, is quite clear about this. The ascetic ideal struggles, against itself, for life's preservation: "The No [the ascetic] says to life brings to light, as if by magic, an abundance of tender Yeses; even when he *wounds* himself, this master of destruction, of self-destruction—the very wound itself afterward compels him *to live*."[62] Bataille claims that "in principle the means are always double. On the one hand, one appeals to the excess of forces, to movements of intoxication, of desire. And on the other hand, in order to have at one's disposal a quantity of forces, one mutilates oneself (through ascesis)."[63]

The ascetic will is, as I have remarked, extraordinarily powerful; it is ultimately tragic—in the highest and strongest sense of tragedy, the pleasure of pain and discord. Again, I quote Nietzsche at some length:

> For an ascetic life is a self-contradiction: here rules a *ressentiment* without equal, that of an insatiable instinct and power-will that wants to become master not over something in life but over life itself, over its most pro-

found, powerful and basic conditions; here an attempt is made to employ force to block up the wells of force; here physiological well-being itself is viewed askance . . . while pleasure is felt and *sought* in ill-constitutedness, decay, pain [*Schmerz*], mischance, ugliness, voluntary deprivation, self-mortification, self-flagellation, self-sacrifice . . . we stand before a discord that *wants* to be discordant, that *enjoys* itself in this suffering and even grows more self-confident and triumphant the more its own presupposition, its physiological capacity for life, *decreases*.[64]

An oddly concordant discordance, this. This triumphant will holding on to a whole cluster of contradictions is oddly like that of the strong, proud, classical type, the Nietzschean noble ideal.[65] The ascetic will, however, is unified *against* the very conditions of its own *possibility*, turning its strength against all that ordinarily constitutes life. In asceticism we again find ourselves up against the pronounced difference between unpleasure (*Unlust* to both Freud and Nietzsche) and pain (*Schmerz*) that may be exceptionally pleasurable. Saint Teresa provides us with a number of vivid descriptions of this possibility: "from the deeper enjoyment of that blessing which gave her such sweet pain, she complained of it to God. She would gladly have cut herself to pieces, body and soul, to show the joy that she felt in that pain."[66] One of the most famous passages in mystical literature occurs in Teresa's chapter in which "She Embraces Her Pain":

It was our Lord's will that I should see this angel in the following way. He was not tall but short, and very beautiful; and his face was so aflame that he appeared to be one of the highest rank of angels, who seem to be all on fire . . . In his hands I saw a great golden spear, and at the iron tip there appeared to be a point of fire. This he plunged into my heart several times so that it penetrated to my entrails. When he pulled it out, I felt that he took them with it, and left me utterly consumed by the great love of God. The pain was so severe that it made me utter several moans. The sweetness caused by this intense pain is so extreme that one cannot possibly wish it to cease, nor is one's soul then content with anything but God. This is not a physical, but a spiritual pain, though the body has some share in it—even a considerable share. So gentle is this wooing which takes place between God and the soul that if anyone thinks I am lying, I pray God, in His goodness, to grant him some experience of it.[67]

Asceticism produces exhaustion. And yet, paradoxically, it combats exhaustion by its very stimulation and overstimulation—the escape from the dull nagging torments of unpleasure into the ecstasy of pain, a pain whose cessation one cannot desire. Thus Nietzsche again: "I would discern in self-contempt (which is one of the signs of saintliness) and likewise in self-tormenting behavior (starvation and scourges, dislocation of limbs, simulated madness) a means by which these natures combat the general exhaustion of their life-force."[68] "Sometimes," Nietzsche says, the saint "wants the complete cessation of all bothersome, tormenting, irritating feelings, a waking sleep, a continuing repose in the lap of a dull, animal-like or vegetative indolence; sometimes he seeks out battle and provokes it in himself, because boredom holds its yawning visage up to him."[69] Nietzsche does not allow his anti-Christian bias to blind him entirely to the paradoxicality of ascetic sainthood. The saint's is one of the strongest wills, but it has willed its own denial. The very impossibility of the ascetic quest fuels the intensity of the will's effort.

The role of pain in asceticism is to create the ec-static state. Pain, says Bataille, can "carry me nearer to the moment when horror will seize hold of me and bring me to a state of bliss bordering on delirium."[70] It is no accident that such violent pleasure seems pathological; like Sade's acceleration and Masoch's suspension, pain throws one outside of reasonable time's orderly duration. The discordant pleasure of ascetic discipline in its extreme form takes one outside the order of the everyday world, inartistic and profane.

repetition and seduction

Know what rhythm holds men.
—Archilochus, cited in Blanchot, *The Writing of the Disaster*

Asceticism, like the literary forms of Sadistic or Masochistic perversion, manifests repetition. In the works of Sade and Masoch, repetition bursts boundaries and transgresses limits. In ceaseless and frenzied acceleration the Sadist in the Sadean narrative impossibly bursts through the bounds of reason and the foundational limitations of institutions; in layers of frozen images the Masochistic narrative and its protagonist defy time's motion and desire's satisfaction, make a mockery of contracts and invert positions of power. The ascetic version of repetition is again different. Deleuze remarks upon repetition that occurs just *before* life (linked, as Freud shows us, to death's tranquillity) and that which occurs *at* life's origin (with the binding power of Eros).[71]

Ascetic repetition is the impossible effort to get behind, before, or beyond the origin of desire—motivated utterly by desire itself. For Freud, the gratifying object is always inadequate; it fails to restore the primal condition of need-less satisfaction. Desire itself comes about for the first time in the dismaying realization that one is separate from one's caretaker and cannot feed oneself by oneself, but in this realization the deepest desire is not to be fed but to be one again. Unfortunately, this separation is also the beginning of subjectivity; one's self cannot be *one* again with another without that self's being lost. Desire's continuation is insured because its satisfaction is impossible.

The ascetic drives desire to its limits as an utterly implacable seduction of the entire worldly order, undermining its power. At the same time asceticism is a seduction of the divine, drawing it ineluctably to the human soul. Desire is driven further in order to defy it; satisfaction is antisatisfaction. Pain is courted as a way of overthrowing both desire and the profane world order; the normal orders of desire and pleasure (the ordinary and acceptable desire for satisfaction, the ordinary and accepted pleasure of gratifying release) are instantaneously undermined by the ecstatic triumph of the powerful will. Nietzsche is unquestionably right to see in asceticism's triumph the enigma of seduction.[72] Seduction is a drawing toward; according to Baudrillard, it undermines the entire model, the entire order, of desire, pleasure, and power.

For the ascetic, divine grace is a response to the possibilities of (all sorts of) subtle seductions. The ascetic goal is in fact a quest for the grace of God. It is seductive both as undermining and as drawing. God, the ultimately desirable other (the ultimate object of an utterly implacable love), is drawn through a violent defiance of all other possibilities of desire and pleasure; the ascetic challenge to death is an ultimate act of faith. "Faith in the religious sphere is similar to seduction in the game of life. Belief is turned to *the existence of God* . . . while faith is a *challenge to God's existence*, a challenge to God to exist. . . . One *seduces* God with faith, and He cannot but respond, for seduction, like the challenge, is a reversible form."[73] Seduction here is *brought about* by the very overthrowing of the world order that it *accomplishes*. This inherence of the seductive in the ascetic accounts for the peculiarly potent voluptuousness of asceticism, captured in Bernini's St. Teresa, or in the many accounts by female ascetics resembling this from Hadewijch: "And he came himself to me, took me entirely in his arms, and pressed me to him, and all my members felt his in full felicity, in accordance with the desire of my heart and my humanity. So I was outwardly satisfied and fully transported."[74] It accounts for its supreme arrogance; what could be more presumptuous than to lure God?

Christian asceticism has lost its place in modern Christianity precisely because of this disturbing, arrogant seductiveness; it is too *pagan*: "[The Greek gods] provided the image of a world order ruled not by laws, as in the Christian universe . . . but by a mutual seduction. . . . That universe where gods and men sought to please each other—even by the violent seduction of sacrifice—has ended."[75] It is this "violent seduction of sacrifice" that forms the heart of the ascetic paradox—sacrifice constituting the sacred, humility out of arrogance, life out of death, affirmation out of denial. It is profoundly perverse, self-denying and yet self-overcoming. The desire that drives it at once turns against the body and demands (and glorifies) the presence of the body as a space of suffering. The seduction of the sacred by the delighted (and thus mocking, even if utterly serious) sacrifice of pleasure reembodies God: it repeats the sacrifice of the first incarnate Word, God's body; it draws the divine back into the body and transports the body in the intensity of its pain to the divine. It is unquestionably powerful, subversive precisely in its conformity to religious demands.

PART TWO

CONTEMPORARY PRACTICES AND PLEASURES

I really felt that you were shattering the atmosphere around me, that you were creating a void in order to allow me to progress, in order to offer the expanse for an impossible space to that which within me was potentiality only, to a whole virtual germination that must be sucked into life by the interval which offered itself.

—Antonin Artaud, *Le Pèse-Nerfs*

5

theoretical displacement

But joy demands eternity.
— Friedrich Nietzsche, "The Drunken Song"

With the move to twentieth-century practice, the demand for placement, even in the service of displacement, takes a different turn. This
is due, I suspect, to the double nature of these pleasures as bodily
and contemporary. Despite the strength of various censorship movements, nobody cares too much what theorists read, unless it makes
them misbehave—and the misbehavior that Sade or Masoch might
engender will be so linguistic or theoretical that few will understand
enough to object. Pleasures of the body, on the other hand, are more
visible and so more prone to others' valuation. Whatever value one
might place on medieval ascetic practice, it is, as noted in the introduction to the discussion of those practices, resolutely medieval: that
is, it occurs within a religious context not directly available to us,
though we may and do appropriate various elements of it. Practices
that belong to our time demand some placement in that time, and
some placement, therefore, of oneself.

This demand is in fact something of a challenge. It is a theoretical challenge, because I would insist that one of the key strengths of
the counterpleasures is their disruption of the stability of identity,
their very real problematizing of the subject. Postmodern, perverse,
queer subjectivity is in many ways a refusal, or minimally an ac-
knowledgment of the problematic nature, of such placement. As Judith Butler writes:

> And if identity is a necessary error, then the assertion of
> "queer" will be necessary as a term of affiliation, but it

will not fully describe those it purports to represent. As a result, it will be necessary to affirm the contingency of the term: to let it be vanquished by those who are excluded by the term but who justifiably expect representation by it, to let it take on meanings that cannot now be anticipated by a younger generation whose political vocabulary may well carry a very different set of investments. That it can become such a discursive site whose uses are not fully constrained in advance ought to be safeguarded.[1]

Perverse identification is a practical challenge as well. Terry Hoople remarks upon this in the opening passage of his article "Conflicting Visions: SM, Feminism, and the Law. A Problem of Representation":

> Practitioners are forced to suffer the weight of cultural representations (and not just "popular representations") of "the sadomasochist" as sexually perverted, morally depraved, physically and mentally abusive, obsessed with power, fascistic, racist, paedophilic . . . in general very scary people to be around. Telling "vanilla" friends, or even your own parents, that you are a sadomasochist is not only difficult, it is simply unwise: there is too much to lose and nothing to gain by letting the word out. . . . It was suggested to me by at least one of the journal's reviewers that coming out in this paper might have repercussions, and that I should consider the matter thoroughly. So, upon that seemingly sound advice, I will bracket that possibility.[2]

This is indeed sound advice, but as Hoople suggests it cannot always be followed, however one might wish to do so. Again, to place these pleasures of one's own time is to place oneself, as well, in relation to those pleasures.

This is by no means to suggest that here we abandon theory for auto/biography. Foucault, ever a source of wise remarks, told his interviewer in "An Ethics of Pleasure," "As far as my personal life is uninteresting, it is not worthwhile making a secret of it. By the same token, it may not be worth publicizing it."[3] Aside from making note of the important fact that Foucault (as his various biographies indicate) was lying (that is, that his personal life seems to have been quite interesting), I might note that there is still not much worthwhile in secretiveness or publicity. Theory as autobiography is limited and not, I think, very interesting (though each may play an interesting partial role in the other).

Foucault's construction of asceticism tells us something more important: theory is not some outpouring of self but may be its own transformative practice, as he suggests in the same interview: "I am not interested in the academic status of what I am doing because my problem is my own transformation. . . . This transformation of oneself by one's own knowledge is, I think, something rather close to the aesthetic experience. Why should a painter work if he is not transformed by his own painting?"[4] Theory, then, is already transformative of identity; thus to theorize out of identity is problematic.

But neither is it "worthwhile making a secret of it." These experiences of joy and power are indeed my own, or more precisely, because such "experience" shatters subjectivity, the experience of returning more powerful from such joy is my own. The frustration of finding the very existence of such joy and power denied is unquestionably my own. While I do not wish to value these practices over those of literature or of medieval Christianity—a hierachization that must be meaningless—their contemporaneity means that their transgressiveness will be more directly apparent. And the transformation wrought by writing has been to strengthen, by attempting to meet the complex demands of "self"-representation, all that I have found good in such practice. Ideally, the act of reading may be similarly, however slightly, transformative.

This transformation might be assisted by a more precise placement—not of the person of the author but of the act of writing. These reflections arose not only from critical and theoretical concerns but as well from a more "practical" tension between joy and frustration. The demand made by joy was less straightforward; reactivity remains a constant temptation. Joy does demand expression, though— it overflows; it is excessive, too much to remain entirely internal (especially when external opinion sometimes denies even the possibility of that joy's existence). The particularly intriguing element of the joy in the practices described below is that it is not simply an excess of pleasure; it is an overflow of *power*, a power that initially makes no sense—especially within good sense, which moves only in one direction. It is a power that one is repeatedly and disquietingly assured does not in fact exist—or, if it does, *should* not, and this of course is the corresponding frustration.

We can begin placing these contemporary pleasures by their relation to other counterpleasures. That there is vast powerfulness in asceticism I hope to have suggested already. In the final chapter I shall elaborate a bit on some of the more specifically contemporary implications of that claim. Sade and Masoch turn our attention to the power of language to subvert itself. Here we come to see that there is also, in what is probably a more common contemporary experience, vast powerfulness in s/m practice, most peculiarly in bottoming (that is, in the experience of the masochistic or submissive position)—a power that makes little sense to good sense. It is because of this sense of power found in practices of the body that I would suggest that s/m is importantly continuous with, though by no means identical to, ascetic practice.

Its continuity with Sade and Masoch is less direct, relying on the common desires for disruptiveness. More unexpectedly, it is in many respects discontinuous with what would seem its own literature, s/m erotica or pornography. Such literature is not infrequently sentimental, every bit as romantic as Masoch, and free of portrayals of the kind of power I shall argue is created by practice. (There are some rare exceptions, such as the fiction works of Pat Califia and Laura Antoniou.) Though I would hardly argue that body and language do not call to one another, we still must be cautious about conflating literature with practice; to do so here would be approximately as accurate as making an assessment of vanilla sex on the basis of mainstream pornography. S/m *literature*—much of it, anyway—is much closer to classical Masochism than are the practices to which Masoch has given his name. (We do, however, find a trace of Masoch's theatricality in practice, in the exhibitionistic and voyeuristic love of the view and the gaze.)

I have urged caution here because these two are so easily conflated. In part this is no doubt our familiar terminological problem— the terms "sadism" and "masochism" are made to stand for both bodily and textual practices. Further problematizing the issue is the fact that fantasy may well resemble literature, and psychoanalysis has concerned itself with fantasy. Carol Siegel writes:

> As Kaja Silverman has observed, in the accounts offered by patients of their fantasies and sexual behavior [much more, I suspect, the former than the latter] on which Reik and Kraft-Ebbing as well as Freud and Gilles Deleuze base their influential theories of masochism, the male masochist consistently differs from the female masochist in showing an openness verging on exhibitionism. . . . "He acts out in an insistent and exaggerated way the basic conditions of cultural subjectivity, conditions that are normally disavowed; he loudly proclaims that his meaning comes to

him from the Other, prostrates himself before the Gaze
even as he solicits it, exhibits his castration for all to see,
and revels in the sacrificial basis of the social contract."[5]

In fact, as well, both fictional and factual descriptions of female
masochists indicate the solicitation of the Gaze, and that gaze is in
some cases female, in others male, in others transgendered and
sometimes multiple. Gender divisions are not simple here, a point to
which we shall have cause to return.

In terms of any ordinary understanding of the economies and
sources of either power or joy (economies that should be well problematized for us by now), there is little place for a notion of
masochistic power or for a positive understanding of sadistic
strength (sadism is generally conceded to be powerful but dismissed
as hostile and immoral). The claim that these are real and powerful
pleasures makes still less sense given the fact that one hears not infrequently, still, that such acts are precisely as they appear at the out-
sider's first glance to be: forms of disempowerment (masochism or
submission) and oppression (sadism or dominance), whether they
are voluntary, involuntary, or the product of false consciousness.
(This assumes that the bottom is somehow disempowered or weakened by participating in s/m activities. On the other hand, among
s/m practitioners a more common question is "what's in it for the
top?"—who, from the outside, seems to have it all, to be the triumphant oppressor.) It still seems to be true that the predominant intellectual sentiment is s/m-negative, although—academia being far
from immune to fashion—this is changing.[6] Even for those who
share an unrepentant aestheticism, with no particular desire to politicize pleasure, the negative sentiment can be troubling; one may not
wish to politicize what one will nonetheless not allow to be denied.
(And, as has been pointed out to me, whenever one deals with
power, one has already gotten into politics.)[7] These pleasures have
been most insistently politicized by those who believe they should be
abolished.

The s/m-negative feminist literature has provided the steadiest
continuing source of this frustrating insistence. This literature continues to make the same arguments that were being made more than a
decade ago, in the seminal collection *Against Sadomasochism*, but the
fault is not all on one side. In fact, though this collection is an important marker and common reference point, the debate is even older:
"Since at least as early as 1976, there has been debate among feminists

about the politics of sadomasochism. (See, for example, issues of *Big Mama Rag*, *Lesbian Tide*, *Hera*, and *off our backs* published during 1976)."[8] Those who favor or tolerate s/m have not, in general, responded to the critique of patriarchal power—a radical critique, which essentially holds that s/m practices echo and thus reinforce existing power structures—but have instead repeated liberal arguments for freedom of practice.[9] I do not believe that it is useful to respond by keeping the discussion in these terms. I hope that I have provided a sufficiently radical perspective, a "new" take on power as something other than control, to somewhat alter this repetitive discussion, though in my analysis I shall of necessity take on some of the old objections.

The intellectual (as opposed to either erotic/pornographic or practical) discussion of s/m includes much impassioned argumentation on issues of consent and on the problematic possibility that erotic violence is the reinforcement-by-reenactment of a broader cultural violence (as opposed to its playful undermining by parodic simulation). Proponents argue that consensual activity is no one's business but that of those directly involved; that such activity is fun, possibly cathartic, even a way of reclaiming one's power or sexuality following, for example, childhood trauma.[10] Opponents argue that consent to violence is impossible in a free subject and can only be a cultural construct, a form of false consciousness (an "attempt to replicate the phenomenology of oppression through role-playing")[11] or perhaps a crippling addiction.[12]

I shall not be arguing for catharsis, nor for the ability of simulation or parody to undermine the reality it seems to repeat. (Though s/m is often understood as simulation, as all an act rather than a reality, I am most interested in what is served by the play acting: in the pain and restraint and control inflicted and received, whatever role one may take on for this infliction and reception.) I shall not discuss issues of privacy nor of reclamation, not because any of these issues or arguments is unimportant, but because all matter within the realm of the good subject, within the order of subjectivity. For the same reason, I shall not present the libertarian argument. Once subjectivity is ruptured, which is one of the most important elements of power-play, the issues are different. However, as I shall suggest below, there remains a sense in which consent is relevant and in fact essential, in the issues of the will following its own direction and of the notion of playing-with-desire. Consent is a vital starting point, not a final goal. This is less obvious, more complicated, infinitely more problematic than political issues of yes-or-no consent.

Before we can turn to a discussion of these pleasures, we should note that in many ways it would be inaccurate to treat s/m as if it were a single phenomenon (or pair of phenomena). The community of practitioners is divided, most notably across gender and orientation and "old leather" versus "new leather" lines. Though there are important commonalities across this diversity, we should note these differences—and then note why they make *less* difference than one might suppose.

Gay men have perhaps the longest history of established leather communities, and often seem to be more comfortable with s/m than others do. Gayle Rubin remarks upon this history in her essay "The Leather Menace":

> Gay male sadomasochists are less numerous than hetero-sexuals, but they are much better organized. Gay men have developed an elaborate technology for building pub-lic institution for sexual outlaws. When the gay male leather community emerged, it followed the organiza-tional patterns of the larger homosexual community.[13]

Further on, she notes:

> The average gay man is not into leather or S/M. But the average gay man is probably more aware of sexual diver-sity and erotic possibilities than most heterosexuals or les-bians.[14]

Pat Califia notes the importance of the gay male community for the establishment of other, especially lesbian, s/m groups: "It is his-torically important to remember that the first people who supported lesbian sadomasochists were gay leather men and professional (usu-ally bisexual) dominatrixes."[15]

As many theorists note, heterosexual practitioners probably out-number gay or lesbian sadomasochists[16] (though, especially within "new leather," the bisexual or pansexual component is substantial). Heterosexual sadomasochists too form a fairly marginal community, as Rubin notes: "contrary to much of what is said about straight S/M in the feminist press, heterosexual S/M is *not* standard heterosexual-ity. Straight S/M is stigmatized and persecuted. . . . They are consid-ered to be perverts, not normal."[17] Even in gender terms, such heterosexual practitioners may not be "straight"—consider the pop-ularity of gender-role reversal in female-dominant heterosexual couples. This is not a simple inversion; much of this pleasure seems to belong to simulation, part to the very fluidity of identity that identity-rupture makes possible. Dominant women may enjoy dominating other women as well as men, and it seldom seems that trading roles with men, with its echoes of vengefulness, is a primary motive. More often the pleasure of such role trading is that of not having to continue to be (solely) oneself, a pleasure that may serve (though it need not) as a starting point for a more radical disruption of any subjectivity at all. This possibility may be borne out by the popularity of gender play among nonheterosexual couples; "daddy-boy" play, for example, occurs among lesbians as well as gay men.[18] The pleasure of going beyond oneself may well be helped by not having to remain within one's everyday role. Though role-play is not identical with s/m, it too may serve to destabilize rigidly identified subjectivities.[19]

But despite the gender range among practitioners, most of the theory both supporting and opposing s/m practice has come from the feminist lesbian community. In part this is no doubt due to a unique sense of the role of theory in this community, exemplified in the claim "feminism is the theory, lesbianism is the practice."[20] Much feminist theory, especially from the cultural feminist movement of the 1980s, is explicitly opposed to what it sees as the masculine elements of s/m practice. Steven Seidman (not a part of this movement but an excellent commentator on it) writes in *Embattled Eros* that "S/M would seem inevitably to promote instrumental, aggressive, and objectifying orientations. Do not these values contradict feminist values (e.g., nurturance, person-centeredness, tenderness, sharing, nonhierarchical relationships)?"[21]

Because lesbians are still a marginalized and often disempowered community (lesbian chic notwithstanding), the sense that lesbian sadomasochists have embraced the masculine eros and false consciousness of mainstream heterosexuality is particularly distressing.[22] Because lesbian identity is still intertwined with feminist theory, objections to lesbian sadomasochistic pleasures easily take a theoretical turn. Correspondingly, in their determination to preserve and to understand the power of their pleasures, lesbian sadomasochists have given us some of the strongest writing on the subject. Much has been negative. Gayle Rubin's 1981 remark that "current radical (mostly feminist) writing on S/M is a hopeless muddle of bad assumptions, inaccurate information, and a a thick-headed refusal to accept evidence that contravenes preconceptions"[23] is still accurate. So too is her analysis that "like the social discourse on homosexuality, the social discourse on S/M sets up phony issues and poses phony questions. At some point, we need to step out of this framework and develop an alternative way to think about sexuality and understand its politics."[24] One of the earliest and most important collections to take an s/m positive stance was also lesbian: *Coming to Power*, edited by San Francisco's Samois collective. Much, though not all, lesbian s/m theory seems to me applicable to s/m more generally, and it is perhaps not accidental that both Califia and Rubin do not always put gender first in explaining their sexuality.

Whatever the stance of the community at large, the academic gay and lesbian discourse has been at best ambivalent about s/m. I should mark as a particularly inspirational source a panel on consensual sadomasochism, sponsored by the Gay and Lesbian Philosophy Association, at the December 1993 meeting of the American Philosophical Association (Eastern Division).[25] The panel was generally, though not entirely, critical of such practices. (A 1996 panel from the same group, though not on the topic of s/m, proved to be just as inspiring, with two of three panelists—in a discussion of lesbian theory—casually and somewhat gratuitously dismissing s/m as an immoral possible practice.) More frustrating than the criticism, however, was the hesitant, reluctant, and limited *defense* of s/m in this session, without any sense of an affirmative, aesthetically and politically transgressive *value* to be found in such practices. The combination was sufficiently depressing and annoying to lead me to the conclusion that I needed to write something myself—in response, but less reactive, in an effort to avoid reactivity's tendency to let others do the representing. Since writing, I have been delighted to find others prompted by a similar frustration.[26] Because the criticisms forced me to think about the extraordinary difficulties, as Terry Hoople has remarked, of self-representation, I am in fact grateful to them for their very hostility.

I emphasize the importance of lesbian theory because it will arise with what would otherwise seem undue frequency in the work that follows. In fact, though, here we must be less interested in identities (on which, I would remark once more, the counterpleasures have, in any event, a somewhat destabilizing effect, problematizing as they do the place of the individual) than in pleasures. Some pleasures, with their accompanying sense of power, cut across the subcommunities of those who find pleasure in s/m. In fact, the destabilizing of identity is politically quite important: "The individual . . . is not the *vis-à-vis* of power; it is, I believe, one of its prime effects. The individual is an effect of power . . . precisely to the extent to which it is that effect, it is the element of its articulation."[27] Thus I would disagree with Kaja Silverman's argument that "For Foucault . . . perversion has no subversive edge; it merely serves to extend the surface upon which power is exercised."[28] Foucault's "new asceticism" and "new pleasures" unquestionably incorporate perversion, subversive edge and all.

One more community distinction should be noted, because it may apply more directly to the approaches to pleasure—the distinction in terms of old versus new leather. Sometimes this distinction reflects a disgruntled or alarmed sense that s/m has become infiltrated by the "stand and model" crowd, fetishists who like the fashions but largely disdain the rest of the practice.[29] This consumer fetishism is conspicuous, as a 1993 article in the women's fashion magazine *Mademoiselle* noted: "S&M has emerged even further out of its closet: not only leering from the pages of Madonna's dopey *Sex* or being touted by its sleazy practitioners on Geraldo's junk-TV talk show, but . . . in the window of an upscale department store . . . in a Versace-inspired bondage dress. And it is no great shock that in a recessionary consumer economy, yet another form of sex is being marketed."[30]

The marketing of this sex is what some practitioners fear, as it is likely to bring an influx of the uninformed or purely fashionable; on the other hand, it has had the advantage of lessening certain stigmas. There is of course considerable overlap among the s/m and fetish communities, and the terms are sometimes used interchangeably. (Elizabeth Grosz refers to lesbian s/m as a "quasi-fetishistic variation[] of lesbianism," though noting that it "cannot be regarded as [a] fetish[] until it can first be shown that female fetishism is possible.")[31] In fact, however, fetish may imply a purely theatrical desire, without any particular pleasure in pain or otherwise recognizably unusual practice. On the other hand, fetishes may well serve as an immediate contextualizing factor, putting practitioners into "scene space" or readiness for the kind of play I shall describe; or certain sights, scents (such as leather), or sounds (such as the rasp of metal) may serve as an immediate reminder much as lasting marks do, as I shall discuss in more detail below.

More interestingly and more often the old/new leather distinction refers to a move from a carefully, even rigidly, hierarchized and demarcated community of masters and slaves, tops (who undergo careful apprenticeships) and bottoms, to a more fluid community in which many members identify as switches (playing either top or bottom)[32] and may be polysexual or play across gender preferences.[33] The distinction is dramatic, but alters the pleasures less than it might seem:

> One can say that S/M is the eroticization of power, the eroticization of strategic relations. What strikes me with regard to S/M is how it differs from social power. What characterized power is the fact that it is a strategic relation that has been stabilized through institutions. So the mobility in power relations has been limited, and there are strongholds that are very, very difficult to suppress because they have been institutionalized and are now very pervasive. . . . All that means that the strategic relations of power are made rigid.
>   On this point, the S/M game is very interesting because it is a strategic relation, but it is always fluid.[34]

Old leather places its emphasis on the strategic relation, the *organization* of strategy; new leather on fluidity. But both in fact play with power and with boundaries, both establishing and breaking them. In attempting a pancommunity commentary, I have taken seriously Rubin's remark, "There is a lot of separation between the straight, gay, and lesbian S/M communities. But there is a also pan-S/M consciousness. As one wise woman who has been doing this for many years has said, 'leather is thicker than blood.' "[35] I do not wish to deny the existence of real differences across straight, gay, lesbian, and bi- or pansexual s/m communities, nor between old and new leather. But some pleasures *are* shared here, and these I think are quite important, and do cut across these subcommunity boundaries, and do belong to a discussion of counterpleasures more generally, even one that avoids the postmodern tendency to a "relentless contemporaneity"[36] by its inclusion of counterpleasures beginning in the Middle Ages.[37]

However, working across these boundaries also displays a theoretical trait that greatly troubles s/m negative (especially lesbian) feminists, one that has been a factor in some condemnations of s/m as antifeminist: its playfulness with and about gender.[38] Other writers cling to gender divisions that current writings, both fictive and first-person factual, suggest are outmoded. Thus Silverman:

> Reik suggests . . . that even the clinically masochistic woman does not really exceed her subjective limits; she merely stretches them a bit. The male masochist, on the

other hand, leaves his social identity completely behind—
actually abandons his 'self'—and passes over into the
'enemy terrain' of femininity. . . . The sexual fantasies cited
by Reik fully bear out these characterizations, as do those
included by Kraft-Ebing.[39]

On the other hand, Parveen Adams sees s/m as a sexuality beyond gender, emphasizing its "choice," "mobility," "consent," and
"play with identity and . . . genitality."[40] Gayle Rubin, besides being
one of the original and formative voices in the current s/m-positive
discourse, has argued for the need to conceive of sexuality beyond
terms of gender and gender divisions. Pat Califia stirred up lasting
trouble with her remark in a 1979 *Advocate* article "A Secret Side of
Lesbian Sexuality" that if she had to be marooned on a desert island,
she'd prefer the company of a male masochist to that of a "vanilla
dyke."[41]

This is not to argue that gender is now an irrelevant, socially dis-
cardable category. But s/m is not a set of practices or experiences distinguished primarily by gender. Indeed, recent theory suggests that
gender may be another of the boundaries with which it delights in
playing[42]—it becomes not only gender-bending but what the artist
Bob Flanagan gleefully labeled "gender demolition."[43] This playfulness with gender, here as elsewhere, is unsettling to more traditional
feminisms, which require a firm sense of gender boundaries if they
are to be supportive of women. Thus s/m takes its place among the
practices of the postmodern, in which the identity of the subject becomes a performance, sometimes fluid, sometimes an open question.
Practices can deconstruct as well as construct identities; these practices of pleasure do both.

6

m-powerment

Foucault's body

And yet whoever says flesh also says sensibility. Sensibility, that is, assimilation. But an intimate, secret, profound
assimilation, absolute in relation to my own suffering
—Antonin Artaud, "Situation of the Flesh"

A mere disciplining of thoughts and feelings is virtually
nothing . . . one first has to convince the body.
—Friedrich Nietzsche, *Twilight of the Idols*

I attempt here a reflection on the pleasure and power of pain and of
restraint, which would seem to be in opposition to power (or at any
rate to be used *by* power *against* opposition)—with the idea that both
entail an exceptionally forceful enhancement of the always unexpected resistant power of the body, specifically a resistance to the
seemingly irresistible disciplinary power of contemporary culture.
Despite the foregoing discussion, it still seems very strange to speak
of "pleasures of pain," or "of restraint," and it seems even more
strange when one recognizes how closely I would ally pleasure and
a politically subversive form of power—and in what follows their
entanglement will be apparent.

The oddness of the alliance of pleasure with pain and restraint is
apparent even before we undertake a consideration of power. Here a
review of a more customary understanding, a return to Freud to see
his cultural pervasiveness, provides a helpful contrast. Generally we
understand by "pleasure" that which soothes stress, relieves tension—that which eases or releases us. We may take quiet and gently

soothing pleasures (long walks, bubble baths, good meals), or noisy and boisterous pleasures of quicker release (which amount to sex, sports, war, and beating the crap out of things—which pleasures, of course, we are not supposed to get mixed up with one another). The former we might count as restrained pleasures—soft, slow, even refined. Or we might argue, as both Aristotle and Epicurus did in their quite distinct ways, that the carefully moderated (in that sense restrained) life is less painful, more virtuous, more rewarding, *happier* (in that sense more pleasurable).[1] But even before approaching the paradox of pleasurable pain—pleasure *in* restraint, pleasures *of* restraint? Restraint already implies resistance, tension, the inhibition of pleasure (and especially of noisy or fast-paced pleasures). Along with pain, then, restraint would be pleasure's opposite. What makes s/m interesting in this context is its forthrightness about the pleasure of these paradoxes.

To understand the perverse pleasures of restraint and restrained (ritualized, ceremonial, and especially *stylized*) violence (including the pleasure of pain), we must remember what Foucault has told us: that it is always the body that is at issue, especially in pleasure. And it is perhaps in restraint that the body comes into its fullest pleasure. (And unlike the restraint of asceticism, this is a consciously pleasurable physicality.) As I shall argue, this is a pleasure taken in the body's strength against power—not merely the power that restrains it, but power in much more pernicious and insidious forms. This force of the body against power, as Foucault has suggested, has startling implications of resistance—and, I would add, implicit possibilities of equally startling (and, again, strikingly subversive) pleasures, in restraint, discipline, resistance itself. Restraint and pain play, that is, between two terms I shall discuss below, *plaisir* and *jouissance*, at once grounding and destroying the cultured subject. Against all appearances, the pleasure of pain and restraint is the joyful triumph of the body. It is the pleasure of Barthes's "anachronic" reader, who "enjoys the consistency of his selfhood (that is his pleasure) and seeks its loss (that is his bliss). He is a subject split twice over, doubly perverse."[2] It is Bersani's "subject-shattering jouissance,"[3] which the subject desires with self-exceeding intensity.

Here, of course, we are concerned specifically with the excesses of restraint and pain, which mark, beyond the usual restraints of culture, the approach to the erotic (dealing specifically with pain and restraint as opposed to, for example, role-play or other fetishes). Both are intriguingly counterintuitive; neither ought to be as forceful, nor to entail such a sense of strength and power, as each nonetheless does.

In arguing for the joy inherent in power, I should make it explicit that I reject two important claims. The first is that it is at once possible and desirable to find or construct an erotic space outside power. This means rejecting the myth of "a pure and natural pleasure uncontaminated by power,"[4] or even the claim made by some lesbian theorists that lesbian sex represents a power-free alternative to other sexual relations.[5] This sense of impossibility I take from Foucault, and develop in what follows here. The second is that masochism is in fact what John Stoltenberg calls "the eroticization of powerlessness."[6] Masochism does not give one power over anyone nor does it provide a utopian, egalitarian "power-with"—it is instead a sense of power as *strength*, an extraordinary relation to one's own self, flesh, and subjectivity, to the world as a space of possibility, an openness to the outside.

My claim is that these pleasures are at once extraordinarily potent and politically subversive forms of embodiment. This will not be an easy claim of which to make sense. Human bodies are deeply problematic philosophically, and have been at least since Plato urged us to turn away from the beautiful boys whose bodies we must, nonetheless, be able to appreciate if we are even to begin the ascent of Diotima's ladder.[7] They have remained problematic even when we have turned our exploration of them away from the explicitly value-judgmental toward the metaphysical. Reductive materialism (or, for that matter, reductive idealism) is no solution at all, arising as it does from the annihilation of one-half of what remains a fundamentally dualistic position. Metaphysics fails the body. The phenomenological effort to get at a lived or living body is certainly less reductive, but too easily slides into a sense of the body as lived *by*: by the ego, or by the subject, that persistent metaphysical malingerer. Alternatively, the body itself *becomes* subject or ego, a subtler variation on the metaphysical reduction.

Judith Butler writes, "If the formulation of a bodily ego, a sense of stable contour, and the fixing of spatial boundary is achieved through identificatory practices, and if psychoanalysis documents the hegemonic workings of those identifications, can we then read psychoanalysis for the inculcation of the heterosexual matrix at the level of bodily morphogenesis?"[8] And if we can, then might the explosivity of bodily pleasure beyond ego boundaries already queer the self?

And yet to approach the body outside metaphysics, physics or phenomenology seems at first glance absurd—what sense can one make of a body that is neither a clear-cut *thing*, a good solid object whether or not inhabited and manipulated by a subject; nor a proper *subject* itself, grounded right here in a real live lived world? What sense can we make of Foucault's body?

Foucault's is the body in history, bearing the inscriptions of the powers that impinge upon it, and it is as constructed as any other manifestation of power. And yet there are always, for Foucault, possibilities of resistance—even necessities for resistance, and these arise, necessarily, in and through these constructed bodies. This is intuitively odd: if *we* the subjects are socially and historically *constructed*, even in or as our bodies, what on earth resists power; what *can* resist? (What would it even mean to resist?) Does anything exceed power, when power and the relations of power construct existence and identity, construct the very *notion* of the body, down to its most minute level?

It would seem not. "It seems to me that power is 'always already there,'" Foucault writes; "that one is never 'outside' it , that there are no 'margins' for those who break with the system to gambol in."[9] There are no margins, and so the body cannot stand in the nonexistent realm outside power. Thus it would not appear to make sense to speak of the body's resistance to power. In this event, the anti-s/m movement would appear correct in attributing to masochism either a wan passivity or a mere delusion of strength.

This impression of powerlessness is enhanced by Foucault's emphasis on the body as the locus of the inscription of power. Power, "the materiality of power," "operate[s] on the very bodies of individuals."[10] The exercise of power is always *material*, philosophical prejudices to the contrary: "One must set aside the widely held thesis that power, in our bourgeois, capitalist societies, has denied the reality of the body in favor of the soul, consciousness, ideality. In fact nothing is more material, physical, corporal than the exercise of power."[11]

Power is exercised on bodies; it constructs individual bodies *as* those bodies and those individuals, it is altogether corporeal. There is nothing outside power, no space beyond power in which the body might cavort free and uninscribed. Yet it is precisely where power seems to be both strongest and most insidious, where the body seems most irrevocably inscribed, that something rather extraordinary happens:

> Mastery and awareness of one's own body can be acquired only through the effect of an investment of power in the body. . . . All of this belongs to the pathway leading to the desire of one's own body, by way of the insistent, persistent, meticulous work of power on the bodies of children or soldiers, the healthy bodies. But once power produces this effect, there inevitably emerge the responding claims and affirmations, those of one's own body against power, of health against the economic system, of pleasure against the moral norms of sexuality, marriage, decency. Suddenly, what had made power strong becomes used to attack it. Power, after investing itself in the body, finds itself exposed to a counterattack in that same body.[12]

This sudden exposure does not, as Foucault points out in the same passage, eliminate power or prevent its return—power doesn't disappear. But power's persistent return also means that resistance reemerges: "there are no relations of power without resistances; the latter are all the more real and effective because they are formed right at the point where relations of power are exercised; resistance to power does not have to come from elsewhere to be real . . . hence, like power, resistance is multiple."[13]

Some force, some . . . power, perhaps? resists power, a force brought into existence *by* power. Relations of power, says Foucault, "are capable of being utilized in strategies."[14] What, then, of a possible strategy of resistance (though certainly not the only possible strategy in this multiplicity), one that deliberately invokes power only to break it?[15] What kind of resistance is that—and what kind of pleasure emerges in that resistance?

the discipline of desire

> And what [the poem] tirelessly affirms, what it cannot silence . . . is what René Char echoes when he says, "The poem is the realized love of desire still desiring." And André Breton: "Desire, yes, always."
>
> —Maurice Blanchot, *The Space of Literature*

Before a more explicit exploration of the subverting moment, let us look at the strategy. Our exploration of asceticism has already suggested the explosive value of unreleased desire. The practices of restraint (both bondage and control) defy the "natural" (and calming) teleology of the subject's desire; such practice is unnatural, unproductive, inefficient, self-destructive—and powerful. Whence the power of what seems to be a force of sheer negation, or the pleasure of what seems to be only pain and frustration? The answer lies in two related forms of overcoming: the overcoming of subjectivity and of the discipline of productive efficiency. The pleasure of this overcoming is that of the will—not the autonomous, subject-centered free will with which we are comfortably familiar, but the defiantly unanalyzable force of the incarnate Nietzschean will, itself a force of desire that creates and seeks out resistance in order to have the pleasure of growth, attained only in overcoming (often, in fact ideally, of itself). It is the paradoxically powerful pleasure of the subject pushing toward *and beyond* the transgression of its own limits.

Nietzsche reminds us that free movement of the power of the will is directed toward obstacles—*toward* as much as *against*: the strong will seeks out what resists it, seeks even its own dissatisfaction.[16] Yet this resistance-seeking, too, accords with the will's unspeakable rules, and Nietzsche remarks (almost surprisingly, to those more familiar with his image as the philosopher of choice for assorted fascistic thinkers) that "What is essential 'in heaven and on earth' seems to be, to say it once more, that there should be *obedience* over a long period of time and in a *single* direction—given that, something always develops . . . for whose sake it is worth while to live on earth; . . . —something transfiguring, subtle, mad and divine."[17] (Here it is the strong who obey.) The will's strength is found in deliberate resistance in accord with an obedience to nothing external to itself, an obedience more strict, more difficult, and more free than any compliance with external authority.

Pleasure itself is, as Foucault's remark on "pleasure against moral norms" suggested and our exploration of other counterpleasures has indicated, already potentially subversive, at least where it edges into intensity. But how do restraint, in particular, and pain, as we shall see, enhance the Nietzschean pleasure of the growth of the will to power, and how could the power of this will resist or subvert the (seemingly much greater) power of our disciplinary culture? That restraint provides obstacles is evident. These obstacles allow the enhancement of the sense of power as it exerts itself—but then what? More precisely: Against what power does the resistant force of the restrained body arise? Is a masochist in cuffs only struggling against leather and chain, or against the top who put him there, or, just possibly, against something less apparent and more culturally strong?

It is not the case—it would be too simple—that the body exerts itself only against the power represented by its restraint and that it is against this restraint that its resistance emerges. It this were so, we ought simply to please ourselves by avoiding unnecessary restraint altogether, unless we are merely bellicose enough to want to fight against *something*. After all, restraint enough, it seems, would be encountered anyway, without its deliberate and excessive imposition. Surely it would be more reasonable to exert our energy in fighting harder against everyday restrictions than in imposing more fantastic forms of restraint upon ourselves?

But rather than being only something to be resisted, restraint itself is a strategy of resistance. The masochist finds restraint and pain against which to push herself past herself. Restraint is, in fact, a manipulation of the power of desire, a manipulation that neither denies nor undoes that power, but maximizes it to maximize the body's improbable if unlasting triumph against its subjection—its subjectivity—its disciplinary productivity, its "natural" and "moral" order. This is a Bataillean desire, avid for nonsatisfaction.

Pleasurable restraint, restraint that *provokes* the power of joyous resistance, cannot be identical with the power that seeks to *forestall* resistance. Starting in pleasure, masochism is wholly unlike oppression. There may be some political necessity, some form of justice (though I have found this to be a dangerous word) that demands a resistance *directly* to the powers impinging upon one's body. But the body under the restraint that strengthens its power resists, again, not that restraint—which is merely a strategic organizing force—but rather the greater forces that make of it a socially acceptable, productive subject. The value of pain lies both in its intensity (pleasure and pain are alike matters of sensation, though not only of sensation, and at a certain intensity of pleasure/desire/bliss become blurred) and in its unparalleled ability to disrupt the organization of subjectivity (see the last section of this chapter). Restraint, besides forestalling gratification, prevents the release from pain—allows one to stay with the pain where one could not do so alone.

Jesse Meredith marks the critic's disgust at this possibility: "I cannot reconcile Samois' claim that sadomasochism is entirely consensual with the frequent statement that a 'good' sadist takes the masochist to her limits—*and a little bit further*. (What is 'a little'? And who decides? Where is 'consent' then?)"[18] The subject cannot exceed itself alone, and it is past subjective limits that consent, having been a *vital* ground or starting point, alters its meaning radically, becoming the movement of the will with little regard, as I shall continue to argue, for personhood.

At the same time, being twice split, both pain and restraint ground the subject—it is said that asceticism is the root of culture, and there is, of course, nothing like pain to make one fully self-aware. They force attention to themselves, to sensation and desire—and, having thrown the subject both into and out of itself, provide both active and mnemonic techniques of subversion. As I shall suggest, they teach us that our flesh may surpass our subjectivity, that we are stronger and more powerful than our selves.

Here is a significant parallel with asceticism and other excessive forms of restraint (and it is only excesses of restraint that interest me here, not Aristotelian moderation nor even Epicurean abstemiousness). They may undermine physical strength, may literally be deadly (*far* more so for asceticism than for sadomasochistic practices, regardless of one's sentiments about the currently popular "safe, sane, and consensual" requirement). Not everyone, of course, recognizes this.[19] But it remains the case that such excessive restraint and such perversely sought pain undermine the powers that constitute the "good" subject, and do so in the triumph of bodily resistance—which becomes, in the very defiance of subjectivity, a subversive triumph for the "doubly perverse," no-longer-so-good subject.

It becomes so precisely by undermining the production/consumption order of gratification, by perverting and subverting desire. No one should assume (since Nietzsche, no one should be forgiven for assuming) that the denial inherent in restraint is predicated upon the *repression* of desire—recall Bataille's description of the saint as one who "is not after efficiency. He is prompted by desire and desire alone and in this resembles the erotic man."[20] This desire is precisely the desire of (or inherent in) power, power's desire for expansion. Recall as well Nietzsche's description of our awe before sainthood: "In him . . . they sensed the superior force that sought to test itself in such a conquest, the strength of the will in which they recognized and honored their own strength and delight in dominion."[21] The right of mastery, says Nietzsche, is the right to inflict pain—but the highest mastery is that over the self[22] (and may include the choice to have pain inflicted). This triumphant restraint and delight in pain are absolutely corporeal. Self-mastery can itself be transcended in a self-defiance that overcomes the self in the discipline of restraint and the delight of pain.

This is the defiance of *telos*, which as I have suggested several times over will turn out to be quite important. Restraint, as I have said, is a means of intensification: it disciplines the forces of desire so that their expression is both stylized and intensified. Desire is given time to *grow*; its quick release and undoing are prevented. Restraint refuses easy release to the point of altering the very nature of desire. Desire becomes both power and pleasure. At a certain point desire no longer makes good sense; its movement turns paradoxical. Indeed, too early gratification would be masochistically experienced as quite disappointing—one reason to be wary of seeing bottoms as meek, passive, or even particularly undemanding.

This notion of joy in resistance will itself encounter considerable and heartfelt resistance: "Out of the human capacity to perceive and to think these words come to me: *it is an intolerable absurdity to hear that binding is liberation.*"[23] Asceticism, binding, bondage, discipline in the non-Foucauldean sense, restraint, chosen pain—these are not, in point of fact, liberation. With Foucault, I would argue that the liberation of sexual desire in fact fits our culture very neatly. These are instead a play with desire. They are strategically deployed forces of power through which the body resists, not the trivial and momentary restraint nor even, in the case of the saintly ascetic, the entire life of the flesh, but rather, again, the social restraints that constitute the good subject. As I shall suggest, if there is a political value to this resistance, it will not be found where we expect such things, but we may find it all the more powerful in its unexpectedness.

We should perhaps explore the subject further, to unfold more completely these possibilities of resistance.

declining productivity

The twentieth century will undoubtedly have discovered the related categories of exhaustion, excess, the limit, and transgression—the strange and unyielding form of these irrevocable movements which consume and consummate us. In a form of thought that considers man as worker and producer—that of European culture since the end of the eighteenth century—consumption was based entirely on need, and need based itself exclusively on the model of hunger. When this element was introduced into an investigation of profit (the appetite of those who have satisfied their hunger), it inserted man into a dialectic of production which had a simple anthropological meaning: if man was alienated from his real nature and immediate needs through his labor and the production of objects with his hands, it was nevertheless through its agency that he recaptured his essence and achieved the indefinite gratification of his needs.

—Michel Foucault, "Preface to Transgression"

I have suggested a double break through strategic restraint and pain: with subjectivity and with productivity. These are, of course, related. The break with good subjectivity arises in the *useless* and *excessive* nature of deliberately invoked pain and restraint. Foucault's disciplined subject is efficient, productive, working under the imperative of complete use—of time, space, and body. No time must be wasted, no space disordered, no gesture unproductive.[24] "Let us say," he writes, "that discipline is the unitary technique by which the body is reduced as a 'political' force at the least cost and maximized as a useful force."[25] Both efficiency and productivity, enhanced by disciplinary order, take on for us the status of cultural imperatives in the culture that so constructs its subjects.

At the same time, our bodies are identified by and as consumer objects: "The body becomes increasingly *the* stake of late capitalism. *Having* the commodified object . . . is displaced by *appearing*, producing a strange constriction of the gap between consumer and commodity."[26] As efficiency and productivity align themselves with the imperative of teleology—that is, with the need for an aim or goal, an effect or product—they align themselves both with the morally good and with consumer-oriented satisfaction in which even pleasure is a product. Delay and restraint defy culture in a way that strikes many as immorally and unnaturally manipulative.

If we turn this teleological discipline to the organization of the force of desire, we come to value most a quick, efficient gratification (which eliminates the power of desire to distract and render undisciplined) or else a productive channeling in which desire is directed to ends that uphold the established order and secure it in its functioning. The former prospect emphasizes efficiency, the latter, productivity; but both oppose the very different, transgressive discipline of the limit at which we lose the subject itself.

I mentioned earlier the doubleness of *plaisir* and *jouissance*. Our usual and soothing sense of pleasure, the pleasure that Roland Barthes calls *plaisir*, is neatly described by Jane Gallop as "comfortable, ego-assuring, recognized and legitimated as culture."[27] To this

quality of steadiness and preservation Barthes (among others) opposes neither pain nor restraint but the pleasure of *jouissance*, a
French term often regarded as untranslatable, which Gallop describes as "shocking, ego-disruptive, and in conflict with the canons
of culture."[28] In this opposition, pleasure, as *plaisir*, would accord
with and serve the interests of both culture and subjectivity. (It
would thus seem to be on the side as well of the power that is formative of culture and of the subject.)[29]

Jouissance is often associated with the pleasure of orgasm, but
need not be so—and pleasure that disrupts subjectivity becomes especially interesting if it outlasts the relatively brief span of the secular Western orgasm, or at least defies its *telos*, its *directedness*, its
lingering artifactuality. This, it turns out, is its first form of subversion, that of the imperative of result—that is, productivity (and at the
same time the commodification inherent in the artifact of the orgasm). Moreover, in this defiance the pleasure of *jouissance* loses its
socially approved status, the status that allows orgasmic pleasure to
move back into the realm of the culturally accepted, as that which
Gallop calls "the calming teleology of sexual arousal,"[30] a teleology
we've accepted as obvious at least since Freud. We have already seen
such defiance three times over. Sade and Masoch defy the build up
and resolution that gratify us in literature. Asceticism defies the ease
that keeps the body profane. But, perhaps because of its contemporaneity, s/m seems to be an exceptionally evident case of this defiance.

While ego and culture so often come together, whether in soothing *plaisir* or teleological *jouissance*, pleasure that disrupts both ego
and culture is dangerous; it is the pleasure Baudrillard calls seduction: "sexual pleasure too is reversible, that is to say that, in the absence or denial of the orgasm, superior intensity is possible. It is here,
where the end of sex becomes aleatory again, that something arises
that can be called seduction or delight. . . . No one knows to what destructive depths such provocation can go, nor what omnipotence it
implies."[31] It is in this pleasure of seduction (again, tantalizingly similar to asceticism) that we begin to see the pleasure of restraint—and,
even, though less directly, of pain. Seductive delight for Baudrillard
is always linked with restraint, with a ritualized but violent delay of
the gratification of desire.

This delay, this ritualized and sometimes ceremonial seeming violence of restraint, opposes both the productive and the teleological.
It breaks the subject, and so it is impossible for this provocation to be

morally or politically correct—such rectitude demands a sovereign subjectivity. The pleasures of pain and of delay become instead what Gallop, expressing an evaluation not her own, calls "tainted pleasure, bad, sick, masochistic: perversion." She points out that, though "liberated from subjection to biologico-Christian standards [of procreativity], pleasure must now be politically correct."[32] (As orgasmic, *jouissance* comes back under the heading of gratification and can be made to serve political if not egological correctness.) The politically correct pleasure is gratifying; pleasure is gratification.

Unless one happens to be some sort of pervert, or saint. . .

It is in defiance of any "calming teleology" that both pain and restraint enter into their odd alliance with pleasure (both, or neither, *plaisir* and *jouissance*). *Restraint* encompasses various forms of delay and of gratification's denial, the rerouting of desire away from speedy satisfaction. (It is a commonplace among masochists to remain in a state of desire deliberately intensified by themselves or their tops.) Like pain, restraint takes in (or is taken in by) both the ascetic and the erotic, encompassing both an excessive discipline or self-discipline and the very literal restraint of movement (whether as bondage or in response to the challenge of the command).

In their deliberate turning away of desire from its *telos* toward gratification and release, both restraint and pain, whether self-imposed or invoked, make of desire a subversive force. Such restraint is a means not to desire's repression or elimination, but to its intensification; pain too is a means not to the ultimate denial of desire but to its subversive rerouting away from release to an explosive increase.

If we take the first perspective—that desire ought to be directed toward its gratification—then we find ourselves in the realm of Gallop's teleological calm. This is the space of politically correct pleasure, especially for women. Gallop, among others, has remarked upon the Hite report brand of feminism, which celebrates masturbation for its efficiency and reliability in the teleological pursuit of climax.[33] This is the politically correct morality of gratification,[34] oddly close, as we with Gallop have already noted, to the Christian and biological (or psychoanalytic) paradigms of productivity. That is, both insist upon a directed desire, not to be intensified by delay nor altered by violence in its straight, rapid, and efficient projection toward its goal. Perversely, though, s/m seems to fit with a cultural feminist sexuality in at least this respect: it diverts energy and desire away from the goal oriented genitality so often labeled masculine.

Under the imperative of the productive channeling of desire, we are back to conditions of external restraint, the position of the disciplined subject. Here it is tempting to say that desire is *repressed* so that the subject, undistracted by irrelevant urges, takes on the factorylike efficiency of an automaton. Foucault, however, suggests that repression is too easy, and in many ways inadequate, as an explanation of power.[35] So we seek another explanation: if the power of external restraint is *not* repression, then perhaps it is the construction of very efficiently, productively channeled desire in the efficient, productive desiring subject. The imposition of such restraint may well, of course, provoke resistance; on the other hand, it may continue unchallenged if its mechanisms are good enough. That is, desire may be neatly channeled into productivity, such that efficiency itself becomes cathected, productivity itself gratifying. This description suggests a more stable system than does the hypothesis of repression, though of course there remain possibilities of resistance. (And the repressed, after all, invariably *returns*, disrupting the productive order.) In either case, productivity cannot be entirely secure.

Freud would call the opposition to efficient gratification *perverse*.[36] Baudrillard, as we have seen, calls it seductive, and he sees delightful seduction, the ritualized strategizing of the force of desire, as capable of undermining the power of productivity. In seduction, in delight, the force of desire restrained asserts itself against the economic structuring of power. ("It is never an economy of sex or speech," he writes," but an escalation of violence and grace."[37]) Thus what is perverse for the Freudian, seductive for Baudrillard, is also subversive, and so it acquires a Foucauldean interest as well. At the level of the body, it is restraint that is at issue, with its extended, often violent intensification. Bondage is not liberation; it is resistance, it is power, and it is joy.

Thus, in its way, an excessive and useless restraint is *already* a form of resistance—to power as the disciplinary force of efficiency and productivity. Whether power has constructed desire or channeled it; whether we see desire *as* power or as a bodily force that may, as the body always may, collude with the powers that inscribe it or defy them in resistance (even by using them against themselves), we find a powerful defiance of power in the pleasures of pain and restraint. If the cultural norm is desire-directed-toward-production, or even the repression of desire in favor of production, then the intensification of desire in an unproductive direction (more: a direction without a *telos*) is a form of resistance. If the norm is the efficient gratification of desire, then the deliberate, sustained, and intensified arousal of desire is, again, a resistance to an institutionalized form of power. If we once discover the intensity of the pleasure possible in desire's intensification under restraint, the more socially manipulable pleasures of gratification lose some considerable degree of their force. Perhaps this is the fear of those who describe s/m as addictive.

We have already noted how nearly the ascetic denial of efficiency approaches the self-sacrificial—the ultimately unproductive. (The saint, we recall, is not after efficiency.) The nonascetic excesses of restraint are equally unproductive, defying gratification in favor of an extravagant spiraling of intensity at the cost of an absurd expenditure of energy.

Thus far I have noted primarily the power of restraint, but something similar happens in the pleasurable eroticization of pain. Where pain is *not* something to be overcome (where pain and pleasure, without being the same, have become entangled), we find ourselves without an evident *goal* for erotic activity (hence, perhaps, the sense that s/m is erotic rather than sexual—not because it is less "down and dirty" but because it is less strictly genital, certainly less orgasmically preoccupied, than vanilla sex. It is in this sense that Foucault can call it a "desexualization" of pleasure).[38] More strikingly, the sensation of *pain*, which remains painful even when it is eroticized, provokes a double response: at once a sense that it *must stop*, not infrequently accompanied by a reflection along the lines of "what was I *thinking*?" (some newcomers are startled to find that the pain is in fact real and fairly intense), and a sense that it *must not* stop: both its cessation and its continuation are at once entirely intolerable and unspeakably desirable. (This is one reason that restraint is often a helpful supplement.) There is nowhere that one might "get to." Here, too, desire, taken beyond the orderly economy that would allow it to produce relaxation, explodes.

The argument against sadomasochism sees restraint quite differently. Here the idea is that the sadist gratifies her desire (like a stereotypical man) and ignores the masochist's. The masochist, because he voluntarily submits to restraint, must have abandoned desire, as Jessica Benjamin suggests:

> The master's denial of the other's subjectivity leaves him faced with isolation as the only alternative to being engulfed by the dehumanized other. In either case, the mas-

ter is actually alone, because the person he is with is no
person at all. . . . The masochist increasingly feels that she
does not exist, that she is without will or desire, that she
has no life apart from the other.[39]

Further:

The masochist's self is '"false" because . . . he has not been
able to realize the desire and agency that come from
within. He has not experienced his impulses and acts as
his own, arising without direction from outside.[40]

That one could want to play these incendiary games with desire does
not make sense where desire's multiplicity is refused, where all pleasure must return to the security of the subject.

In the face of pain and restraint the body as desire, in desire, still
desiring defies subjection to the economic order that power is not,
but that power constructs and enforces, which our culture sees as
both natural and morally correct.

A greater and more dangerous—that is, more profoundly subversive—form of defiance, however, remains to be examined: we
must finally take a closer look at subjectivity.

imploded subjectivity

How can it be understood, unless we go right back to the
inevitable agony of the discontinuous creature doomed to
die, that violence alone, blind violence, can burst the bar-
riers of the rational world and lead us into continuity?

—Georges Bataille, *Erotism*

While we are in Foucauldean (or perhaps Nietzschean) territory, let
us remark a bit more carefully upon the construction of the subject.
The subject, on this view, is not pregiven, ahistorical, disembodied,
nor existentially free (though this last by no means absolves it of responsibility). Rather, the very concept of the subject—and the very
existence of subjectivity, which strikes us as too intimate to be a construct—is, in fact, constituted by the body's subjection. (I do not
mean by this to exclude language from this constitutive process.
Body and language never exist for us unmediated by one another.
Nietzsche's claim that the "I" is a grammatical fiction, a mistaking of
syntax for metaphysics,[41] does not mean that this fiction has not been

inscribed on the subjected body.) The contemporary body is subject to the intellectual disciplines of the human sciences, which construct their subjects in studying them and gain power through their knowledge of the subject, knowledge through their power over the subject. The body is subject as well to the omnipresent and ultimately internalized gaze of these sciences and the institutions that give rise to them (schools, factories, hospitals, prisons), ultimately of the entire social sphere; under this gaze, through these disciplines, in its carefully structured and divided space, the subject emerges—in, as, and through the body. It seems as improbable that one could move outside this subjection as that one could move outside power.

But under restraint, and, further, in pain the subject itself is undone—and thereby acquires an aesthetically subversive power of resistance (and we once more note that the very fact of subversion, itself resistant, is not infrequently pleasurable). This is a statement that will seem at once immorally apolitical and politically appalling. Immorally apolitical, because it lacks the political value of giving power to the disenfranchised subject—by it, in fact, the *subject* is subverted, becoming subversive only in the most indirect fashion. In my emphasis on pleasure I will seem to be too individualized, yet I shall be arguing that this pleasure, valuably, defies the boundaries of the individual subject. On the other hand, it might seem that I am presenting and arguing for a message that is clearly politically dangerous: that it is pleasurable to be restrained and to be subject to violence—which would seem to go against all manner of very fundamental convictions that most of us hold regarding human rights.

The human rights argument has in fact been raised against s/m. Margaret Hunt reports on Janice Raymond's presentation at an important conference on feminism and power:

> The gist of her remarks was that lesbian S/M recapitulates and reinforces the oppressive structures of the atrocity. . . . At one point, she compared people with tolerant attitudes toward . . . S/M to those who deny the Holocaust ever happened. This was very distressing not only to some of the people in the audience who did S/M (including several who were Jewish) but to a prominent feminist historian of the Holocaust who was attending the conference. . . . Julia Penelope focused on what was to become a recurrent theme of the conference, the accusation that the S/M community . . . was insensitive to the victimization of

women and girls as represented in . . . rape, battering and the like.[42]

I shall begin my counterargument with a return to the politics of the subject. Generally, when subjectivity is considered as a political issue, it is considered a form of "empowerment" to be *recognized* in all of one's likeness and Otherness.[43] Some writers have, not unreasonably, suggested that this recognition should permeate the intimately interpersonal as well as the more obviously political: "The secret of love," writes Jessica Benjamin in "Master and Slave: the Fantasy of Erotic Domination," "is to be known as oneself."[44] This implies, of course, that there is one self to be known. Judith Butler writes on the contrary of "the impossibility of a full recognition, that is, of ever fully inhabiting the name by which one's social identity is inaugurated and mobilized, [which] implies the instability and incompleteness of subject-formation."[45]

Obviously enough, Benjamin's Hegelian emphasis on *recognition* is quite opposed to the loss of subject status. And in fact, one common reason for the opposition to restraint and violence, even s/m's stylized violence, and to the infliction of pain in particular, is that there seems to be no *love* involved. Somehow we have come to have a rather pastoral and sanitized conception of love.[46] (In the next and final chapters I shall try to present an alternative image of love, which is in fact crucial to both s/m and asceticism, and at least relevant to Sade and Masoch.) Benjamin's analysis in this essay claims that violence, including violent restraint, *reinforces* the subject (or tries to), and that even violence is an attempt at love under her definition; that is, the recognition of subjects by one another: "Violence, we may generalize, is an attempt at differentiation . . . The fantasy of erotic domination, the play with violence, is an attempt to relive an original effort at differentiation that failed."[47] Erotic violence, then, is an attempt to *establish* more firmly those shaky subject- or ego-boundaries, so that we may *recognize* one another's subjectivity and thus try to love one another—though for her violence always fails in this attempt.

I would argue against this claim, not with Hegel but after him, with Bataille, who finds in both violence and restraint, in both the erotic and the sacred, the *disruption* of differentiation. It is here that subjectivity begins to come undone, still more radically than in the alteration of the direction of its desire or even itself as desire. Masochism is not, as Benjamin argues, an inability to deal with paradox;[48] it is an overwhelming pleasure in the paradox of a desire that wills beyond itself.

Bataille emphasizes the ability of both excessive asceticism and violent eroticism to disrupt subjective discontinuity, to undo isolation—not so sweetly reassuring a move as one might at first think. A major element of our understanding of subjectivity is the subject's discontinuity or separateness. There can be, to put it crudely, no understanding of "this is me" without the corresponding sense "that is not me." Under the intensification of impersonal desire provided by restraint, discontinuity is overcome. One loses a sense of the bounds of oneself—though not to be replaced by any sort of perfect continuity, any loss of otherness or sense of cosmic union. In the loss of the discontinuous subject sense, paradoxically, is a touch of the loss of subjection: the emergence of the force of the will of the body under a quite different inscription, the body's freedom from its own unavoidable subjection under an other subjection fully sought.

As Benjamin rightly notes, "Life means discontinuity, the confinement of each individual to a separate, isolated existence. Death means continuity."[49] What fascinates Bataille, who presents a quite similar distinction (particularly in *Erotism* and his *Somme Athéologique*), is the *discipline* of overcoming individual discontinuity—particularly through the body and the delight of that flirtation with the edge of death. Benjamin writes that "the body stands for discontinuity, individuality, and life,"[50] but she is speaking of the embodied *subject*; Bataille's' fascination is with the body of the shattered subject, the transgression of the seemingly insurmountable boundary between discontinuous living and the continuity of death. It is not the death of the *body* but of the *subject* that is sought—a "death" invariably followed by a return quite possibly undesired.

Here is one of the most important sources of the sense of masochistic power. The subject, oneself, retains *in the body* the memory of this transgressive rapture: "The spot where I have earlier known ecstasy, memory bewitched by physical sensations, . . . together have an evocative power greater than the voluntary repetition of a describable movement of the mind."[51] These spots can be quite literal, and may explain the importance many bottoms place on marks both temporary (bruises, aching spots, shallow cuts) and permanent (body modifications such as piercings or brands).

That the subject can retain this knowledge suggests that there is indeed some nonmomentary power to this resistance to unbroken subjectivity; "As soon as I emerge from [rapture], communication, the loss of myself cease; I have ceased to abandon myself. I remain there, but with a new knowledge."[52] This is the knowledge, impossible without a subject, of a possibility beyond subjectivity. Thus there is an odd movement in this rupture of subjectivity, captured in a remark from Bataille's *Inner Experience*: "The subject—weariness of itself, necessity of proceeding to the extreme limit—seeks ecstasy, it is true: never does it have the *will* for its ecstasy. There exists an irreducible discord between the subject seeking ecstasy and the ecstasy itself."[53] At once an irreducible discord and a mutual strength—this is the paradox of m-powerment.

Restraint, in its intensification of desire and its impersonal disregard for gratification, already begins the explosive movement of desire beyond subjectivity. But we must note the role of pain in this transcendence or transgression as well. "Pain," writes Benjamin, "is the violent rupture of the self-organization."[54] Proponents of moderate asceticism as well as the more conciliatory proponents of s/m tend to deemphasize pain. Pain makes it hard to present a picture of mere self-discipline and strong character, or of ironic simulation, innocent role-play (both role-play and simulation may be at work, but neither is innocent—rather both serve as background to pain and restraint), any sort of healthy normality. Whatever else may be purely simulated, the *pain* remains real, and as it increases the order of the ego is broken. Indeed, the sensation of this breakage is one of the most remarkable aspects of s/m play. As pain continues, repeats, and builds (and desire, as I remarked earlier, explodes), there is a sense of being slammed, repeatedly, into the wall of oneself, against one's own ego boundaries until these break, and, with them, shatter the descriptive capabilities of language. Pain thus reinforces and amplifies the power of restraint. This breaking of limits is a source of power and joy, readily subject to misreading: "There's supposed to be no coercion in S&M, yet there's clearly pressure to keep going further. How can anyone who's sexually excited by the inequalities acted out in S&M be trusted to respect limits?"[55]

This too is easily read otherwise. Opponents of restraint's excesses often point to the claims of lost self among ascetics as well as submissives and masochists—a loss that is less a disappearance that a giving over of the self, a voluntary enslavement, whether this takes the form of an impassioned Augustinian insistence that freedom comes in turning the will over to God, or the less transcendent form of leather collars with rings for leads. If we assume—and as good rational subjects we would have to assume—that freedom and autonomy are to be desired, this is pretty clearly not a good thing. But stepping outside this version of the autonomous subject we encounter the Nietzschean will and its corresponding sense of freedom—very different from that of Augustine, or for that matter (more rationally) Descartes or (less theistically) Kant. Here it is the movement of the will against resistance sought and created by its own force that is freedom—a subversive freedom in an aesthetic resistance. It is the aesthetic itself that subverts, beyond any directly "political" implications of s/m. It is in this mnemonic embodiment of the outside, the space beyond the edge of the self, that the remarkable strength of sadomasochistic subversion becomes apparent: freedom from subjectivity is freedom from the forces of subjection, and the body knows that such things are possible.

Sought and created by its own force. . . . Though the existence of safewords[56] is one of the most common points raised in defense of s/m, I have no intent here of returning us to issues of consent, which so preoccupy those who cannot understand why anyone would "voluntarily" undergo restraint, and who assume in such cases an excess of cultural conditioning *denying an authentically free subjectivity.* (I would only note that if masochists are too conditioned by patriarchy to consent freely to their pleasures, then it is unclear how anyone else acquires the freedom to consent to hers.) I would say rather that at a sufficient intensity of power, a sufficiently impassioned desire turns the body against the restraint of subjection, yanks the body beyond the subject—institutes the body's rebellion against its subjection to subjectivity, beyond that realm in which consensuality has any tidy meanings.

Here where we cannot be sufficiently precise we must be extremely careful. The strong will seeks out what resists it, attains ecstasy in exertion, exaltation against impossibility—but this does not make all restraint good. Without seeing in Nietzsche (and Foucault after Nietzsche, and all of us after Foucault) some sort of voluntarism[57] we must nonetheless see in their work the description of a will that follows its *own* absurdly difficult rules—the rules that are its own for its own growth and its own sacrificial expenditure (the Nietzschean forms of joy, recelebrated by Bataille). Restraint by or under another set of rules can as easily weaken and break the force of the will as its exuberant search for resistance can push it to further power. Such restraint and such violence are closer to repression than to seduction. Violence and restraint imposed against desire fail entirely to be the strategic manipulation *of* desire (by desire . . .) which is at once provocative and intensifying. *A disregard for desire cannot be a means to its explosive intensification.* Pain, alone, may lead to a loss of subjectivity, but not to a pleasurable *abandon* of the subject, in which the subject freely breaks its own limits and is lost in pleasure. An assault is without the power of the subject's paradoxical move against its own limits. Desire can be explosively intensified by restraint, but *not* if there is no desire at the outset. Pain's play with pleasure can explode our exchange-oriented economic sensibility, but not if there is no pleasure. To be pushed beyond oneself is not the same as being torn away from oneself; the violence of sadomasochistic eroticism is not rape, but requires extraordinary sensitivity and attentiveness.[58] Without this, the anti-s/m movement would be right. We must begin in consent if we are to go to a place in which it has no meaning, or in which all its meanings are made strange.

Not everyone was meant to be a saint, and perhaps not even everyone is a pervert, but where discipline accords with the force of the will the implosion of subjectivity in a sudden boundary loss is more freeing than Kantian autonomy can ever be, more pleasurable, and a stronger force of resistance. Freedom *of* the subject is not the concern under restraint; this is what consent arguments on both sides, preoccupied with power-as-control, miss. Pain and restraint provide us not with an *overtly* political subversion but with the aesthetic subversion of the subject itself—prior to political possibilities, and thus all the more capable of subverting them. It is because the personal *is* the political—and, more to the postmodern point, because we can and must only resist power at the same microlevels at which it manifests itself—that the aesthetically shattered, postsubjective, ascetic, erotic, sadomasochistic body becomes politically subversive.

If this seems politically unsatisfying, it is perhaps for a reason that Foucault, again, has made clear. We tend still to analyze politics in highly centralized, sovereign terms. Subversion, in these terms, must have some direct effect, if not upon the Person of the King, at least upon the activities of The Government. But it has been a long time since power was purely sovereign; disciplinary power (power exercised over bodies and not over goods)[59] *is* so powerful precisely because it is so widely dispersed as to be internalized. To rupture subjectivity is an act of remarkable defiance: "The individual is an effect of power, and at the same time, or precisely to the extent to which it is that effect, it is the element of its articulation. The individual which power has constituted is at the same time its vehicle."[60]

The effects of this subversion will ripple beyond the no longer individual; at a minimum they affect intersubjective relations. This is not the defiance of repression but the joy of power—and "If one wants to look for a non-disciplinary form of power, or rather, to struggle against disciplines and disciplinary power, it is not towards the ancient right of sovereignty that one should turn, but toward the possibility of a new form of right, one which must indeed be anti-disciplinarian, but at the same time liberated from the principle of sovereignty."[61] This is the "liberation" not of the sovereign subject but of the joyful body.

Frank Browning neatly summarizes the incompatibility of this joy with our more customary sense of correctness in *The Culture of Desire*:

> The pursuit and recovery of the sacred and the ecstatic in contemporary life is a journey separate from the path to equity, democracy, and justice. It promises only a quality of knowing unavailable to the Rousseauistic mind of social contracts. The impulse toward the ecstatic speaks of neither good nor evil, neither protection nor redemption. It speaks only to remind us that the permanent human condition is exposure, and it reveals that the new activist demand for sexual "safe space" is little more than a silly oxymoron.[62]

And yet in this dangerous move outside the space of safety we find the possibility of freedom *from* subjection. What stronger rebellion of the body against power, what stronger show of the power of the body, what more joyous corporeal triumph is imaginable? (And, we might add, just how doubly perverse can you get?)

7

switch/hit
taking it from the top

the seduction of control

There's so much pleasure in taking orders, and there's so
much pleasure in giving orders.
            —Michel Foucault, interviewed on a French talk show

The reduction of power to law . . . enables power never to
be thought of in other than negative terms: refusal, limitation, obstruction, censorship. Power is what says no.
            —Michel Foucault, "Power and Strategies"

A switch in perspective brings us to a surprisingly similar vision, to
another disruption of subjectivity. It is evident already that sado/
masochistic power must go beyond control, in more than one sense
of that phrase. Still, power as we have seen it so far finally seems
rather one-sided, though the side has switched from our initial expectation. That is, the theory remains stubbornly bottom-heavy.[1]
Mandy Merck, in her carefully noncommittal analysis of "the feminist ethics of lesbian s/m," asks of feminist writings, "Where, then,
is sadism in these accounts? (One could complain that a good top is
as hard to find in the theory as it reputedly is in the practice.) A few
cruelties may be alluded to . . . but the subjectivity which enacts
them is never examined. Nor is its philosophy."[2] This seems an accurate observation, and one that holds from the more positive per-

spective as well. (Pat Califia, who plays and writes as a top, is a valuable exception.)

Rather than seeing power as identical with control (thus in the top's "possession") we have seen it as a delightfully disruptive *dis*-possession. The problem is that in the theory we've explored so far the force or strength of this destabilizing, even desubjectivizing power seems to linger (as incarnate memory, or as Bataille's "new knowledge") with or belong to the returned, problematized but still in some fashion singular (discontinuous) subjectivity of the bottom. Does the top become purely instrumental? Is *she* the one objectified?

This notion of the bottom as extremely powerful is, as I hope I have shown, already subversive in a cultural context that valorizes the forces of productivity and control and sees any relinquishing of control as a form of victimization. But at least some anti-s/m theorists believe that opprobrium is appropriately focused not on the bottom (who is relegated to the status of a victim at most collaborative in her own abuse) but on the top—the evil sadist.[3] While it should be clear by now that bottoms are *not*—or at a minimum are not disproportionately—victims, an important question remains. Power, after all, moves *between*, and this is as true for subversive as for hegemonous powers. So we must inquire after another part of the relation; we must in fact inquire into relationality. What, after all, *is* in it for the top?

When the bottom's body bears the inscriptions of power, holds the unknowledge (the impossible Bataillean unknowing) of burst subjectivity, remembers impossible joyful knowledge, the subversive joy of m-powerment is evident—and still, we don't know what's in it for the top. Being purely instrumental would certainly not be particularly gratifying. Unsurprisingly, in certain ways (though by no means in every way) top- and bottom-pleasure mirror one another; that is, both productivity/teleology and discontinuous subjectivity are undermined for the top as well; and for him too this undermining occurs as the escalation of strength. The sense of this strength, however, is somewhat different for each of them.

It is true, as s/m-positive writers have often pointed out, that there is a sort of "contact high" for the top, a concept that, though it may not go a long way toward explanation, does describe pretty well. (It also fits well with the emphasis on the sharing of both pleasure and power across subject-boundaries.) Others suggest that there is something magical—or "magickal"—in the s/m exchange. In chemical terms, one might even claim the endorphin rush of the bottom is somehow shared—but it's fairly clear that the reductivism of chemical terms will not get us much further than the vagueness of the occult. (Are the endorphins absorbed through the top's skin, or what?) How, without resorting to either magic or neurochemistry, might we grasp this sharing? How is it that in some real fashion the top and bottom *share* the same joy, take joy in the sharing—since, to quote Jean-Luc Nancy quoting Lucretius, "I say it again and again: pleasure is shared?"[4]

I would suggest that the relationality is more obvious (not, importantly, more genuine) from the top side. Power's relationality is not more *genuine* from one side than another, because power in any case is and *must be* relational. Nietzsche had already made this clear: his will to power is a will to overcome, but what exists to be overcome is itself only will, force, power. As Deleuze puts it, the struggle is always between active will and reactive will.[5]

Foucault makes the point still more strongly when he suggests that we might be better off never speaking of "power" at all, given the noun's tendency to reify, but only of "relations of power": "Power in the substantive sense, *'le' pouvoir*, doesn't exist. What I mean is this. The idea that there is either located at—or emanating from—a given point something which is a 'power' seems to me to be based on a misguided analysis. . . . In reality power means relations."[6]

Power's relegation to a prepositional phrase, "relations *of* power," reminds us that its position is always between, among, with, against, not determinately *at* one pole or another. Power-as-such would not exist, then, only power as (and not merely *in*) the relations of force, relations at once discursive and embodied, at once structural and explosive. Two such relations, seen this time from the top's perspective, show us once more the emergence of the subversive power of embodied pleasure against more hegemonous disciplinary powers.

extravagant expenditures

One morning [Zarathustra] rose with the dawn, stepped before the sun, and spoke to it thus: "You great star, what would your happiness be without those for whom you shine? For ten years you have climbed to my cave: you would have tired of your light and of the journey had it not been for me and my eagle and my serpent. But we waited for you every morning, took your overflow from you, and blessed you for it. Behold, I am weary of my wis-

> dom. . . . I need hands outstretched to receive it. I would
> give away and distribute."
>
> —Friedrich Nietzsche, *Thus Spake Zarathustra*

Embodied will, we have already seen, links joy to desire in the Nietzschean *Lust*, the will that demands eternity (*die Lust will aber Ewigkeit*), bursting time with subjectivity—repeating, accelerating, freezing, exploding.[7] It is important to recognize that joy and desire are not automatically or necessarily linked in this way, in this fashion that demands their co-occurrent intensification. In the everyday (nonecstatic) economy of investment, expenditure is loss (and desire is lack, founded upon the need to fill what is empty, replace what is lost). This is precisely the economy of productivity, the teleological economy found in the security of the center. The transgressive economy of excess links joy to desire such that one cannot increase without the other, and joy becomes not gratification (the teleological artifact of the orgasm) but intensification. (It is interesting, particularly in light of critiques of s/m as unethical, to note that for Foucault this is an ethical eroticism: "The relationship that I think we need to have with ourselves when we have sex is an ethics of pleasure, of intensification of pleasure.")[8] For the top, the relation between *autonomy* and *communication*, rule-giving and responsivity, creates the paradoxical tension that spirals into the intensification of pleasure. The center cannot hold securely when the boundaries have been burst. Desire becomes pleasure and pain at once, undeniable on either side. And joy itself, joy as pleasurable/painful desire, as the will to eternity in the passing moment, transgresses productive order as a subversive force: joy is power, a relation of power.

Power, we recall, is not merely relational but always *material*. Within the economy of joy, power seeks expenditure; materially, as force, the body expends itself. But in expenditure is its increase; the more it expends itself (its energy, its vitality, its strength) the more powerful it becomes. In the epigraphic citation from Zarathustra we recognize a new peculiarity of this expenditure—peculiar, at any rate, until we recollect the always relational quality of power. The peculiarity is this: it will do the sun no good to shine unless it shines upon the people; it will do Zarathustra no good to descend the mountain, full of the vigor he has drawn from his healthy solitude, unless he descends into the ranks of human beings who *need* his wisdom. The expenditure of force which is power, it seems, demands that it not be expended at random nor into a void, but rather that in its expenditure it meet some *receptivity*—something, some other force, must exist to *respond*.

It is because of this demand that most hostile perceptions of tops miss the point, assuming that the sadist or dominant wants to deny the bottom's existence or at least subjectivity: "If I completely control the other, then the other ceases to exist. . . . A condition of our own independent existence is recognizing the other. True independence means . . . both asserting the self and recognizing the other. Domination is the consequence of refusing this condition."[9] But both must begin in subjectivity, if only so that both have the freedom to exceed it (an *object* cannot delightedly burst its boundaries).

The need for responsivity—for, that is, an *active receptivity*—already emphasizes the relationality of power from the top's perspective. This is so both in the sense that the "top's" power demands a powerful bottom, and in the sense that in some fashion the "bottom's" power belongs to the top—though ultimately, and in a deeper sense, this power, in exceeding subjectivity, will exceed altogether the possibilities of possession.[10] The need for a powerful bottom will be explored below. The latter sense is again dual. First, fairly straightforwardly, the bottom, in ceding title to or control of "her" power (perhaps more precisely: her power *as control*) to the top, thereby *increases* that power (though not as control); this is the paradox of m-powerment. Second, more subtly, the transgressivity that is the power of m-powerment we also find, albeit perspectivally shifted, in or as the "top's" power—that is, much of this is the sheer power of limit-breaking.

What's more, responsive receptivity is not just a bottom's trait. Everyone in the sadomasochistic spiral defies the conservative, nonresponsive economy of investment and return, the Freudian economy of libidinal gratification. While it may be more obvious that the teleology of this economy is defied by ceding control (giving over one's desire in the act of giving oneself over *to* desire), we must be aware that *taking* this control can also be a giving over. Awareness is also receptivity, an openness to the responsivity of the other, which is at the same time and in both directions an enabling. Thus all roles in the s/m scene have this subversive potential for undermining our culture's disciplinary demand for productive pleasure.

We should guard against the easy conflation of receptivity with passivity. True receptivity is *active*; we might better see it as *responsiveness*. Nietzsche writes of active receptivity as a defining trait of the best and strongest spirits, which are in fact incapable of withholding responsivity, being so *susceptible* to joy. They are open to the world and must respond to it, which is neither to endure stoically nor to react defensively.[11] This openness is that love which is the love of fate, of what the world brings, an embracing—not a passive—openness. But openness too can *give*; it does not only take in but also opens outward, directs itself outward, sometimes with force.

Responsive openness is engagement. Left to itself, as Bataille tells us, an organism folds down, closes in upon itself, and goes to sleep; left to itself it becomes solely itself. This defiance does not resolve the problem of its insufficiency, its discontinuity from the rest of life. Rather, it intensifies that discontinuity and ceases to seek the impossibly sufficient. Responsivity, on the other hand, defies this individualistic discontinuity; it is an active opening up, not a passive undergoing of a barrage of stimuli—and yet it must play between activity and passivity, it must be an openness to what comes. It both seeks the sufficiency of continuity and maintains the insufficiency of the subject. It is responsivity, we shall see, that openness plays off of control to render dominance and sadism subversive. Eva Feder Kittay sees the ideal erotic exchange as "the mutual and reciprocal giving and receiving of sexual pleasure, such that the other's desire and pleasure are constitutive of our own"[12]—but in fact this, at an unusual level of intensity, is precisely what the sadomasochistic relation manifests.

Again, it's too easy to think of responsiveness as solely the bottom's responsibility. With more care, it's here that we can begin to understand the *double* generosity of s/m responsivity. To take delight is also to give it. To (try to) top to no response is to expend one's force into a void. If this expenditure meets with an obstacle, with an explicit resistance, the only ethical response is redirection—"ethical" not in the more customary sense of autonomous responsibility but in the sense of response-ability or responsivity, a sensitiveness to genuine opposition. This is the kind of opposition that would pit the top's dominating will against the strongest or dominant will of the bottom.

This will make more sense if we recall the Nietzschean argument behind the "unity of domination," which constitutes subjectivity—his claim that we must regard "the subject as multiplicity." No one is one; no one is singular. Each "one" of us is a multiplicity of forces, of often divergent and not infrequently contradictory wills and desires. Foucault suggests that we may even need a politics of "sub-individuals." The strongest people are those in whom a single will is strong enough to harmonize this diversity—not to render it singular, but to put its multiplicity to work under a single direction—a disharmonious set of forces is weakened by being dissipated in a multiplicity of directions. (Of course, the harmonizing will, if indeed it pushes for growth, must always be prepared before discord and may thrive on the intensifying pull of paradox; its harmony will not be static.) Each "one" of us is , to use language explored more fully below, both active and reactive, both negating and affirmative, in varying mixtures and degrees. An *opposition* between two strong wills would mean that the top could impose her will only by a repressiveness that would create resentment, founded on a desire to destroy the strength of the bottom. This, of course, is many people's unreflective take on power and especially on sadism. As Foucault notes, this is a relatively weak sort of power. In fact, power is stronger where it has desire on its side: "power would be a fragile thing if its only function were to repress, if it only worked through the mode of censorship, exclusion, blockage and repression . . . exercising itself only in a negative way. If, on the contrary, power is strong this is because, as we are beginning to realize, it produces effects at the level of desire."[13] To impose repressive power is to top nonresponsively. Under such conditions there will be no joy to share, no high with which to come into contact. It is conspicuously dull and depressing to top someone who is annoyed, resentful, or uninterested. Intensity requires making others want the pain imposed on them, without its ceasing to be painful.

We will have occasion later to return to the power struggles inherent in obvious clashes of wills. But opposition and resentfulness take subtler forms as well, such as an utterly passive nonresponse. Power, without being reducible to repression, nonetheless requires resistance. The distinction is approximately this: good tops know how to direct the play of power so that they and their bottoms overcome to some considerable degree the same resistance, the same weakness, though its manifestation may be very different for them (most obviously, it will usually begin as "mine," for the bottom; "yours," for the top). Thus I would disagree with those whose respect and fondness for s/m leads them to suggest that s/m power is only collaborative, a "power-with" rather than a "power-over."[14] Power plays not merely between but against. The top really does take pleasure in controlling, and in the intensification of sensation that is pain; *and* she takes, simultaneously, pleasure in overcoming the very resistance to control and pain that makes it possible in the first place to impose them (that is, we can neither control nor hurt where no resistance meets us).

The often missed point is that, because it is not centrally or ultimately localizable, it cannot be said to be the power of one subject
against another subject. It can instead be the power, as I shall argue
in more detail in the next section, of strength and affirmation against
weakness and resentment, *across* subjects. That good tops must be
empathic, aware, and tuned in in their generosity is a commonplace,
but good bottoms (however greedy, as many are) must be equally
generous in their responsiveness, in their active receptivity that *enables*, makes space for, the top's self-strengthening excessive expenditure. Their necessary strength is often overlooked from the outside,
though seldom from within.

Part of the story is apparent even at an obvious level, in the ability to enter into the spiral of desire, to take on the pleasure "as if" it
were one's own—and to let the "as if" become all. And in fact, given
the power of joy to rupture subjective boundaries, it must in some
sense be true, as I've already suggested, that the power is the top's.
Empathy cannot be the whole of the story, however; the experience
of topping is not the same as the experience of bottoming; exerting
and inflicting are not the same as undergoing. Howevermuch the
participants may feel together, they do not feel the same. The joy of
these practices belongs neither to the bottom alone nor solely to the
top, nor is it wholly true that each has her own power—rather, the
power, being relational, begins in the relation, the space between
these two (or more) subjects, a space between boundaries that this
movement of power will rupture. (The relation between subjects is
not the only power-relation at work. As we shall see, relations of
power *within* the subject are at least as important. The onset of most
s/m scenes, however, is intersubjective, though like all modes of
eroticism s/m does have its autoerotic forms.) Generosity and empathy, the ability to be deeply aware and mindful of another's state,
will both be of the utmost importance, but each goes beyond any obvious sense, and indeed may appear as its contrary.

When desire meets with desire—in, as Blanchot has put it, "a col-
lision of lights"[15]—a space is created for the "contact high" of the top,
an increase in power, unquestionably an increase in her sense of
power, but, like the spiraling ecstatic desire of the bottom, an increase in a power that overflows the boundaries of subjectivity.[16]

We have already seen that joyful desire, the power of m-powerment, subverts the power of control as exerted by the disciplinary
mechanisms of our culture, by using control against control, making
of it a power beyond control. But joy does not escalate in a vacuum;

as a form of power it must be a relation. Here what is overcome is re-sistance, reluctance, the subjectivization of the flesh. What over-comes is a subjection beyond the subject, a greedy and generous joy. The greed for intensity, even if it may begin as the bottom's, is power's greedy demand for an expansion that may exceed subjectiv-ity. In joy greed and generosity meet at the generative point of the paradox, with joy and desire, pleasure and pain, explosion and im-plosion, acceleration and suspension, time and eternity. The generos-ity of the bottom lies in her ability to give up resentment, to give herself up to the control of the top, to *respond to* rather than to *react against*. Responsivity is the movement of power-with-power, in the sense of active-with-active, against reactivity, overcoming selfishness while necessitating greed. The top's corresponding generosity lies in giving that-to-which the bottom's power responds, and in having the power to make that gift. (And this may be a considerable expendi-ture; lectures in s/m groups deal with "tired tops." Bob Flanagan re-marks that "usually it's the top that's burdened; usually it's the master who says [groan] 'Oh, I gotta whip her *again.*' . . . Or, 'I'm so sick of giving orders!' " Bottoms seem to be less satiable; "a real masochist *never* gets enough; they want it to go on 24 hours a day.")[17] This power to give, however, cannot *belong* to him; without sacrific-ing control he is yet as dispossessed by his generosity as the bottom is by his greed.

Already we have seen this counterproductive joy from below, from the masochistic/submissive perspective. In fact, though, it is readily apparent that the top just as strongly declines productivity: it is his role to continue control and restraint against gratification, to play pain against pleasure, to intensify joy and desire beyond com-prehension's limits. But if this were a purely facilitative role—if the power thus increased *belonged* (even as a relation between disparate elements of the subject) or even returned (mnemonically, say) solely to the bottom—then there would surely be even fewer tops than there are. There is more than work at work here.

Here we recall the obvious: control is not the only form of power, but it is a form. And it is control that the top not only exerts but ef-fortfully *expends*—yet, by expending, takes. This control, however, is forced by its very responsivity outside its usual orderly paradigm—it is control that cannot be finalized. First, because it controls an ever-shifting situation, a fluctuating play of forces, and *depends* for its exertion upon the desire to *keep* those forces at play, to escalate them beyond control. That is, because this is the joyful *desire* that *seeks its own perpetuation*, control must always be just out of control, always pushed just beyond the limit of security, in order that it may be further sought. No top, except in play (that is, as part of a continuing scene), puts a scene into order and calmly departs, thus fully satisfied. We might similarly make this point by seeing joyful control as self-subverting because it contains within itself, as I have said, a responsive generosity that exceeds the boundaries that control, and even the orderly delimitation of the ego, would set. This is therefore not control that would repress or destroy, but control that would respond and strengthen, even where such strengthening entails breaking. It is control at play in play, and as was the case for masochism, in sadism the context of the desire makes all the difference. In an interview, Bob Flanagan notes that good sadists "only do it with people who *like* it. Then that becomes a positive experience: you're not overpowering someone, you're *melding* with someone."[18] This is control, the autonomy of being master, the one who makes the rules—already played against communication.

Sadism is the seduction of control, and the image of seduction suggests a further attribute of this power-play. Seduction, as we have seen Baudrillard point out, subverts power structures by making a game of them. Games, however, are by no means without rules. The important distinction is between rule and *law*: to transgress a law is to incur a penalty (ultimately, where the law is The Law, or divine, death)[19] without recourse; but to refuse a rule, to break a rule, is to be removed from the game. (If one accepts a standardized penalty for rule breaking, one is still in some sense playing by the rules.) To take oneself out of the game is to place oneself back under the order of law. To play with full devotion to the rules is to suspend for a moment the seemingly greater force of law before the seductiveness of serious play, serious enough to treat the rule as if it were law.

And if the law of desire is gratification—the death of desire—then the rule of seduction is intensification—the eternalization of desire. The sensitive sadist seduces not merely the bottom's desire but her own as well. She desires control *and* its subversion (precisely the sort of subversion-by-intensification that we find in play across all the counterpleasures). She is "in control" of the situation only so long as she keeps it in motion (and not "under control"). She desires gratification not merely to have it but, like the saint, *in order* to postpone it. She desires empathically the bottom's pleasure, and so plays it off against pain; desires more pain and so plays it off against pleasure, perhaps staying just this side of the safeword, pain and pleasure both

becoming greater than ordinary gratification makes possible. She desires to inflict pain, and restraint, right up to the edge of the impossibility of control.

The rule is intensification. Intensification demands that seduction, the always distancing of gratification, be impossibly sustained.
("For a distance is necessary," Blanchot writes, "if desire is to be born
of not being immediately satisfied.")[20] Uncontrolled, desire will rush
to satisfaction. The vanishing point of pure control is the constant retreat, the unovercomable otherness of the subject/object of control.
("There is no longer subject-object, but a 'yawning gap' between the
one and the other and, in the gap, the subject, the object are dis-
solved; there is passage, communication, but not from one to the
other: *the one* and *the other* have lost their separate existence.")[21] The
impossibility of unity keeps desire in its spell. The disunified subject's dual demands for autonomy (rule-giving) and communication
(order-breaking)[22] maintain the tension. In autonomy we see control;
in communication, responsivity.

And subjectivity's tidy order, imploding from the bottom, explodes from the top. The top abandons herself to *communication*; she
cuts across herself and is one self no longer. But she intensifies as
well her *autonomy*, her rule-giving, here where her rule is wholly self-
legislated and indeed legislates beyond her very limits (taking over
the will of another), limits broken by communication. She is in
charge, master, first of herself (as we shall see), then of other subjects,
always before the unknown, at the edge of control.

In its empathic, responsive generosity and the very violence that
the *intensification* of that generosity implies, the act of topping is an
increase of power in its expenditure, as much as the life-giving glow
of the sun. Like the power trip of masochism, it therefore plays
against the disciplinary paradigms of efficiency, productivity, and
their related teleological constructions of power. It expends itself
with no thought to its own loss, yet without expectation of return.
The sadist too knows that all bruises fade: "The mark, it is to be absent from the present and to make the present be absent. And the
trace being always traces, does not refer to any initial presence that
would still be present, as remainder or vestige, there where it has dis-
appeared."[23] The *presence* of control, the lasting mark, the settled
order, has always already vanished. In this first sense the joy of topping is the joy of the pure gift, the joy of the potlatch, of an extravagant outpouring of energy that feeds upon itself to its own
gain—and its own triumphant annihilation. Good tops *need* to give,

though what they give is pain. This goes beyond the "normal" generosity of good lovers, because sadists and dominants need to give greater intensities of sensation in mind and body. Vanilla eroticism certainly involves autonomy (each party involved can construct, make, grant and refuse requests), but not at the *intensity* of sadistic control. It involves communication (between the requesting parties, and perhaps even to the extent of boundary-problematicization at orgasm), but not at the subjectivity-defying intensity of the responsive power-play of control, pain, and restraint. Inattentiveness in most situations is unpleasant; in s/m, disastrous. One critical essay remarks, "when the activity is S&M, it just ups the stakes."[24] So it does—but not all the stakes are bad, and care can put the odds in your favor.

It is odd to see the enabling of an expenditure as an act of generosity, though it is. It is equally odd, from another perspective, to see restraint, pain-infliction, and even contextual "enslavement" as acts of generosity, but they are, even where generosity is suffused throughout by greed and shatters the "recipient" as well as the "giver." The seduction of control forces control to an expenditure beyond control.

strength and domination

He no longer delimits himself; he fragments himself.
—Maurice Blanchot, *The Step Not Beyond*

Nietzsche writes in *Ecce Homo* of the proper role or use of strength and nobility of will. (This is hardly his only such writing, of course, but the claims appear here in exceptionally succinct form.) Mastery is always, ultimately, self-mastery, the *discipline* of the will, which, remarkably, appears as its own mode of responsivity: "I am always up to dealing with any chance event; I have to be unprepared if I am to be master of myself."[25] One is *not* master of chance but rather of oneself before chance. It is this mastery that grants to those of strong spirit the ability—that is, implicitly, the possibility of the *right* (it is not that any strong spirit will have this right, but that any weak nature will not. Consent is still required)—to extend that mastery beyond the limit of one's own subjectivity, to play with others' forces: "Let the instrument be what it will, let it be as out of tune as only the instrument 'man' can become out of tune—I should have to be ill not to succeed in getting out of it something listenable. And how often have I heard from the 'instruments' themselves that they have never heard themselves sound so well."[26] It is in this section that Nietzsche condemns both resentful enmity (to oneself as well as others, he notes, "however unchristian it may seem . . .") and pity ("I count the overcoming of pity among the *noble* virtues.") The proper role of strength is to strengthen; the strong will does not pity or resent weakness but *transforms and overcomes it*—in oneself or others.

This may be contrasted to ordinary forms of both desire and joy. "Joy and desire appear together in the stronger that wants to transform something into a function; joy and the wish to be desired appear together in the weaker that wants to become a function. Pity is essentially of the former type: an agreeable impulse of the instinct for appropriation at the sight of what is weaker."[27] Pity's desire to appropriate demands that it seek weakness. The transformative control of the strong spirit, however, seeks strength. This is immediately startling to those who would read Nietzsche as a protofascist, but is startling too for more careful readers, in its sense of communal or at least relational responsibility, a theme not often made explicit in Nietzsche's work.

I am not at all arguing that the top is somehow more powerful, more noble in spirit—properly played, again, top and bottom are both positions of great power. And a great many people play both roles. "The idea that masochists are victims of sadists underlies much of the debate on S/M," Gayle Rubin writes. "But tops and bottoms are not two discrete populations. Some individuals have strong and consistent preferences for one role or the other. Most S/M people have done both, and many change with different partners, at different times, or according to situation or whim."[28] Nietzsche's example of an instrument well-played—Heinrich von Stein, "who died so unpardonably young"—clearly has his respect, even his love. Bearing this relation of respect in mind, I shall extend Nietzsche's ideas to a more abstract level before returning to the materiality of embodiment—in the process, I hope, illuminating the passage of power across subjects.

The abstraction is based on Deleuze's reading of the Nietzschean will to power. Deleuze proposes a qualitative distinction between modes of the force activated by the will to power (Deleuze distinguishes these: "force is what can, will is what wills,"[29] but force and will are only analytically separable. It is will that is the motive, obstacle-seeking element in power; force is its strength.) The qualitative distinction itself is based upon a quantitative distinction. Noting the multiplicity of forces within any given body, Deleuze notes that *unity* (not singularity, but coordination) is, as Nietzsche points out, the effect of a dominating or harmonizing will, "a 'unity of domination.'"[30] Within a given body we already find multiple wills in different kinds of relations. Deleuze calls these relational qualities active and reactive: "In a body the superior or dominant forces are known as *active* and the inferior or dominated forces are known as *reactive*."[31]

Most of consciousness, Deleuze points out, is reactive, which is why it's important to note that the body far exceeds consciousness: "What makes the body superior to all reactions, particularly the reaction of the ego that is called consciousness, is the activity of necessarily unconscious forces."[32] These forces, inclusive of the superior and active forces, do not lend themselves to ready comprehension. Deleuze quotes Nietzsche's "What is active?—reaching out for power,"[33] adding "appropriating, possessing, subjugating, dominating—these are the characteristics of active force. To appropriate means to impose forms, to create forms by imposing circumstances."[34] The description will be familiar. Topping increases the power of both top and bottom, the latter in order to have more to take over.

But power cannot make unpowerful. Power *appropriates*, takes over, and the form that it imposes, like God's, is its own. Strength, active power, *seeks out obstacles*; it imposes on the world the sign of its own joy in itself. Deleuze remarks that for Nietzsche "active and reactive designate the original qualities of force but *affirmative* and *negative* designate the primordial qualities of the will to power."[35]

Affirmation is the act of joy, of love, of freedom (including, importantly, freedom from resentment). The active force of the affirming will reaches out to other forces, other wills. They may react, obey, be subjugated (rendered inferior, reactive), or they may be transformed, appropriated, and join in the battle against reactivity. The active and affirmative power in Nietzsche's noble subject, our ideal top, *seeks out what resists it*, wherever that may be found—and overcomes weakness, wherever *that* may be found. It intensifies and sustains resistance precisely in the familiar movement of pain and resistance. It is joyous active affirmation in both top and bottom that seeks to overcome weakness, whether in one or both of them. But because this affirmation is not a *reaction*, it does not depend upon finding weakness. Thus it does not depend, for its continued pleasure, on sustaining weakness (as pity does). To seek what is weak and "transform it into a function" would be pity. (To see the masochist as a victim is to pity him.) To seek what is strong and to bring strength into play is joy.

Power grows by overcoming, says Nietzsche. Power exists only in action, adds Foucault: "We have in the first place the assertion that power is neither given, nor exchanged, nor recovered, but rather exercised, and that it only exists in action. Again, we have at our disposal another assertion to the effect that power is not primarily the maintenance and reproduction of economic relations, but is above all a relation of force."[36] Relations exist only in action. The *activity* of overcoming is the manifestation of the affirmative will to power. Power grows by assimilation, suggests Deleuze, and these are not opposing claims. Nietzsche sees self-construction as already a form of domination:

> *One thing is needful.*—to "give style" to one's character—a great and rare art! It is practiced by those who survey all the strengths and weaknesses of their nature and then fit them all into an artistic plan until every one of them appears as art and reason and even weaknesses delight the eye.[37]

Hence, again, "What is essential 'in heaven and on earth' seems to be, to say it once more, that there should be *obedience* over a long period of time and in a single direction."[38] That is, strength is not assimilated by being transformed into a function of the strong will, but rather by being brought into harmony with that will—a harmony which, like that of the tones of a chord, radically alters our notions of identity without each element's becoming the same. Even what was weak takes strength from its role in this play. And when obedience is imposed beyond the self, it creates for the one who imposes it still further strength.

Certain points bear emphasizing. To overcome force is not (cannot be) to eliminate it. (Recall Foucault here, and the pleasurable power of subversion.) Rather, one *form* (one shape, one direction) of power overcomes another; power is always relational. In overcoming, power takes on power by making that-which-is-overcome into its own form, manifesting "the necessity . . . of imposing one's value upon the universe."[39] But this play of power, of the relations of power, cannot simply be interpreted as the power of one subject against the power of another subject. Rather, power works both within and across subjects, sometimes with little regard for their boundaries. The noble spirit who responds to weakness or disharmony not with pity but by putting even weakness in the service of strength and, more importantly, strengthening what is already noble, increases active force and affirmative will against reactive resentful-ness. Insofar as the ruling will, the dominant force, within the noble spirited subject is joyful, as opposed to resentful, that subject in-creases her own power, even in strengthening others (and even in breaking them, and strengthening them again). In turning others to-wards life (in strengthening their affirmative force, through her own subversive use of violence) she increases her own vitality.

That is, it is not the active, joyful *strength* of the bottom that is overcome. The role of the top is not oppressive. Rather, it is weakness in the senses of limitation, reactivity, the force of consciousness (and conscious subjectivity) that comes up against the active corporeal strength of the top, enabling and feeding off of the bottom's strength. One profound reason that many masochists prefer such engagement to autoeroticism is this ability of the top to find, draw out, and sup-plement the bottom's strengths. Limits one cannot break alone can be broken in this way. (This is the "a little bit further" to which we have seen anti-s/m theorists objecting.) In overcoming these limits, both top and bottom emerge triumphant, for the question of the will is not "whose?" but "which one?"—and when subjectivity implodes under the force of twisted desire, the one that wins is joy. The top's subjec-tivity is problematized by an intensification of the two functions of the subject: autonomous rule-giving and responsive communica-tion—such that their inherent paradoxicality destroys their custom-ary order.

It would be quite a surprise to such tops to hear that "in the masochistic attitude toward life there is generally no object dis-cernible that imposes the suffering and is independent of the ego. It is certainly extant in phantasy, but it does not appear in reality and remains in the twilight where it merges into the ego. This type of masochistic character behaves almost auto-erotically."[40] There is in sadistic desire a powerful need to be needed, to give, to break, though to break only those who are paradoxically willing to exceed themselves. Elizabeth Grosz gives a much more apt depiction, in late Deleuzean terms:

> Modes of greatest intensification of bodily zones occur, not through the operations of habitual activities, but through the unexpected, though the connection, conjunc-tion and construction of unusual interfaces which re-mark orifices, glands, sinews, muscles differently, giving organs and bodily organization up to the intensities that threaten to overtake them, seeking the alien, otherness, the dis-

parate in its extremes, to bring into play these intensities. . . . The subject ceases to be a subject. . . . Its borders blur, seep, so that, for a while at least, it is no longer clear where one organ, body or subject stops and another begins.

She adds:

These sites of intensity—potentially any region of the body including various internal organs—are intensified and excited, not simply by pleasure, through caresses, but also the force and energy of pain. . . . This may help to explain some of the appeal of sadism and masochism.[41]

One might ask why the sadistic or dominant "need to give" couldn't manifest itself more calmly, in a nurturing rather than an explosive fashion; why caresses aren't enough. Aside from the inherent impatience of human beings, there is a more serious answer to this question. Intensity has its temporal aspect; it is the rapidity and the sustaining of the build up of power that makes possible the kinds of strength, the responses to restraint, that the bottom experiences and the top grants. Moreover, to build up control gently is almost certainly to keep it stable, not at play on the edge of uncontrol, which is essential in an economy of excessive desire. The top plays the edge as mobile, always at the boundary of a sudden abyss—or simple failure.

Power can be drawn forth by receptivity, seduced by possibility—intensified precisely by that which *seeks it in order to resist it*, seeking in turn this resistance in order to intensify itself. The play against resistance runs both directions, and the strongest tops seek out powerful bottoms, those who won't break too easily. The resistance that the bottom subversively seeks is the restraint, pain, and intensified desire, provided by the top whose desire responds to that desire's movement. The resistance that the top seeks is the movement (against restraint), the reluctance (against the pain), the intensification (with and against desire) overcome in, as well as by, the bottom. This is not the zero-sum game often supposed by those who still think that power is bad. The spiral of power is a relation of power, and all those engaged here are caught up in its escalating expenditure.

This force expended can take on any number of forms, a wide variety of appearances. Again we must not deny, in stretching power beyond control, that control is one of its forms—whether the control is exercised as bondage-restraint or in submission with a more apparently psychological dynamic (in either case, control of one body in accordance with desire that begins as that of another, though it rapidly exceeds possession). A good top is not a dictator, malevolent or indifferent—the distinction between dictator and dominant is precisely the operation of this control in an economy of joy. That is, without the affirmative, joyful *response* of the bottom, the top's control (where it is not simply lost, because after all this is, with all its seriousness and intensity, *play*)[42] becomes at one unpleasurable and useless. This does not eliminate from the list of potentially desirable scenarios either smart-ass (nonsubmissive) masochism nor any form of resistance scenario.[43] Smart-ass masochists ("Sams," aka "uppity bottoms") tend to be quite explicit about having entered voluntarily into s/m situations that may involve restraint; they play off and against that restraint without even an apparent submission, but crucially (and knowingly), governed by the rule of intensification, *they play*.

And difficult as it unquestionably is to formalize the distinctions between "real" resistance and a resistance scene (particularly since bottoms may "use" such scenes to work through "real" emotional or psychological resistances that they want to overcome, risky though such efforts are), both prior and posterior negotiation and a genuine but not remarkably exceptional level of sensitivity do in fact make these distinctions possible, if not always as clear-cut as we would wish. It is thus that the *response* may as readily entail resistance as submission, but a *pleasured* resistance, a resistance already informed by a double desire. Otherwise, we might say, the control encounters not *response* but *reaction*: One subject or the other will have to *lose*. Granted, this kind of taking-control may mean an increase in power for the "winning" side (whichever this might be), but it is a dead-end increase, leaving no more force to assimilate or surmount. It is not an excessive spiral.

Contrast may provide clarification, so we return to the scene of genuine reluctance, a different dynamic with a similar outward appearance. Suppose, as can readily happen even within consensually structured situations, that the bottom resents the control or the sensation being exerted or inflicted upon her—even masochists and submissives are subject, after all, to bouts of human sullenness. Her response may be no response at all, or irritable snapping, or the early use of the safeword (an attempt, in its way, to take *back* or *repossess* control). In any event she will then not be able to *respond* positively to this power, to soak it up like the warmth of the sun and grow from it, and her annoyance will escalate simultaneously with the top's frustration. Power expended and unmet by active responsivity is blocked from the possibility of the joyous spiral. Under such circumstances reactive resentment, a will to negation, is more likely to emerge triumphant: would-be generosity meets refusal, and power finds no place to "pour out" its force. Again, it can only change form or direction (probably meaning a removal from the s/m context, or stopping the scene) or else turn against itself (as frustration or further resentment, a reactivity leading to real hostility and pain-infliction unconcerned with pleasure—the sort of reactivity that anti-s/m theory seems to see as standard), the latter meaning that what negates has won.

This turn is not subversive; it is instead repressive. That is, it is the power of withholding against the joy of giving. And a very similar dynamic is created by a resentful, ungenerous, or unresponsive (not merely tired!) top: that is, desire is not seduced into subversive escalation but ignored or turned away until in frustration it becomes not a desire-with-this-force but a desire-against, not responsive but reactive. Hence the degree of trust and sensitivity often remarked upon as essential to the s/m relation.[44] Without these, what we have is not subversive power but two or more people annoying one another, a resentful form of power already too much present in the world. It is because so many external critics view power relations in this zero-sum fashion that the sadist seems to them such an intolerable human being.

And as we both aligned and distinguished pain and restraint in viewing m-powerment, we note that what goes for control here goes for pain as well, though we might more precisely speak of *sensation*. Sensation properly inflicted and received blurs the opposition of pleasure and pain. The former, as even Sade realized, can be *inflicted* as much as the latter. Where the play is performed with attentiveness, where all involved are caught up in its rhythms, sensation in its intensification goes beyond these oppositional boundaries—or more precisely sustains both terms without resolution. Thus, from the top side, infliction meets at once greed and the reluctance it seeks as resistance, the doubleness of desire; and the force of that infliction is drawn into, drawn in by, the responsive grace of joy. The top's is the power of control already self-subverting, the greedy generosity of the sun, the need to give and expend in order to grow and expand. Again: it is not the bottom (the confluence of forces and wills in his body) who is overcome; it is reactive, resentful power. Under the control of a dominant will, in the force of a desire that cuts across

both subjects, active joy triumphs over repressive control. The desire
of strength is strength transformed and enhanced.

to give and to receive

> the way hands
> want pleasure from you disregarding your pleasure—
>   there
> is something limp in fingering the other to give them
> pleasure you must actively and virilely take pleasure in
> giving it in watching it destroy the face of the other it is a
> scurry between sadism and sainthood and worth waiting
> for and worth working for
>
> —Mary Fallon, "Sextec"

I have emphasized the need to take our conception of power beyond
the narrow limits of control, power over. But control, too, can be a
starting point for subversion—provided it contains within itself the
generosity, the responsiveness, that is the seed of its own disruption
(because to give responsively is already to give over control). Control
can be responsive and hence self-subverting, instead of repressive
(and hence self-limiting). It is by making itself ultimately impossible
that control keeps itself in play.

And caught up in the intensity of the escalating spiral of control,
the top disregards any pleasure no longer her own—because it is all
her own, all and none of it. *Self-mastery*—the most fundamental and
most important form of mastery for both Nietzsche and Foucault—
demands that one meet that for which one can never be prepared,
one's own loss. Controlling and dominating power need not be hostile; one can play an instrument as well as smash it, almost certainly
to one's own greater joy, one's delight in the ability to make music—
to the extent of losing oneself in the melody.

To see "what's in it for the top," we look to power's relationality,
its movement between and across subjects; and to the intensification
of control, of autonomy, of communication. This relationality is the
acausal, multidirectional movement between giving and receiving.
Like the bottom, who cedes her control, the top too cedes some of the
privileges of subjectivity—the rights of closure, of selfishness, the
discontinuity of individuality, the right not to give:

> Since the gift is not . . . the sublime act of a free subject,
> there would be no gift at all if not the gift of what one does

> not have, under duress and beyond duress, in answer to the entreaty which strips and flays me and destroys my ability to answer (*dans la supplique d'un supplice infini*), where there is nothing save the attraction and the pressure of the other. . . . To speak of loss seems, even though speech is never secure, still too facile.[45]

Too facile, because loss is least pure when it seems purest. The top must be powerful and actively responsive enough to give and to *take* both power and joy. Giving is not more blessed than receiving: it is receiving; it is joy's gift to itself. The top's pleasure is that of an expenditure so great as to take him out of himself; he too is opened to the outside of pure desire.

8

unspeakable pleasures
love is a series of scars

Speak—
But keep yes and no unsplit.

> —Paul Celan, "Speak, you also"

What is strangest is that non-knowledge should have the ability to sanction. As if from the outside it had been said to us, "Here you are at last."

> —Georges Bataille, *Inner Experience*

A description of the structures and movements of pleasure risks, however great its theoretical enjoyment, a certain removal or detachment from the pleasures described. This is doubly so when the moments of pleasure are as elusive—as aporetic, transgressive, paradoxical, and disorienting—as those touched upon here.

Context, as we have seen, is vital. Dworkin's descriptions of Sade's scenes fail because they take those scenes out of Sade's razor-sharp prose and accelerating narrative. His language is not a disguise for those descriptions, but a radical transformation of their meaning. Attempts to enact the scenes of submission depicted by Masoch, to decontextualize them from the literary, can only fail, because their power depends upon a refusal of endings, an ability to suspend, that is a textual possibility not transferable to enactment.

An asceticism that seeks to seduce the sacred, reincarnating the Word that is nonetheless supposed to lie beyond the world of flesh, has a power that all external refusals of bodily need would repress and deny. The "new knowledge" made possible by masochistic pleasure is at an extreme remove from the oppressive, disempowering, and often disembodying experience of pain and restraint unsought or assaultive.[1] And the sadist's "contact high" is possible only in a mutual escalation of sensation impossible in a truly repressive context. We have seen common, as well as significantly distinguishing, traits across these pleasures, especially in their ability to disrupt the orders of subjectivity. They are pleasures that shatter us; in the end, even Masoch's brittle frozen images break at the reader's touch. Is there any common ground in their multiple contexts? Where do we begin to end up in such ecstatic fragments?

The question is related to the problem of detachment: Where are we with these pleasures? I would suggest, rather reluctantly, that we are in a context in which delight and pain are not readily distinguishable, and that, in another sense and from another angle, this is not unfamiliar to us after all. In its way this is a too familiar line of thought, upon which Bataille remarks: "Hence love spells suffering for us insofar as it is a quest for the impossible, and at a lower level, a quest for union at the mercy of circumstance."[2] Jean-Luc Nancy, however, has an important warning:

> The thinking of love, so ancient, so abundant, and diverse in its forms and in its modulations, asks for an extreme reticence as soon as it is solicited. It is a question of modesty, perhaps, but it is also a question of exhaustion; has not everything been said on the subject of love? Every excess and every exactitude? . . . as to speaking *about* love, could we perhaps be exhausted?[3]

Which is, after all, the source of my reluctance to make this suggestion—"love" has become an appallingly hackneyed concept, and I am indeed suggesting it as a key to counterpleasure. The counterpleasures begin in a love of pleasure that, like Augustine's love of God, always wants *more*. Like love, they are pleasures of dispossession. They are pleasures in which the sense of freedom comes in a power that may not be a matter of choice.[4] They are pleasures in which the unquestionably erotic is in no way reducible to the genital (retaining the "sacramental character" that for Bataille characterizes the erotic)[5]; thus they resemble Foucault's understanding of non-Western sexuality: "In the West (in societies endowed with an erotic art, the intensification of pleasure instead tends to desexualize the body), it was this codification of pleasure by the 'laws' of sex that ultimately gave rise to the whole arrangement of sexuality."[6] I must note that the analysis of love is both more evident for and more applicable to the trio of pleasures of the flesh than to the pair of pleasures of the text. In some respects, though, it is a love of pleasure—and a love of the ways in which life in its sheer force can take up death as fragmenting or stilling force—that structures these strange texts, and where appropriate I have noted this as well.

The essential connection has already been made: each of these is a pleasure that pushes subjectivity to an extreme, beginning in some element of the subject especially important in the context of that pleasure: rationality for Sade, emotivity and imaginal beauty for Masoch, the duality of body and spirit for the ascetics, the individuation of the productive individual for sadomasochism. In each case there is a force of intensification derived not from loathing or reluctance but from its own joyous insistence.

Some of the connections that follow may seem improbable, and yet they are all traditional: the connection of love to God, to death, to the abandonment of self. They look very different here, in the refusal of certainty and steady positions. The common context of the delights of displacement can only be the shifting edge of the opening space; it is, as I shall argue, a gesture of love that makes the cut. This "love" is not the answer, even an answer, but a constant refusal of answers, our constant dislocation, the constant cut across the boundaries of our schemes of comprehension, a series of scars. Perhaps foolishly, I shall attempt here to mark them.

what now, and how?

> Pain is a sensation that I attempt to avoid. I derive no pleasure from it—if I did, it would no longer be pain. To advocate pain for its own sake is, at best, incomprehensible to me, sheer evil at worst.
>
> —Jesse Meredith, "A Response to Samois"

> There's a fine line between pleasure and pain.
>
> —The Divinyls, "Pleasure and Pain"

Having written of pleasure and power and resistance, I find that there is more that remains unsatisfyingly unsaid. This is that "more," rather more strange and even less logically defensible than what preceded it. It requires us to consider joy as it is caught up in love, and it takes us back to the strange intersection of counterpleasure and the sacred upon which we touched in exploring asceticism; it requires us to consider love as it cuts open spaces for the possibility of joy.

I have already suggested that in pain and restraint the power that is the joyful body's bursts the limits of the productive subject, whatever that body's position; that in the ecstasy of mortification the saint attains to the violence of the sacred; that the force of repetition may burst even narrative subjectivity. The intensification of power—including the power that is at once delight and desire—is itself pleasure, a particularly strange pleasure that I have been calling joy. I make this claim, or rather draw it from Nietzsche, in the place of a starting or foundational point, as a metaphysically arbitrary but aesthetically elegant, unoriginal point from which to depart again.

But even if we acknowledge these strange pleasures—whether or not we go on to acknowledge them as our own—how can we write of them? How can we speak a pleasure that breaks us; what can be said of a subject (perverse reader or ecstatic body) broken by pleasure?

Not, to begin with (to begin again), at once honestly and directly. What transgresses the subject is a pleasure that likewise transgresses language, forcing us to find our meanings in the interstices and twists, the absences and silences, the rhythms and rushes of words. I shall seem at the end to have said too much that is not enough; that is, to have spoken only around and never quite to the point. I can only assure the reader that I am not without frustration at what I nonetheless see as necessary; if the description becomes elliptical, we must recall that the ellipsis is the open space of textuality. I cannot, *one* cannot, describe such joy properly, saying, "It feels to me like this." It is a pleasure that already exceeds the possibility of pleasure, which by our usual thinking ought by rights to belong to a subject, as we saw in the general introduction. This means that we are speaking of that which exceeds discontinuity, that we are into the space of nonknowledge. (What does it mean if we cannot answer the question "Who is pleased?" It means, for one thing, that we can answer neither the Socratic question "What is pleasure?" nor the phenomenological question "What is the experience of pleasure?" And what then is left of an answer?)

And yet we can speak and write *about* it, even if ours is a roundabout speaking, circling and returning. The pleasure of pain and restraint, from any side, is a pleasure in the play between finitude and infinity, the invocation of an absent divinity, with love and grace as with fear and pain, dangerous and unwise. It is joy—the pleasure of abandon. "Abandon" because we cannot attain to this joy and remain in ourselves, but can only come back to it from outside ourselves.

As such it is at once pleasurable and terrible: such an abandoned joy is sublime. This is perhaps another way of finding its dis/placement within the tradition. Traditionally we love what is beautiful, but the sublime may draw us more strongly still. That is, it seems to share in the aesthetically *pleasing*, even in some element of what we think of as beautiful (unless we have been trained to distinguish the two) and the pleasure that beauty brings. At the same time, it includes an element of pain or (and) fear, made intriguing and attractive in its admixture with the aesthetically pleasurable.

That which is sublime, and the joy of the sublime, carries with it a sense of *excess*, the excess of intensification. Jean-Luc Nancy writes: "There is the sublime in art. . . . It signifies: to feel the fainting away of the sensible, to border on the furthest extreme of presentation, on the limit where the outside of presentation offers itself, and to be offered up to this offering. And there is divine sublimity. . . . In this case it is the presence of God insofar as it overwhelms the sensible."[7] In both, sense is overwhelmed, surpassed—but not, not ever, ignored. Sense because it is so profound, so potent becomes nonsense, impossible. We cannot make sense of it by comprehending it within an orderly system—a system of either power or truth, whose inextricability we already know. We can understand it only as unwise.

wisdom at the limit

> When she could not achieve her purpose . . . [Wisdom] stretched herself forward, and was in danger of being absorbed into [the Father's] sweetness and dissolved into His absolute essence, until she encountered the Power that sustains and preserves all things, called "The Limit," by whom, they say, she was restored and supported.
>
> —Valentinus, cited by Iranaeus,
> *Libros Quinque Adversus Haereses*

Limit: of self, of life, of tolerance.

I have repeatedly remarked upon the counterpleasures' play with boundaries and edges. The conception of limit as the power that sustains and preserves all things is not restricted to early Christianity. Limit establishes discontinuity; things are what they are because they are not everything else—because they have limits. We as the subjects we are are necessarily preserved by our own limits as well. (This is our discontinuity.) It is wise to preserve oneself, to stop at the limit—without it, we are in danger not only of losing wisdom, but of dissolving our selves. Bataille writes of our security in our own limits:

> There is always some limit which the individual accepts. He identifies this limit with himself. Horror seizes him at the thought that this limit may cease to be. But we are wrong to take this limit and the individual's acceptance of it seriously. The limit is only there to be overreached. Fear and horror are not the real and final reaction; on the contrary, they are a temptation to overstep the bounds. We know that once we are conscious of it, we have to react to the desire ingrained in us to overstep the limits. We want to overstep them.[8]

In the joy that is rapture and rupture we forget limit and so are lost: "a sort of rapture—in anguish—leaves us at the limit of tears: in such a case we lose ourselves, we forget ourselves and communicate with an elusive beyond."[9] The temptation to normalize this violent communion is overwhelming; one cannot help thinking that there is bound to be some way of making it sound sane and healthy and, ideally, even commonplace (appealing to some common sense). But such communion is not fully compatible with our understanding of normalcy. In sanity we are back to doing what is wise, back with wisdom safely restored (established and preserved) at the limit.

It is unwise to risk abandoning oneself (cutting oneself out of oneself in the openness to the outside); it is *dangerous*. Danger may be, sometimes certainly is, as uninteresting as safety, but at other times it is (at least potentially) much more fascinating and seductive. Generally we are wise enough to resist seduction and fascination, but it is when we are not that we find joy. This too counters a bit of common sense, which would oppose pleasure and danger.

Carol Vance notes this opposition within the realm of the erotic: "For some, the dangers of sexuality . . . make the pleasures pale by comparison. For others, the positive possibilities of sexuality . . . are not only worthwhile but provide sustaining energy."[10] But the most powerfully positive possibilities may be in the danger itself. We must be careful, though, to avoid an adolescent approach, a cocky assuredness of ourselves before danger. We must be prepared to be unprepared.

I am not interested here in the real but more mundane and readily intelligible dangers of prosecution, persecution, disease, back strain, or the purely physical risks of asceticism, its strain and toll on physiological well-being (by which I by no means wish to attribute unimportance to any of them), but in the extremes of abandon/ment. Is this wise? On the contrary, it is incautious and unproductive. But this incaution, heedless of *consequence*, is by no means unresponsive, heedless of what is, of what is other. In it we find a love beyond subjectivity, even in the intensification of subjection.

Joy is loving and unwise not merely in its transgression of subjective limits, but in the *carelessness*—the lightness—of its transgression. Bataille writes: "There exists . . . an affinity between on the one hand, the absence of worry, generosity, the need to defy death, tumultuous love, sensitive naiveté; on the other hand, the will to become the prey of the unknown. In both cases, the same need for *unlimited* adventure, the same horror for calculation, for *project* (the withered, prematurely old faces of the 'bourgeois' and their cautiousness)."[11] This affinity will prove crucial. Such carelessness implies no lack of strategy or artifice, but rather a disregard for consequence. It is incautious—one cannot enter into a careful abandon, though one's abandon may be (in the Nietzschean rather than in the Foucauldean sense) disciplined—under the directive of an overwhelming will.

If I abandon myself to joy that crosses the limit of my self, if I abandon myself *in* joy at the limit, the limit which is my-self, then I abandon myself to, or in, or as my own loss. This is to assent at once to death and to life, to life up the point of death.[12] (That is, to life as exuberance and playfulness, as overcoming and joy, and not as simple self-preservation.) It is thus the fullness of assent, not a "yes to this but not that," rather a Nietzschean *yes* to everything. To assent here is to assent, with Nietzsche again, to return: to the loss and the recuperation of the subject, with its new strength. The assent is not only to this strength but to this loss as well; the abandon is, again, careless (insouciant—without worry) and not calculated, even if it is strategic.

I can only abandon myself to joy and in joy, in acceptance, in return, which is to say that it is a sacrificial joy. In this claim I insist on the double sense of abandon: it is at once the sense of being lost or left and the sense of "wild abandon," of un-self-conscious freedom. In its divine form it is the impossible, the utter openness of possibility, which, as we shall see, sacred space implies.

What is abandoned? My self, my care and caution, my productive subjectivity. But *to* what am I abandoned?

the double cutting of the body unsouled

If only through the violence that operates in our bruised space.

—Maurice Blanchot, *The Writing of the Disaster*

It caresses, it grates, it cuts, it comes: that is bliss.

—Roland Barthes, *The Pleasure of the Text*

Recall the sublimity which is joy's, the combination of beauty and pain: sense and the senses are overwhelmed. Though sensation, beginning as pleasure, becomes pain at some level of intensification, it is also the case that pain and pleasure cross in the affirmation of intensity, become uncontainable, impossible. Where the will moves with pain, into pain, strategically intensified in its own restraint, it affirms intensity by saying yes, by its desire for intensification, its intensification as desire. The approach to the sublime is precisely through sensation that is overwhelming before being overwhelmed, self-overwhelming sensation. It is thus that the subjectivity of the sadist eludes control at last, or that of the masochist exceeds the possibility of restraint. It is thus that asceticism seduces the divine. It is through intensification in a process of refusal that Sade and Masoch, without rejoining the body, subvert our sense of the meaning of narrative.

Such an intensity and intensification of sensation are cultivated most conspicuously in the pursuit of pain and restraint. Susan Griffin, taking the *Story of O* as a prototypical study in masochistic behavior, writes of O that "Will in the form of bodily response is carefully schooled out of her, so that she is no longer connected to her own feelings."[13] This Griffin sees as an expected, if not inevitable, effect or outcome of erotic pain and restraint (and we ought to note the deliberate continuity of *Story of O* with works of mystical renunciation, drawing us back to asceticism as well). Yet we cannot forget that O is a work of fiction, better written than most pornography but hardly great or extraordinarily insightful literature. On the other and nonfictional hand, we have this interpretation of sadomasochistic eroticism: "I am a person who trusts her body and its sensations more than her mind and its thoughts. This is a difficult discovery after years of formal schooling designed, presumably, to make my mind a well-trained, highly reliable tool. Still, my body serves me better . . . . For one thing, thoughts are censored: some things are simply unthinkable. But a body that is freed to do whatever feels right will do the undoable."[14] Once the embodiment—more, the full *bodiliness*—of will is recognized, an extraordinary *connection* between feeling and ability emerges, not a careful *elimination* of either one.

Given that both ascetics and sadomasochists tend to be rather intellectual,[15] we may suppose that the turn to the body is probably not motivated by any inability to use the brain. (Nor, for that matter, can very many people be reading Sade and Masoch for purely prurient purposes, or at any rate most people cannot be reading very *much* by these authors for such purposes.) That is, this turn is not an anti-intellectualism or a nature-cult defiance of intellectual culture. It is hardly the case, as Judith Butler argued in a very early essay, that "sadomasochism takes a non-reflective attitude toward sexual desire."[16] Rather, the recognition that "desire is equal only to excess,"[17] accompanied by a strong[18] and sensuous embodiment and a strong, impatient, and careless will, is a force for the pleasure of abandon, of pain, of restraint, improbable or impossible as these may be. One must recognize desire and be willing to manipulate it strategically; must attend carefully, thoughtfully, and reflectively to the desiring body or the pleasures of reading, to reach these pleasures. The very nature of the pleasure of pain is likely to provoke reflection; it is improbable that one would not stop to wonder what was going on in this paradoxical state of affairs. "Normal" pleasure is more likely to remain unreflective, fitting much more neatly into our common *telos* of subjectivity and production, posing no evident paradoxes, encountering little or no cultural opposition.

It is common but trite to see in asceticism or in s/m a hatred of the body, some pathological rage against physicality. Instead we should see here an intensified awareness of the physical and especially of physical sensation: and, even for asceticism, a *joy* in that sensation, even if it is perceived as the mortification of the flesh. (In this respect s/m is perhaps more direct, acknowledging the bodily pleasures of pain and restraint themselves. But the saints have been blunt enough: "She would gladly have cut herself to pieces, body and soul, to show the joy she felt in that pain," is, we recall, a line from the autobiographical *Life* of St. Teresa of Avila, not the *Story* of the fictitious O.) Thus it is a love of body or text that is intensified.

And so we must begin, again, with the body. The first cutting of the body is that which ensouls or subjects it, that which creates the subject. We may recall the link between the body and discontinuity, the inescapable condition of the subject and the necessary effect of limit. (This, as I remarked in the discussion of asceticism, accounts as well for the ultimate impossibility of satisfaction; we cannot be one again.) Bataille writes: "We are discontinuous beings, individuals who perish in isolation in the midst of an incomprehensible adventure, but we yearn for our lost continuity. We find the state of affairs that binds us to our . . . individuality hard to bear."[19] In joy the subject is abandoned to a sort of continuity, however imperfect. Discontinuity is itself at once necessary and anguishing. The self is found in and founded by this cut across and apart, in this sudden powerlessness of not being all. "Pure" or "real" overcoming of discontinuity by continuity, a real *merging* of subjects, or of some sort of cosmic consciousness, is utopian and definitionally impossible: merged selves are selves no longer. The overcoming of discontinuity is not continuity of selves but rather a violent, sacrificial loss of self.

But while discontinuity may be anguish, as Bataille tells us, continuity is death. Its pleasures are themselves rending, a reversal of the solid, reasonable, ego-reinforcing pleasures of the subject. Thus I am rent once in my beginning, taken out of the wholeness in which I never was; and again in the second cutting, overcoming this discontinuity, when I am ripped out of myself in the transgression of my limits and abandoned to the continuous. The desire for continuity is the desire of loss, unimaginable and unattainable: "The pure and simple desire for the abyss is scarcely conceivable; its aim would be immediate death."[20] *Would* be but *is* not; loss is as aimless as it is careless. I cannot aim at my own loss, even if I desire it. *I* cannot lose myself; I can only be lost, can only be abandoned. Thus, perhaps, the ultimate frustration of both Sade and Masoch, who must remain within language to narrate their tales of intensified pleasures. Sade's "greatest" text, the *120 Days*, remains incomplete, perhaps necessarily, while Masoch's *Venus in Furs* ends with an unconvincing and unimaged role reversal. The reader's anachronic pleasure may exceed gratification, but the narrators' cannot.

Again, we must recognize that perverse or counterpleasure is not grounded (we could perhaps end this sentence here, but let us continue) in a bodily self-hatred. Abysmal, anguishing and abandoned, this pleasure of loss is nonetheless *not* a purely negating pleasure but a joy that now cuts across limits to reverse the effect of the first cut, which established the discontinuous subject, a joy in the cutting. "Joy," writes Jean-Luc Nancy in his discussion of love, "is the trembling of a deliverance beyond all freedom: it is to be cut across, undone, it is to be joyed as much as to joy."[21] This is the undoing of subjective discontinuity; this is the opening to the outside. I have noted already its power as a force of resistance. Now I would note as well its pleasure as a force of power.

Subjective discontinuity is undone by the sacrifice of (at) the limit of oneself. Having indicated the way in which subjectivity, its organization faced with pleasurable pain and restraint, abandons itself, I would emphasize again the careless joy of this gesture, careless and generous—and loving, openly generous with delight in openness. Joy and the generous love with which it is deeply affiliated are movements of insouciant sacrifice—a movement careless and impatient, unconcerned with its transgression of wisdom. And unconcerned with its own impossibility, because here we are lost in reaching it, abandoned at the threshold. "In one sense—and in a sense that will perhaps always conceal the totality of *sense* assignable as such—love is the impossible, and it does not arrive, or it arrives only at the limit, while crossing."[22]

In this improbable and generous love, "the immanence of the subject (to which dialectic always returns to fulfill itself, including in what we call 'intersubjectivity' or even 'communication' or 'communion') is opened up, broken into—and this is what is called, in all rigor, a transcendence. Love is the act of a transcendence (of a transport, of a transgression, of a transparency, also: immanence is no longer opaque). But this transcendence is not the one that passes into and through—an exteriority or an alterity in order to reflect itself in it and to reconstitute in it the interior and the identical."[23] I am undone in this transportive act, not by it neatly restored to my tidily delimited self. And upon the restoration which can only come later, I find my limits stretched, and a new sense of permeability, the "new knowledge" that my subjectivity can be shattered, a new temptation.

It is unwise to love. Joyfully, the containment of the self is abandoned in a joyous cut or thrust, drawn across the limit by an anguish ("at the limit of tears"), which is at the same time an uncontainable delighted laughter, laughter in the face of the terrible, delight bursting out of the center of fear.

I wrote in the earlier exploration of masochistic power of an over sanitized and pastoral conception of love—as recognition, as "I affirm you," as a polite strengthening of discontinuity, as divorced as thoroughly as possible from pain or transgression. I would work instead with an image of love as an impossible joyous abandon—a sense of being without recourse—which opens the self and thus undoes it. Love is exposure to loss, which is the sense of discontinuity overcome; it asks not recognition but, impossibly, abandon: "Nor is love the desire to lose but the desire to live in fear of possible loss. . . . At that price alone can we feel the violence of rapture before the beloved."[24] This is no passive willingness; one-self is not so easily exposed to the outside; it is hard even to *think* of exposing the self to its own loss with joy, carelessness, impatience (which is not to say without fear). This is why one needs an other: reader, god, top, bottom. As Bataille writes, "each being is, I believe, incapable on his own of going to the end of being. If he tries, he is submerged within a 'private being' which has meaning only for himself. Now there is no meaning for the lone individual."[25]

"Learn to think with pain," writes Blanchot, our best thinker of the outside.[26] "Thinking is love," writes Nancy[27]—a facile juxtaposition, but I mean only this: Pain and restraint, as I have suggested, serve exceptionally well for this thought, to throw the subject outside itself, to break the limits of subjection. And to embrace with joy this being-cut-across, this being-ripped out of oneself, is to abandon oneself to and with the sacrificial generosity that love is, painful and unsanitized.

In some sort of perfect (pure, real, impossible) continuity it would be the soul that *joins*, or souls that join: my soul and yours, our souls with the universe or god(s). The soul would be for the purpose of this continuity disembodied. In paradoxically broken discontinuity, though, the body is unsouled, the subject abandoned (set outside itself).

Traditionally, of course, the soul precedes the body, takes chronological and ontological precedence over the body. But the soul—whole, transcendent, unified, and individual—is a variant reading of the subject. It envelops, it is made upon, the body. The body is subject(ed) to the soul of which it is then to be merely the vehicle. One is tempted to say that the body has been, in other words, disciplined to a state of ensoulment, and in rapturous joy is the loss of the soul—but this is inaccurate. The soul is not lost but abandoned—rapture is an entry into divine abandonment.

divine abandon

Eli, Eli, lamma sabachthani?

—Matthew 27:46

Without limit wisdom is lost; we are lost without wisdom. As Valentinus would have it, we are abandoned to the divine—absorbed back into its sweetness. Despite my consistent conjunction here of asceticism and s/m, I think that we must be wary of the association made between the erotic and the spiritual, which more often than not turns to a kind of New Age fluff (veering often, though by no means inevitably, toward the sanitized and pastoral). The concept of the *sacred* is both less fluffy and less essentializing than the spiritual, lacking the latter's tendency to bring us back to spirit, soul, and thence self, subject. *Sacred*, too, does some nice philosophical work for us, as we have seen, via etymology: the sacral is lowest as well as highest, and one makes sacred not merely by sanctifying but by sacrifice. Religious asceticism sacrifices and sanctifies, scars and sacralizes the body, whether or not it is "spiritual"—and so too do the erotic pleasures of pain and of restraint, spiritual or not. The search for the ecstatic and the sacred takes place in the body: here too it is the body that is at issue.

To make sacred is to render, not necessarily godlike, but divine. The more traditional metaphysics of a present or omnipresent divinity would perhaps fit nicely with the spiritual, but we have come too late for such a full metaphysical experience. The divine is not for us an experience of full presence—the cosmic all with which we too might merge. The divine available to us after Nietzsche is instead and at once infinitely generous and infinitely withdrawn. This extraordinarily odd combination, seeming to move between giving and retracting, suggests that our experience of the divine or sacred can only be that of the gift of abandon, the opening to an infinite outside. This, too, is the gift of the text, infinitely withdrawing meaning from the reader. The post-Nietzschean divine is an infinitely open abandon, an unspeakable limitless generosity in which we are lost (one might say that God is still love, but love has changed). This Cabbalistic notion, that God creates the world by withdrawal from it (makes, that is, by making space for existence) is played upon repeatedly by both Nancy (see especially "Of Divine Places") and Blanchot (see especially *The Writing of the Disaster*).[28] The act of utmost generosity—that which gives the very possibility

of existence to creation—is thus identical with the utmost disaster—
the withdrawal of God. This gives to us a sense not only of divine
space but of the divine as space, as the very opening of possibility.
To be abandoned places us perpetually outside security, where possibility opens before us.

Our experience of abandonment is predicated upon death and
returns us to the openness of love. That is: in perhaps the most profound, and certainly the most unalterable, sense I am abandoned by
the death of an other, particularly of an other whom I love—or that
in the other which I love. In this abandonment our discontinuity is
manifest: I cannot die for another, nor with another, and I do not experience my death in that of another—all of this regardless of the intensity with which I might wish to delay or defy that other's death.[29]
But when we seek to understand subject-breaking joy, we are concerned in particular not with the unapproachable finality of the last
death but with the lacerating moments of what Bataille calls communication—especially in the eroticism that is consenting to life up
to the point of death. Love calls us to the abyss of discontinuity, and,
as Bataille also says, "we can experience its dizziness together," discontinuity never being the whole story.[30] At a minimum, we confront together our exposure to the outside. We start as the subjects,
the selves, to which we return, but between us there is loss. It is
never really *he* who abandons *me*; it is only *you*; always the second
person, by whom I am called and to whom I call, never so distant as
the third. I call to, and am abandoned by, *my friend* as by *my God*—as
Christ in our epigraph calls out not to a name or title but to a relation and the space between.[31] It is the loved other who makes love
possible; one "does not say 'I love,' . . . but . . . 'I love you,' a declara-
tion where 'I' is posed only by being exposed to 'you.' "[32] And this
you must be capable of abandoning me, of making the space in that
I can be lost. In the intensification beyond the wise limit of the personal, it is this exposure itself that is loved. Thus ascetic saints often
seem strangely impersonal in their love of both God and humanity,
while s/m eroticism is unusually, and notoriously, comfortable with
anonymity.

To confront exposure, to open to the outside, is to merge neither
with "it" nor with one another. My own death—or even the momentary abandonment of my own subjectivity—is never substitutable for
yours; we are fully discontinuous. By my own death I am not given
any manifestation of my discontinuous individuality. My own death
impends as an unimaginable event, as intolerable perhaps as the death

of my friend but utterly incommensurable with it. And indeed it is my death that will finally unmake my discontinuity, from which finality I cannot return, as I can from smaller deaths, new and more strong.

My death, but also, we recall, my love: what we want is not to die but to, as others have put it, die of not dying. Your death, or in less final (that is, potentially joyous) forms your intolerable individualizing abandon of me, is also the condition of my love for you: we can face the vertigo of death together. To love is to open oneself to possible loss, and to draw upon and reinforce the power of the other to turn both to the outside. In fact some have argued that we can love only in the face of death. What is immortal and never passes is beyond my love as beyond my understanding. But love too cuts across me, cuts back across; by it I am opened to the outside—to you, who are going to abandon me, if only in the sense that we cannot be continuous, and each of us is thrown outside ourselves alone. Yet in this abandon and my return you give me myself, gift beyond giving or receipt, even as you cut across to take me from myself, equally ungivable, irreceivable. The gift is not only loss but its return.

Exaggerate this movement beyond the sustaining power of limit: this is the confrontation with divine abandon. Again, our post-Nietzschean souls could not possibly confront a divinity of full presence—we find now in the divine the ultimate generosity of withdrawal, which we can only experience as abandon. By human abandon we open spaces between one another and then undo the order of those spaces. The withdrawal of a god (not a simple absence or lack, but lack of a Presence) opens an infinite space, a space in which we are given freedom from ourselves (our subjection).

Nancy writes:

> Space is everywhere open, there is no place wherein to receive either the mystery or the splendor of a god. It is granted us to see the limitless openness of that space, it falls to our age to know—with a knowledge more acute than even the most penetrating science, more luminous than any consciousness—how we are delivered up to that gaping naked face. It reveals to us nothing but us—neither gods nor men—and that too is a joy.[33]

(And, as Pascal has told us, a terror.) But finally not even an us is revealed; it is indeed neither gods nor men, but an infinite space of infinite desire, a love open to anything (and this is the perfection of generosity).

Abandon is a gift, with all the generosity that the *gift* carries, generous to the point of sacrifice, an excessive gift that gives everything: this is joy. But this giving is a retraction or retreat as well: all that we are given is an infinite openness, the loss of limit, utter abandon. Joy lacks nothing and so overflows. It is infinitely overfull and fully generous, but it is generous enough to give itself away, to abandon itself to the loss of the subject of pleasure. Nancy finds here, in this double movement, the remaining resisting sacred sense of modern Christianity:

> In the end, something resists. To all of the harshest and most justified criticism of Christianity—of its political and moral despotism, its hatred of reason as much as of the body, its institutional frenzy or its pietistic subjectivism, its traffic in good works and intentions, and ultimately its monopolization and its privatization of the divine—to all of that something puts up a resistance, beneath the horizon of everything: something that, it is not impossible to claim, has (in spite of all the mumbo jumbo) left upon the form of the Pater noster—that prayer which Valéry in his unbelief judged to be perfect—mark that is difficult totally to erase: a generous abandonment to divine generosity, a supplication out of that distress to which the divine alone can abandon us—the divine or its withdrawal.[34]

In pain and under restraint, in the mastery of escalation, in any strategy that throws us outside us, we sacrifice ourselves to perfect abandonment, human or divine—and perhaps, finally, even that definitional last boundary is transgressed. The outside may be equally erotic or sacred. All abandon that returns us to ourselves fits our definition of the sacred. This is as close as we may come to the final desire, to die without dying: "But the death of not dying is precisely not death; it is the ultimate stage of life."[35] Here too we return to fragmentation and stillness, the vitality of the drive to a death that is forbidden to arrive.

Abandoned beyond discontinuity, we are beyond the freedom of autonomous subjects (even gods); we are abandoned to the infinite generosity that cuts across our own limits, and with infinite generosity we abandon those limits. Free from this autonomous and discontinuous freedom, we find the generosity of love as this openness, the creation of infinite space and returning time.

This, then, is the pleasure of the resistant, subject-shattering power of pain and restraint. No doubt there are other ways to break the bonds and boundaries of disciplined subjectivity. I do not mean, by arguing that this is the pleasure of pain and restraint, to say that nothing else could give us sublime joy (which is at the same time a joy that we can never be given because we cannot be there to receive it). This, though, does not give us the right to ignore or to disparage the sublime joy of abandonment that takes place through pain and restraint, in which the body by its subjection to these is freed from its subjection to the self, in which intensity ignores Limit, in which infinite emptiness becomes impossible generosity and anguish at the edge of tears is the same as the laughter of an uncontainable delight.

notes

notes to introduction

1. Georges Bataille, *Theory of religion*, translated by Robert Hurley (NY: Zone Books, 1989), originally published posthumously, in 1973, 9.

2. ibid., 9–10.

3. The SI was "officially" in existence from 1957 to 1972; its best-known member was probably Guy Debord, author of *The society of the spectacle*. For the history and collected short writings of the SI, see *Situationist International anthology*, edited and translated by Ken Knabb (Berkeley: Bureau of Public Secrets, 1989). This relatively short-lived movement exercised considerable influence on French thought, most conspicuously that of Baudrillard, though in the French manner he does not generally say so.

4. Raoul Vaneigem, *Le livre des plaisirs* (Paris: Encre, 1979). *The Book of Pleasures*, translated by John Fullerton (London: Pending Press, 1983).

5. Michel Foucault, "An Ethics of Pleasure," in *Foucault Live*, edited by Sylvère Lotringer (NY: Semiotext(e), 1996), 378.

6. See especially several essays collected in Georges Bataille, *Visions of excess: selected writings 1927–1939*, translated by Allen Stoekel with Carl R. Lovitt and Donald M. Leslie Jr. (Minneapolis: University of Minnesota Press, 1985), especially "The Notion of Expenditure," "Sacrifices," "The Sorcerer's Apprentice," and "The Sacred," as well as the multivolume work *The accursed share: an essay on general economy* (1967), translated by Robert Hurley (NY: Zone Books, 1991).

7. Indeed, Bataille's own politics seem to have been complicated, changing, sometimes undesirable, and sometimes indecipherable.

8. see especially the essays and interviews collected in Michel Foucault, *Power/Knowledge: selected interviews and other writings*,

1972–1977, edited by Colin Gordon, translated by Colin Gordon, Leo Marshall, John Mepham, Kate Soper (NY: Pantheon Books, 1980), and in Michel Foucault, *Foucault live: collected interviews, 1961–1984*, especially the second half, containing interviews from 1975 and later.

9. see Roland Barthes, *The pleasure of the text* (1973), translated by Richard Miller (NY: Hill and Wang, 1975).

10. ibid., 57.

11. see ibid., 51.

12. see Sigmund Freud, "The dissection of the psychical personality," in *New introductory lectures in psychoanalysis* (1933), translated by James Strachey (NY: W.W. Norton, 1965), 100.

13. see Gilles Deleuze, *The logic of sense* (1969), translated by Mark Lester (NY: Columbia University Press, 1983).

14. see most of Nietzsche's works.

15. see Jean Baudrillard, *Seduction* (1979), translated by Brian Singer (NY: St. Martin's Press, 1990).

16. see Sigmund Freud, "The sexual aberrations," in *Three essays on the theory of sexuality* (1905), translated by James Strachey (NY: Basic Books, 1962), especially 20.

17. ibid., 16.

18. Deleuze, 1969, 75 (in the original, 93).

19. Freud, 1905, 16.

20. ibid., 67, see also 75.

21. ibid., 67.

22. Sigmund Freud, *The project for a scientific psychology* (1895), translated by James Strachey, in *Standard edition* volume I (London: Hogarth Press, undated), 312.

23. "The sovereign tendency obeyed by . . . primary processes is easy of recognition; it is called the pleasure-pain principle, or more shortly the pleasure principle. These processes strive toward gaining pleasure; from any operation which might arouse unpleasantness ('pain') mental activity draws back (repression)." Sigmund Freud, "Formulations regarding the two principles in mental functioning" (1911), translated by M.N. Searl, in *Freud: general psychological theory*, edited by Philip Rieff (NY: Macmillan Books, 1963), 22. "The nervous system is an apparatus having the function of abolishing stimuli

which reach it, or of reducing excitation to the lowest possible level which would even, if this were feasible, maintain itself in an altogether unstimulated condition." Sigmund Freud, "Instincts and their vicissitudes," translated by Cecil M. Baines, in *General psychological theory*, 86, see also ibid., 87. "In the theory of psychoanalysis we have no hesitation in assuming that the course taken by mental events is automatically regulated by the pleasure principle. We believe, that is to say, that the course of those events is invariably set into motion by an unpleasurable tension, and that it takes a direction such that its final outcome coincides with a lowering of that tension—that is, with an avoidance of unpleasure or a production of pleasure." Sigmund Freud, *Beyond the pleasure principle* (1920), translated by James Strachey (New York: W.W. Norton, 1961), 1.

24. see Freud, 1920.

25. Freud, 1905, 50.

26. Sigmund Freud, "The economic problem in masochism" (1924), translated by James Strachey, in *Freud: General psychological theory*, 191.

27. Bataille, "The Sorcerer's Apprentice," in *Visions of excess*, 223.

28. Freud, 1905, 70.

29. Freud, 1924, 191.

30. Leo Bersani, *The Freudian body: psychoanalysis and art* (NY: Columbia University Press, 1986), 39; cited in Steven Shaviro, *The cinematic body* (Minneapolis: University of Minnesota Press, 1993), 56.

31. Besides "The economic problem in masochism," the most important text for this idea is one of the essays in *The three essays on the theory of sexuality*, "The sexual aberrations," in which Freud is frustrated in his efforts to make sense not only of masochism and sadism but of perversion generally. Freud distinguishes aberrant sexual object-choices from aberrant sexual aims; only the latter are actually labeled perversions in his text. Aim-perversions include "activities which either (a) extend beyond regions of the body that are designed for sexual union, or (b) linger over intermediate relations to the sexual object"(16). Freud lists oral intercourse (but not kissing, "the point of contact with what is normal"(17)), anal intercourse, various forms of fetishism, lingering over touching, voyeurism and exhibitionism, sadism and masochism (18–26). The perversions are considered "pathological" only if they have "the characteristics of exclusivity and fixation"(20). It is worth noting that

the pair constituted by sadism and masochism is perverse in a way somehow different from the others, as Freud points out; worth noting because the pleasure-pain alliance, raised by these two forms of activity, proves quite persistently problematic.

32. See Freud, 1905, "The sexual aberrations."

33. Judith Williamson, "Woman is an island: femininity and colonization," *Studies in entertainment: critical approaches to mass culture* (Bloomington: Indiana University Press,1986), 14; cited in *Feminist cultural studies*, volume 1, edited by Terry Lovell (Brookfield: Edward Elgar, 1995), xxi.

34. see *Feminist cultural studies*, volume 1: "Of the postmodern focus on consumerism, [Angela] McRobbie comments . . . that this has led 'to an extrapolation of cultural objects out of the context of their usefulness (or their materiality); they have been prised away from their place in history and from their role in social relations, and have been posited instead in a kind of vacuum of aesthetic pleasure and personal style," xxv.

35. Friedrich Nietzsche, *The gay science* (1882), translated by Walter Kaufmann (NY: Vintage Books, 1974), preface to the second edition, section 4.

36. Deleuze, however, develops the link between quantitative and qualitative in the context of his discussion of Nietzsche, and Freud admits only of quantitative distinctions in stimulation.

37. *Feminist cultural studies*, vol. 1, xxvi.

38. In fact, sometimes the pleasure derives in part from enjoying the knowledge of its transgressivity, and diminishes when it is no longer perceived as transgressive to the point of representing a threat. Bob Flanagan, during his installation/exhibit/performance of "Visiting Hours" at New York's New Museum of Contemporary Art, remarked of his own exhibitionistic masochism that it was a bit more fun when it really bothered more people—which did not imply that otherwise the fun was gone altogether.

39. For a more thorough discussion of the distinctions between active and reactive pleasures, see Friedrich Nietzsche, *The genealogy of morals* (1887), translated by Walter Kaufmann, in *Basic writings of Nietzsche* (NY: Modern Library, 1968), and Deleuze, "Active and reactive," in *Nietzsche and philosophy* (1962); translated by Hugh Tomlinson (NY: Columbia University Press, 1983).

40. Michel Foucault, "An Ethics of pleasure," in *Foucault live*, 386.

41. David Halperin, *St. Foucault: towards a gay hagiography* (NY: Oxford University Press, 1995), 37.

42. Carol Queen, "Bisexual perverts among the leather lesbians: some thoughts on border-crossing," in *The second coming: a leatherdyke reader*, edited by Pat Califia and Robin Sweeney (Los Angeles: Alyson, 1996), 71.

43. Lesley Stein, "The body as evidence: a critical review of the pornography problematic," in *Screen*, (1982): unpaginated. Cited in Arthur Mielke, *Christians, feminists and the culture of pornography* (Lanham, MD: University Press of America, 1996), 43.

44. In an interview recently published over the World Wide Web, author and editor Laura Antoniou makes the intriguing suggestion that the current popularity in the s/m community of the slogan "safe, sane, and consensual" may well reflect an urge to stay safely in the center, where sanity and normality are perilously close to identical. "Consensual" is, as she notes, obviously an important element of play—but it is *so* obviously so that its mention in a slogan is either condescending or paranoid. "Laura, leather and life," Crossroads Learning Center, Seattle WA, November 8, 1995. At <http://weber.u.washington.edu/~humsex/l/society/latrans.txt>.

45. *Feminist cultural studies*, volume 1, xv.

46. see Jacques Lacan's "Kant avec Sade," translated by James B. Swenson Jr., *October* 51 (Winter 1989): 55–74, itself heavily indebted to the analyses of Sade in Pierre Klossowski's *Sade mon prochain* (1967), translated by Alphonso Lingis (Evanston, IL: Northwestern University Press, 1991).

47. This quotation from an interview in the influential collection *Coming to power* captures the spirit of this forthrightness: "I *have* gone to my limits a few times. . . . Going to my limits means I go through this door. It's like another dimension. It's like going to the outer limits and *out* of them. . . . *That's* satisfying to me." "Hot and heavy: Chris interviews Sharon and Bear," *Coming to power*, edited by the Samois Collective (Boston: Alyson Publications, revised edition, 1987), 58.

48. see Halperin, 1995, 62f.

49. see Jacques Derrida, *Aporias* (1993), translated by Thomas Dutoit (Stanford: Stanford University Press), 1993.

50. "Friendship as a way of life," in *Foucault live* (translated by John Johnstone), 310. Also see many of Foucault's other interviews, notably including "Body/Power" (in *Power/Knowledge*) and his *Ad-*

vocate interview, "Sex, power, and the politics of identity" (in *Foucault live*).

51. "Friendship as a way of life," 310.

52. see "Language to infinity," in *Language, countermemory, practice*, selected essays and interviews, edited and translated by Donald F. Bouchard and Sherry Simon (Ithaca, NY: Cornell University Press, 1977): "Headed toward death, language turns back upon itself; it encounters something like a mirror; and to stop this death which would stop it, it possesses but a single power: that of giving birth to its own image in a play of mirrors that has no limits." 54.

53. see "Preface to transgression" in *Language, countermemory, practice*: "In effect, do we not grasp the possibility of such thought in a language which necessarily strips it of any semblance of thought and leads it to the very impossibility of language? Right to the limit where the existence of language becomes problematic?" 40.

54. Though this image or notion pervades his work, it is perhaps best developed in Georges Bataille, *Erotism: death and sensuality* (1957) translated by Mary Dalwood (San Francisco: City Lights Press, 1986), and in Georges Bataille, *Inner experience* (1954), translated by Leslie Ann Boldt (Albany: SUNY Press, 1988).

55. " 'Pleasure'—as a feeling of power (presupposing displeasure)." (*The will to power*, posthumous collection, translated by Walter Kaufmann and R.J. Hollingdale (NY: Random House, 1968) sec. 657). "The essence of pleasure: that power increases, that the difference enters consciousness" (*Will to power*, section 695).

56. Judith Butler, *Bodies that matter: on the discursive limits of "sex"* (NY: Routledge, 1993), 90–91.

57. ibid., 241.

58. compare the sentiment that Heinrich Heine attributes to both August Wilhelm and Friedrich Schlegel in *The Romantic school*: "Our emotions are withered; our imagination is dried up"—with Romanticism as the remedy, in Larry H. Peer, editor, The *Romantic manifesto: an anthology* (NY: Peter Lang, 1988), 142.

notes to chapter 1

1. Mielke, 1996, chapter 2. Within traditional Christianity, however, the emphasis is more likely to fall on the sinfulness of carnal pleasure (see ibid., 51).

2. For a discussion of both positions, see Lynne Segal, "Does pornography cause violence? The search for evidence," in *Dirty looks: women, pornography, power*, edited by Pamela Church Gibson and Roma Gibson (London: British Film Institute, 1994), and Mielke, 1996, cited above.

3. see, for example, Eva Feder Kittay, "Pornography and the erotics of domination," in *Beyond domination: new perspectives on women and philosophy*, edited Carol C. Gould (Totowa, NJ: Rowman and Allanheld, 1984), 159. Cited in Mielke, 1996, 70.

4. Susan Gubar, "Representing pornography," in *Feminist cultural studies*, vol. 2, 600.

5. MacKinnon, Catharine, *Only words* (Boston: Harvard University Press, 1993), 17.

6. ibid., 19.

7. See Segal, 1994, throughout.

8. ibid., 9.

9. The film adaptations of their work actually suggest that it is not directly adaptable. While I know of film versions of Sacher-Masoch's work only by rumor, I am aware of at least two film versions of Sade: *Marquis*, done entirely with puppets, and Passolini's *Salo: 120 Days of Sodom*, which is sometimes nearly as unwatchable as Sade is unreadable, but which makes use of Sade's text for twentieth-century political commentary that the author, chronologically, cannot have intended. (This is not, of course, a criticism of the film.)

10. This work was still unpublished when *Take back the night* was printed; it was printed in 1981 as *Pornography and silence: culture's revenge against nature* (NY: Harper and Row, 1981).

11. George Steiner, "Night worlds," in *The case against pornography*, edited by David Holbrook (London, 1972), 229. Cited in Susan Gubar and Joan Hoff, editors, *For adult users only: the dilemma of violent pornography* (Bloomington: Indiana University Press, 1989), 613.

12. from Kathleen Barry, "Pornography: the ideology of cultural sadism," in *Female sexual slavery* (NY: New York University Press, 1984), 174. Cited in Gubar and Hoff, 613.

13. It is more difficult to make a case for Sacher-Masoch's misogyny, since the women in his texts tend to be dominant, the men groveling. It is possible to do what Dworkin does in her understanding of some of the works in Andrea Dworkin, *Pornography:*

men possessing women (NY: Penguin Books, 1980) and simply reverse the roles on the assumption that men in pornography *must* be dominant (see her chapter 1) so that Masoch is writing in a sort of code. It is also the case that Sacher-Masoch's hero Severin, in *Venus in furs*, is a fairly pushy bottom, demanding his domination rather forcefully, and so could be seen as still in charge of what happens to him.

14. *Pornography and silence*, 16. Cited in Mielke, 1996, 44.

15. "The precise object of 'sadism,' Foucault writes, "is not the other, nor his body, nor his sovereignty; it is everything that might have been said" ("Language to infinity," 62).

16. Carol Siegel, *Male masochism: modern versions of the story of love* (Bloomington: Indiana University Press, 1995), 2.

17. Kaja Silverman, *Male subjectivity at the margins* (NY: Routledge, 1992), 266.

18. or, to use Deleuze's term for Sade, "pornological" (in *Masochism: coldness and cruelty*).

notes to chapter 2

1. Honesty compels me to admit that I have cheated in selecting this highly appropriate epigraph, as it was said not of Sade but of James Joyce, in Woolsey's decision to permit *Ulysses*, as a nonobscene work, into the U.S.

2. For this insight I am grateful to John Protevi, who in 1993 allowed me to read a portion of a book about sense on which he was working.

3. All etymologies are from the *Oxford English Dictionary* (Oxford: Oxford University Press, 1989).

4. Bataille, 1957, 191.

5. ibid., 186.

6. ibid., 190.

7. For the best exposition of the death drive (*Todestrieb*), a late theoretical construct for Freud, see Freud, 1920, chapters 6 and 7. On the link between death and silence, see also Deleuze, 1967.

8. This is the starting point of MacKinnon's argument. See MacKinnon, 1993, chapter 1.

9. Jane Gallop, *Intersections: A reading of Sade with Bataille, Blanchot, and Klossowski* (Lincoln: University of Nebraska Press, 1981), 33.

10. Freud, 1924, 193.

11. Donatien Alphonse François, Marquis de Sade, *120 days of Sodom and other writings* (posthumously published), translated by Austryn Wainhouse and Richard Seaver (NY: Grove Press, 1966), 673.

12. ibid., 471.

13. ibid., 485.

14. ibid., 502.

15. ibid., 495.

16. Barthes, 1973, 51.

17. Maurice Blanchot, *The Step Not Beyond* (1973) translated by Lycette Nelson (Albany: SUNY Press, 1992), 53.

18. Where animals do appear, as in *Philosophy in the bedroom* (in *120 days of Sodom and other writings*), they have a purely instrumental value; they are tools, not victims.

19. *120 days of Sodom*, 362.

20. For the most famous instance of this connection, see Jacques Lacan, "Kant with Sade."

21. Baudrillard, 1979, 31.

22. *120 days of Sodom*, 193ff.

23. ibid., 577.

24. ibid., 591.

25. see the *Critique of pure reason* (1781), translated by Norman Kemp Smith (NY: St. Martin's Press, 1965), sections 91ff.

26. Donatien Alphonse François, Marquis de Sade, "Dialogue between a preacher and a dying man" in *The passionate philosopher: a Marquis de Sade reader*, selected and translated by Margaret Crosland (London: Peter Owen, 1991), 28.

27. Donatien Alphonse François, Marquis de Sade, *Justine* (1791), translated by Helen Weaver (NY: Capricorn Books, 1966), 104.

28. Klossowski , 1967, 15.

29. Bataille, 1954, 46.

30. Bataille, 1957, 168.

31. see the formulations of the categorical imperative in Immanuel Kant, *Groundwork of the metaphysics of morals* (1785), translated by H.J. Paton (NY: Harper and Row, 1948).

32. see Kant, 1781, appendix to the transcendental dialectic.

33. *120 days of Sodom*, 595 and 623.

34. René Descartes, *Meditations on first philosophy* (1641), translated by Laurence J. Lafleur (Indianapolis: Bobbs-Merrill, 1951), fourth meditation.

35. see appendices to Kant, 1781.

36. This is the state of absolute knowledge in G.W.F. Hegel, *Phenomenology of mind* (1861), translated by J.B. Baillie (NY: Harper and Row, 1965). Bataille writes, "Hegel attains *satisfaction*, turns his back on the extreme limit (*l'extrême*)." Bataille, 1957, 43.

37. Blaise Pascal, for whom faith itself becomes a matter of reason in his famous wager (*Pensées* (ca. 1660), translator unnamed (NY: E. Dutton and Co., 1958), 233), gives this fear its most vivid articulation: "The eternal silence of these infinite spaces frightens me" (*Pensées*, 206).

38. Bataille, 1957, 173.

39. Jane Gallop suggests that Klossowski's version of Sade is not only much like Bataille's version of Sade but also much like Bataille. Gallop, 1981, 68–69.

40. Klossowski , 1967, 33.

41. Simone de Beauvoir, *Must we burn de Sade?*, translated by Annette Michelson (London: Peter Neville, 1953), 76.

42. *120 days of Sodom*, 535.

43. *Justine*, 93.

44. ibid., 201–2.

45. in Bataille, 1957, 173n: note cites Blanchot, *Lautreamont et Sade*, 258. The essay from which the quotation is taken may also be found as "Sade's reason," translated by Bernard Wall, in *The Blanchot reader*, edited by Michael Holland (Cambridge: Blackwell, 1995), 96.

46. Deleuze, 1967, 29.

47. Gallop, 1981, 32.

48. *120 days of Sodom*, 658.

49. ibid., 662.

50. ibid., 364.

51. ibid., 538.

52. Deleuze, 1967, 118–21.

53. Bataille, 1957, 179.

54. Maurice Blanchot, *The writing of the disaster* (1980), translated by Ann Smock (Lincoln: University of Nebraska Press, 1982), 45.

55. Deleuze, 1967, 30.

56. Bataille, 1957 , 194.

57. Klossowski , 1967, 114.

58. ibid., 116–17.

59. Deleuze, 1967, 31.

60. Bataille, 1957, 195.

61. Silverman, 1992, 275.

notes to chapter 3

1. Deleuze, 1967, 13.

2. ibid., 46.

3. ibid., 16. *Algolagnia* may be an unfamiliar term; it is defined as "sexual gratification derived from inflicting or experiencing pain," *American heritage dictionary* (NY: Dell Publishing Co., 1989).

4. Siegel, 1995, 110.

5. Freud, 1905, footnote added in 1924, 25.

6. Freud, 1924, 192.

7. ibid., 193–95.

8. ibid., 194.

9. Georges Bataille, *Literature and evil* (1957b), translated by Alastair Hamilton (NY: Marion Boyars, 1985), 73.

10. Freud, 1924, 194–95 (in Studienausgabe, 347).

11. ibid., 199.

12. ibid., 201. Here we see one of the strangest instances of instinctual fusion: the triumph of the erotic is the transposition of the death drive into external expression via the musculature, yet this ex-

pression takes the form of hastening the death drive's original, antierotic aim.

13. Silverman, 1992, 198–99.

14. Freud, 1924, 192.

15. For a contemporary instance of this antifetish, see a dreadful film with fine actors: *The comfort of strangers*, directed by Paul Schrader in 1991.

16. Beauvoir, 1953, 45.

17. Leopold von Sacher-Masoch, *Venus in Furs* (1870), in *Masochism*, translated by Jean McNeil (NY: Zone Books, 1989), 240. Compare Friedrich Schlegel, who writes in Athanäum fragment #116 "[Romantic poetry] can ascend . . . on the wings of poetic reflection, midway between the work and the artist. It can even expand this reflection and multiply it as in an endless series of mirrors," in Peers, 1988, 12.

18. Deleuze, 1967, 70.

19. ibid.

20. Friedrich Nietzsche, *The birth of tragedy* (1871), in *The birth of tragedy and the genealogy of morals*, translated by Francis Golffing (NY: Anchor Books, 1956), sections 5f.

21. Annie LeBrun, *Sade: A sudden abyss* (1986), translated by Camille Nash (San Francisco: City Lights Books, 1990), 189.

22. An idea perhaps best expressed by James Joyce's Stephen Dedalus, who renders the "ineluctable modality of the visual" as *nebeneinander*; opposed to that of the audible, *nacheinander*. See James Joyce, *Ulysses* (NY: Modern Library, 1934), "Proteus" (chapter 2).

23. Deleuze, 1967, 101–2.

24. Masoch, 1870, 196.

25. Masoch, contract, 1869, in *Masochism*, 277.

26. Masoch, undated contract, in *Masochism*, 278–79.

27. Masoch, 1870, 260.

28. For Freud, these movements are ultimately organic. The organism's drive to free itself from tension is only satisfied in the utter stillness of being no longer alive, since as long as it lives it must suffer at least internal stimulation. However, the only possible route to

this stillness is the organism's loss of its own coherence, in a physiological and even cellular breaking down and breaking apart. See Freud, 1920, chapters 6 and 7.

29. Deleuze, 1967, 34.

30. see Masoch, 1870, 143, 208, 211.

31. Interestingly, Carol Siegel notes the possibility of the dominatrix as a character well beyond conventional femininity. Responding to Jessica Benjamin's *Bonds of love* (for more on this text here, see the chapters on contemporary practice), Siegel writes, "We are left wondering why the dominant and submissive role that are assigned so differently by Masoch have suddenly (and retrospectively) become so deeply gendered that the men and women who play them can only seek in vain to 'lose' their connections to masculinity and femininity. As Benjamin shows, her reading of female desire is consonant with 'the well-known difference between male and female sexual pleasure' (*Bonds of love*, 120). Because what is 'well known' about female desire seems to be all we know, we cannot recognize a female pleasure not fundamentally different from (masculine) aggression, one that does not confirm the currently dominant visions of both gender and sexual difference." Siegel, 1995, 107.

32. Deleuze, 1967, 70. This idea may also be found, with less philosophical development, in the work of Theodor Reik.

33. Deleuze, 1967, 33.

34. Beauvoir, 1953, 32.

35. Linda Williams, *Hard core: power, pleasure and the frenzy of the visible*, 1989, 277. Cited in Mielke, 1996, 11.

36. Deleuze, 1967, 52.

37. ibid., 70.

38. Masoch, 1870, 153.

39. ibid., 152 (original: 19). Again, compare Friedrich Schlegel: "Indeed, [Romanticism's] unique essence is that it is always becoming *and can never be completed.*" In Peers, 12. Emphasis mine.

40. ibid., 189.

41. ibid., 179. In his use of Christian imagery without its theology, Masoch again echoes a strain of Romanticism, which made particular use of medieval images. See Heine, in Peers, 140–41.

42. ibid., 172.

43. Leopold von Sacher-Masoch, "A Childhood Memory and Reflections on the Novel" from *Revue bleue* (1888), in *Masochism*, 273–74.

44. ibid., 276.

45. In this, Masochism expresses the force of the primary, nonextrajected death drive. The death drive becomes actively aggressive when it is externalized—which is to say already fused with Eros—and in its primary, internal form makes still, silently, the motile life of the organism. See Freud, 1920.

46. Deleuze, 1967, 120–21.

notes to chapter 4

1. Peter Brown, *The making of late antiquity* (Cambridge: Harvard University Press, 1978), 100.

2. Guy Baldwin, "Radical rite," in *Religious sex*, edited by David Aaron Clark and Tristan Taormino (NY: Rhinoceros Books, 1996), 126.

3. vide supra.

4. edited by Pat Califia; further information at <http://www.patcalifia.com>.

5. This is not the only religious imagery thus employed; special note should be made of the wide use of pagan images as well. Both traditions, of course, lend themselves both to the structured ritual and the enduring image.

6. see Baldwin in Clark and Taormino, 1996.

7. Morny Joy, "Incontinent observations: a response to Margaret Miles," in *Broken and whole: essays on religion and the body*, edited by Maureen Tilley and Susan Ross (Lanham, MD: University Press of America, 1993), 20. The quotation is from Grosz's *Volatile bodies* (Bloomington: Indiana University Press, 1994), page unspecified.

8. references in Mielke, 1996, xxii. Mary Jo Weaver's reference from "Pornography and the religious imagination," in Gubar and Hoff, 1989.

9. *Pornography and silence*, 16; cited in Mielke, 1996, 44.

10. In fact, the most antisomatic sects of early Christianity were Gnostic, and were condemned as heretical. See Elaine Pagels, *The Gnostic Gospels* (NY: Random House, 1979), 4–7.

11. Bynum dates the more exclusive focus on the soul to the fourteenth century and later. See Carolyn Walker Bynum, *The resurrection of the body* (NY: Columbia University Press, 1995), 277.

12. ibid., 276.

13. Rosemary Haughton, *Beginning life in Christ* (Westminster, MD: Newman Press, 1969), 38. Cited in "Rosemary Haughton on spirituality and sexuality," Joy Milos, CSJ, in Tilley and Ross, 1993, 194.

14. Carolyn Walker Bynum, *Fragmentation and redemption* (NY: Zone Books, 1991), 177.

15. Bynum, 1995, 109.

16. Margaret Miles, "Desire and delight," in Tilley and Ross, 1993, 11. Miles goes on to note that for Augustine, sex is "consuming, totalitarian" and must be avoided lest it take over his life; but he does not universalize this: "He did not, it should be noted, in the *Confessions* or in his other works, press his own resolution on anyone else or describe celibacy as the norm for 'serious' Christians. Nevertheless, his rhetorical power ensured that his description of his own resolution was powerfully affecting, contributing to the subsequent glorification of the sexless life in Catholic Christianity" (12). Though arguable, this is at least an interesting possibility.

17. Bynum, 1991, 152.

18. ibid., 183.

19. see ibid., 235f.

20. Bynum, 1995, 110.

21. Freud, 1924, 196 (in Studienausgabe, 349).

22. Bataille, 1957, 233.

23. Church officials were well aware of this threat. There was much debate in both cases as to whether the women's practice might be demonically rather than divinely inspired. St. Teresa of Avila was sent before the Inquisition at least six times. See Gillian T.W. Ahlgren, *Teresa of Avila and the politics of sanctity* (Ithaca: Cornell University Press, 1996).

24. Athanasius, *The life of Antony* (ca. 360 A.D.), translated by Robert C. Gregg (NY: Paulist Press, 1980), section 7.

25. Bell, Rudolph M., *Holy anorexia* (Chicago: University of Chicago Press, 1985), 43.

26. ibid., 25.

27. ibid., 79.

28. Athanasius, sec. 47; Bell, 1985, 128, 137, 143.

29. Bell, 1985, 43.

30. ibid., 128.

31. for example, in Bell alone, 92, 137, 143, 175, etc.

32. Bell, 1985, 43, 128, 137, etc.

33. ibid., 25.

34. Georges Bataille, *Guilty* (1961), translated by Bruce Boone (Venice, CA: Lapis Press, 1988), 22.

35. Georges Bataille, "The notion of expenditure," in *Visions of excess*, 119. This claim is true etymologically as well. "Sacred" is linked both to "sacrifice" (from the "Latin *sacrifer*, from *sacri-*, *sacer*, sacred [*sacra* neut. pl, sacrifices]) and to "sacral" (the lowest, as in lowest part of the spine). See the *Oxford English dictionary*.

36. Armando Favazza and Barbara Favazza, *Bodies under siege* (Baltimore: Johns Hopkins University Press, 1987), 1.

37. Bataille, 1957, 256.

38. Geoffrey Galt Harpham, *The ascetic imperative in culture and criticism* (Chicago: University of Chicago Press, 1987), 46.

39. ibid., 56.

40. Athanasius, sec. 5.

41. see especially the chapter entitled "What is religious" in Friedrich Nietzsche, *Beyond good and evil* (1886), translated by Walter Kaufman (NY: Vintage, 1989) and the third essay of the *Genealogy of morals* (1887).

42. Friedrich Nietzsche, *Human, all-too human* (1878), translated by Marion Faber with Stephen Lehmann (Lincoln: University of Nebraska Press, 1956), sec. 142.

43. Nietzsche, 1886, sec. 229.

44. A reminder from the general introduction: though this notion is particularly developed in the discussion of forepleasure in Freud, 1905, the distinction between voluptuous pleasure and release, with the latter always given priority of healthiness and maturity, is present throughout his work.

45. Bell, 1985, 99.

46. ibid., 143.

47. Nietzsche, 1886, sec. 51.

48. Harpham, 1987, 43.

49. Bell, 1985, 28.

50. St. Catherine of Siena, *The dialogue*, translated by Suzanne Noffke, O.P. (NY: Paulist Press, 1988), "Tears" sec. 90.

51. ibid.

52. Athanasius, sec. 5.

53. Nietzsche, 1878, sec. 137.

54. Bell, 1985, 163.

55. Nietzsche, 1887, section III.7.

56. Nietzsche, 1878, section 140.

57. Bataille, 1957, 264.

58. "The notion of expenditure," 119.

59. see Nietzsche, 1886, section 188.

60. ibid., section 229.

61. Bataille, 1957, 23.

62. Nietzsche, 1887, section III.13.

63. Bataille, 1954, 23.

64. Nietzsche, 1887, section III.11.

65. See Nietzsche, 1886, part nine; and Nietzsche, 1887, first essay. I imagine that Nietzsche himself would have been appalled by this suggestion; Christianity was perhaps still too near for him.

66. St. Teresa of Avila, *The life of St. Teresa of Avila, by herself* (1562), translated by J.M. Cohen (NY: Viking Penguin, 1989), 113.

67. ibid., 210.

68. Nietzsche, 1878, section 140.

69. ibid., section 142.

70. Bataille, 1957, 267.

71. Deleuze, 1967, 116f.

72. Nietzsche, 1887, section III.11.

73. Baudrillard, 1979, 142.

74. from *Hadewijch: the complete works*, translated by Columba Hart (NY: Paulist Press, 1980), 280. Cited in Caroline Walker Bynum, ". . .'And woman his humanity'," in *Gender and religion*, edited by

Bynum, Stevan Harrell, and Paula Richman (Boston: Beacon Press, 1986), 271.

75. Baudrillard, 1979, 177.

notes to chapter 5

1. Butler, 1993, 230.

2. Terry Hoople, "Conflicting visions: SM, feminism, and the law. A problem of representation," in *The Canadian journal of law and society* 11 #1 (Spring 1996): 179–80.

3. Michel Foucault, "A Ethics of Pleasure," 381.

4. ibid., 379.

5. Siegel, 1995, 142; citing Silverman, 1992, 206.

6. This may, however, only intensify the negative responses. Pat Califia notes in her essay "Some Notes on Some Women": "Unfortunately, the feminist tendency to judge sadomasochism more harshly than any other sexual identity has gotten more elaborate and more popular in recent years" (*Some Women*, edited by Laura Antoniou [NY: Rhinoceros Books, 1995] 23).

7. For this point, graciously made, I am indebted to Bruce Milem.

8. Robin Ruth Linden, introduction, in *Against sadomasochism: a radical feminist analysis*, edited by Robin Ruth Linden, Darlene R. Pagano, Diana E.H. Russell, and Susan Leigh Star (East Palo Alto, CA: Frog In the Well Press, 1982), 3.

9. Sandra Bartky makes this point clearly in her antimasochistic chapter, "Feminine masochism and the politics of transformation," in *Femininity and domination: studies in the phenomenology of oppression* (NY: Routledge, 1990).

10. This argument may be made on the "other side" as well: here the repetition of the trauma is likely to be seen not as catharsis but as entrapment in a pattern of abuse begun in childhood, perhaps an association of love or attention with pain, much as it is said that abusive parents were themselves abused children (presumably the top takes on the "abusive parent" role and the bottom the "abused child" role). Linden presents a version of this hypothesis: "The catharsis hypothesis maintains that unexpressed impulses will build up . . . and that people will suffer damage by being prevented from acting out these feelings" (introduction to *Against sadomasochism*, 9).

11. See ibid., 7.

12. Claudia Card's argument in *Lesbian choices* mingles the catharsis and addiction hypotheses: "Without the catharsis of sado-masochism, participants' hostilities might have been directed against social oppression. But, if we become addicted or compulsively fix-ated in sadomasochism . . . whatever hostility spills over the bounds of contracts seems more likely to be directed against those who would resist oppression" (Claudia Card, *Lesbian choices* [NY: Colum-bia University Press, 1995] 237). Cited in *Some women*, 32. See also *Against sadomasochism*, 9; and Bev Jo, Linda Strega, and Ruston, *Dykes loving dykes: dyke separatist politics for lesbians only* (Oakland: self-published, 1990), 197.

13. Gayle Rubin, "The leather menace," in *Coming to power*, 221.

14. ibid., 222.

15. Pat Califia, "A personal view of the history of the lesbian S/M community and movement in San Francisco," in *Coming to power*, 249.

16. see, e.g., Rubin, 220–21.

17. Rubin, 221. At least one recent (1997) legal case, that of the Houghtons in New York, supports this view.

18. For evidence of the popularity of such play, see the remark-able variety of stories collected in Pat Califia, editor, *Doing it for Daddy* (Boston: Alyson, 1994).

19. Role play may be, in its seductively playful simulation of dominance and subordination, itself subversive of more pervasive power structures. While this has not been my focus here, and does merit further consideration elsewhere, I believe that role play may act as an aid to the loss of identity I discuss. However, I am most in-terested in that which cannot be "faked," in pain and restraint—even where this is aided by dramaticization. Compare Bataille on religious drama: "from the moment that the drama reaches us . . . we attain au-thority, which causes the drama. (In the same way, if there exists in us an authority, a value, there is drama; for if it is so, one must take it seriously—totally." Bataille, 1957, 10). See also Califia (editor), 1994, 15. I am indebted to Terry Hoople for helping me to think about the role of theatricality and role playing. For an excellent discussion of theatricality and performance in s/m, see Lynda Hart, *Between the body and the flesh: performing sadomasochism* (NY: Columbia University Press, 1998).

20. This claim, of course, is hardly uncontroversial. Some heterosexual or bisexual feminists are put off by a sense that they are thus excluded from the feminist movement. Some lesbians are dismayed by having their happily carnal pleasures rendered matters of abstract theory, and speak disparagingly of "conceptual lesbians."

21. Steven Seidman, *Embattled eros: sexual politics and ethics in contemporary America* (NY: Routledge, 1992), 121. The short answer to Seidman's rhetorical question is that, again, by a shift in the context of power, these orientations are in many ways undermined—and that these are, as contemporary feminists sometimes note, by no means universal female or feminist values.

22. Consider the following: "Throughout *Against Sadomasochism* it is argued that lesbian sadomasochism is firmly rooted in patriarchal sexual ideology, with its emphasis on the fragmentation of desire from the rest of our lives and the single-minded pursuit of gratification, sexual and otherwise" (Linden, *Against sadomasochism*, 4). "No-one appeared to wonder whether this S-M proliferation was a lesbian copy of a faggot imitation of patriarchal backlash against feminism" (Morgan, *Against sadosmasochism*, 122). "The male and heterosexual bias of S&M is obvious. . . . How can *any* Lesbian convince herself that S&M could ever be anything but male?" (*Dykes loving dykes*, 190–91).

23. Rubin, 224.

24. ibid.

25. Not identifying as gay or lesbian, I have previously attended these meetings with some concern for intruding upon others' space—though with, I have felt, a sufficiently legitimate interest in the topics addressed, and, perhaps more importantly, in the absence of other queer philosophical venues. Recent changes in this association have made it more inclusive, making some of the rest of us more welcome. (To avoid a sense of coyness, I note here that in terms of gender my own orientation is omnivorous.)

26. I must mention in particular Jacob (then Susan) Hale (Cal State Northridge), whose 1994 response to Claudia Card included a nonexhaustive list of 32 reasons, none of them "pathological," to practice s/m; and Terry Hoople (Concordia University), whose work on the subversive potential of s/m I have found both stimulus and supplement to my own thought.

27. Michel Foucault, "Two lectures," in *Power/Knowledge*, 98.

28. Silverman, 1992, 186.

29. The practitioners' corresponding disdain for this crowd (the name comes from a sarcastic suggestion that perhaps these fashion fetishists have misunderstood the initials s/m) may imply a disdain for the consumer orientation of which postmodern culture in general is, as we have seen, accused.

30. Barbara Grizutti Harrison, "Hurting the one you love," *Mademoiselle* (Feb. 1993): 60.

31. Elizabeth Grosz, *Space, time and perversion: essays on the politics of bodies* (NY and London: Routledge, 1995), 142.

32. Some critics see these labels as marketing hypocrisy, noting "SM's presentation of itself as a hip new lifestyle inhabited by 'tops' and 'bottoms' rather than 'sadists' and 'masochists,'" (Reina Lewis and Karen Adler, "Come to me baby or what's wrong with lesbian SM" in *Women's studies international forum* 17 #4 (1994): 435). In fact the labels "top" and "bottom" are used here precisely because of their flexibility; a top (generally a dominant or sadist) may enjoy receiving pain as part of a service; a bottom may be submissive but not masochistic, or vice versa, and so on. The authors of this article also criticize s/m as just another mode of consumerism: "In the Reagan and Thatcher era of conspicuous consumption, the (secret) purchase of new consumer durables . . . is in itself one of SM's main sites of pleasure." (ibid.)

33. Interestingly, this may not change the players' sense of identity. Pat Califia, describing her s/m experiences with gay men, writes, "I have sex with faggots. And I'm a lesbian. You think *you're* confused?" "Gay men, lesbians and sex: doing it together," from 1983, in *Public sex* (San Francisco: Cleis Press, 1994), 183.

34. "Sexual choice, sexual act" from *Foucault live*, translated by James O'Higgins, 331.

35. Rubin, 220–21.

36. *Feminist cultural studies*, vol. 1, xxvi.

37. Of course, any number of authors could defend against this criticism better than I—Foucault's studies in antiquity, Derrida's works in classical philosophy, and Bataille's medieval obsessions all argue against this claim.

38. I should note that an affirmation of strong differences between genders and between orientations is found in less negative works as well. Elizabeth Grosz writes in *Space, time and perversion*, "In

lesbian sadomasochism . . . the status, value, and control of the female body are at stake, as are the implements of sexual desire that serve as fetishes. . . . The fantasy scenarios . . . are always a restaging of the loss or abandonment of the female body. This distinguishes lesbian desire from the structures and desires that mark stereotyped heterosexuality" (166). While much of Grosz's work in the text is quite intriguing, my suspicion is that gender is seldom primary for sadomasochism, and that s/m play deals in "the status, value, and control" of all manner of bodies.

39. Silverman, 1992, 190.

40. Parveen Adams, Per Os(cillation), *Camera obscura* 17 (1988): 28–29. Cited in Mandy Merck, *Perversions: deviant readings* (NY: Routledge, 1993), 243.

41. see Califia, 1994, 14.

42. for example, Pat Califia and Robin Sweeney, editors, *The second coming: a leatherdyke reader* (Los Angeles: Alyson, 1996). This sequel to *Coming to power* includes a 4-article section on playing with the boundaries of gender.

43. Re/Search, People series, volume one, *Bob Flanagan: Supermasochist* (NY: ReSearch Publications, 1993), 63.

notes to chapter 6

1. See Aristotle, *Nicomachean ethics,* translated by Terence Irwin (Indianapolis: Hackett Publishing, 1985), and Epicurus's *Ethics* and *Sovran maxims* in Diogenes Laertius, *Lives and opinions of eminent philosophers in ten books,* Book X, translated by R.D. Hicks, Loeb Classical Library (NY: G. Putnam's Sons, 1925) Book X. Compare this remark: "Let us assume, as contemporary sadomasochists would have us do, that the submissive partner is not coerced by violence or threats, but undergoes his or her treatment, as declared, by choice. Are all choices equally commendable? Nearly every historic form of hedonism, from that advocated by Protagoras to that of the French 'decadents,' has promoted a strategy of enlightened pleasure seeking even while exalting pleasure as the ultimate good. Many have counseled discipline and moderation, meaning discipline not in the sense of whips and chains, but of orderly conduct and self-restraint. As they observed, limited desires are more easily satisfied than extravagant desires. Even those hedonists scorned by Plato, who condoned a

more extreme range of experiences, regarded pain as a necessary consequence of and an inevitable retribution for pleasure. But contemporary devotees of sadomasochism want to excise that causal connection between restraint and pleasure" (Hilde Hein, "Sadomasochism and the liberal tradition," in *Against sadomasochism* 86–87). Perhaps, I cannot resist suggesting, if we redefine restraint. . . .

2. Barthes, 1973, 14.

3. Bersani, Leo, "Is the rectum a grave?" *October* 43 (Winter 1987): 217, cited in Tania Modleski, *Feminism without women: culture and criticism in a "postfeminist" age* (NY: Routledge, 1991), 152.

4. Linda Williams, 1989, 20.

5. Amber Hollibaugh makes note of this utopia in "Talking sex," Deirde English, Amber Hollibaugh, and Gayle Rubin, *Socialist review*, 11 #4 (1981): 44.

6. John Stoltenberg, "Eroticized violence, eroticized powerlessness," in *Against sadomasochism*, 126.

7. See Socrates' speech in the *Symposium*, Plato, translated by Michael Joyce, in *The collected dialogues of Plato*, edited by Edith Hamilton and Huntington Cairns, Bollingen Series 71 (Princeton: Princeton University Press, 1989).

8. Butler, 1993, 14.

9. Michel Foucault, "Power and strategies," in *Power/Knowledge*, 141.

10. "Body/Power," in *Power/Knowledge*, 55.

11. ibid., 57.

12. ibid., 56.

13. "Power and strategies," 142.

14. ibid.

15. It will be obvious by now that this is linked to the construction and breaking of boundaries, important, as Foucault points out, to the workings of power in our culture: boundaries are crucial to disciplinarity and so to the construction of the individuated subject.

16. *The will to power*, section 696.

17. Nietzsche, 1886, section 188.

18. Jesse Meredith, "A response to Samois," in *Against sadomasochism*, 98.

19. Carl Stychin, in analyzing the Spanner decision (a British and later European high court decision that argued that sadomasochistic play was a form of assault, regardless of consensuality), quotes the majority opinion of Lord Templeman: "Sado-masochistic participants have no way of foretelling the degree of bodily harm which will result from their encounters" (506) and further: "Society is entitled and bound to protect itself against a cult of violence. Pleasure derived from the infliction of pain is an evil thing. Cruelty is uncivilised," in Carl F. Stychin, "Unmanly diversions: the construction of the homosexual body (politic) in English law," *Osgoode Hall law journal* (1995): 507.

20. Bataille, 1957, 256.

21. Nietzsche, 1886, section 51.

22. Friedrich Nietzsche, *Ecce homo* (1888), translated by R. J. Hollingdale (NY: Penguin Books, 1979), "Why I am so wise," section 4.

23. Susan Griffin, "Sadomasochism and the erosion of self: a critical reading of *Story of O*," in *Against sadomasochism*, 185.

24. see Michel Foucault, *Discipline and punish: the birth of the prison* (1975), translated by Alan Sheridan (NY: Pantheon Books, 1977).

25. ibid., 221.

26. M.A. Doane, "The economy of desire," in *Feminist cultural studies*, vol. 1, 381.

27. Jane Gallop, *Thinking through the body* (NY: Columbia University Press, 1988), 121.

28. ibid. See Barthes, 1973: "Text of pleasure [*plaisir*]: the text that contents, fills . . . comes from culture and does not break with it, is linked to a *comfortable* practice of reading. Text of bliss [*jouissance*]: the text that imposes a state of loss, the text that discomforts . . . unsettles the reader's historical, cultural, psychological assumptions." 14.

29. On this see particularly Foucault, 1975.

30. Gallop, 1988, 75.

31. Baudrillard, 1979, 17–18. It is worthwhile to look at this passage in the original, to note the sometimes unexpected play between *plaisir* and *jouissance*: "*la jouissance est elle aussi réversible, c'est-à-dire qu'il peut y avoir une intensité supérieure dans l'absence ou le déni de jouissance. C'est même là, quand la fin sexuelle redevient aléatoire, que surgit quelque chose qui peut s'appeler la séduction ou le plaisir. . . . Nul ne sait à*

quelle profondeur destructrice peut aller cette provocation, ni quelle tout-puissance est la sienne" (29–30).

32. Gallop, 1988, 108.

33. On this point compare Baudrillard: "Increasingly, all seduction . . . —which is always a highly *ritualized* process—is effaced behind a *naturalized* sexual imperative, behind the immediate and imperative realization of desire. . . . Henceforth one no longer says: 'You have a soul and it must be saved' but: 'You have a sex, and you must put it to good use.' . . . . 'You have a body, and you must derive pleasure from it.' 'You have a libido, and you must expend it,' etc." (Baudrillard, 1979, 38).

34. Here I cannot resist the following citation: "I would like to move the debate over sadomasochism out of the realm of what is "politically correct" and into the realm of what is "politically desirable." The question is not what *should* our sexual desires and interactions be (we've already had enough of that), but what do we *want* our sexual desires and interactions to be?" (Karen Rian, "Sadomasochism and the social construction of desire," in *Against sadomasochism*, 47). To separate these two strikes me as absurd: surely what we believe our desires *should* be will impinge upon what we *want* them to be.

35. see "Two lectures" in *Power/Knowledge*, and Michel Foucault, *The history of sexuality, volume I (an introduction)* (1976), translated by Robert Hurley (NY: Vintage Books, 1990).

36. See Freud, 1905, "Sexual aberrations."

37. Baudrillard, 1979, 81–82.

38. see Halperin, 1995, 88.

39. Jessica Benjamin, *The bonds of love: psychoanalysis, feminism, and the problem of domination* (NY: Pantheon Books, 1988), 65.

40. ibid., 72.

41. See *The will to power*, section 484, etc.

42. Margaret Hunt, "Report of a conference on feminism, sexuality, and power: the elect clash with the perverse," in *Coming to power*, 86.

43. The desired or desirable *form* of this recognition may vary, from the Hegelian recognition of the other as like oneself and therefore a full subject, to the more "postmodern" notion that it is difference itself that we must recognize and, without assimilating, respect.

44. Jessica Benjamin, "Master and slave: the fantasy of erotic domination," in *Powers of desire: the politics of sexuality*, edited by Ann Snitow, Christine Stansell, and Sharon Thompson (NY: Monthly Review Press, 1983), 280.

45. Butler, 1993, 226.

46. Leo Bersani, in "Is the rectum a grave?" uses "pastoral" in this context; both the article and the term have been important in my understanding.

47. "Master and slave," 292.

48. Benjamin, 1988, 12.

49. "Master and Slave," 285.

50. ibid.

51. Bataille, 1954, 60.

52. ibid., 53.

53. ibid., 60. compare Maurice Blanchot: "The relation of the Other to me would tend to appear as sadomasochistic, if it did not cause us to fall prematurely out of the world—the one region where 'normal' and 'anomaly' have meaning" (Blanchot, [1980], 19). Here the world is the world of the subject, individual and discontinuous.

54. "Master and slave," 298.

55. *Dykes loving dykes*, 196.

56. A "safeword" is a context-breaking word used to call a halt to (or to express a problem within) a sadomasochistic or dominant/submissive scene. Usually these words are available to and used by the bottom in the scene, the one who is serving or undergoing pain and who may find the stimulation too intense. They may also be used by tops (dominants or sadists) who find a scene difficult in, for example, an emotional sense. Such words allow players to avoid to a considerable extent the confusion that both role-playing and paradoxical desire may present, such as whether "no" or "stop" means in fact that the action should end. It is sometimes argued that a bottom who has a safeword is necessarily in control of the situation.

57. This avoidance of an account based on voluntarism echoes a similar point in Judith Butler's account of gender performativity. In *Bodies that matter* she writes, "gender performativity cannot be theorized apart from the forcible and reiterative practice of regulatory

sexual regimes; . . . the account of agency conditioned by those very regimes of discourse/ power cannot be conflated with voluntarism or individualism, much less with consumerism, and in no way presupposes a choosing subject." 15.

58. In this context I should note that Terry Hoople has shared with me in correspondence his ideas for an s/m ethics of *care*, marking the difference between ethical and unethical violence, and that though I am not primarily concerned with ethics here, I have found these ideas quite helpful.

59. see "Two lectures," from *Power/Knowledge*, 104–5.

60. ibid., 98.

61. ibid., 108.

62. Frank Browning, *The culture of desire: paradox and perversity in gay lives today* (NY: Crown, 1993), 104.

notes to chapter 7

1. I fear that this brief chapter will not exactly remedy that situation, though it may be a contribution to that remedy. There has been much more work on bottoming from which I might draw, and my own experience is also quite bottom-heavy.

2. Merck, 256.

3. see, as one of the most vivid examples, Lorena Leigh Saxe, "Sadomasochism and exclusion," in *Adventures in lesbian philosophy*, edited by Claudia Card (Bloomington: Indiana University Press, 1994): "Too much attention has been paid to masochists, as if settling the question of consent will settle the entire issue. All too little attention has been paid to sadists. . . . Some ways of interacting with another Lesbian are not acceptable, regardless of whether she has consented to that treatment. . . . Sexual sadism is one of those unacceptable ways of treating a Lesbian. . . . To show a basic disrespect for a woman is unacceptable."65. On the basis of her ensuing arguments, we may presume that Saxe would find heterosexual, polysexual, or gay male sadomasochism no more acceptable.

4. Jean-Luc Nancy, "Shattered love" (1986), in *The inoperative community*, edited by Peter Connor, translated by Peter Connor, Lisa Garbus, Michael Holland, and Simona Sawhney (Minneapolis: Uni-

versity of Minnesota Press, 1991), 99. Nancy, being French, does not further specify the quotation's source.

5. see Gilles Deleuze, *Nietzsche and philosophy* (1962), translated by Hugh Tomlinson (NY: Columbia University Press, 1983).

6. Michel Foucault, "The confession of the flesh," in *Power/ Knowledge*, 198.

7. The link between time and subjectivity is hardly a novel concept—Augustine suggested that time might be the human perceptual equivalent of God's eternal omniscience. (See *Confessions* [ca. 397], translated by Henry Chadwick [NY: Oxford University Press, 1991][especially Book XI]). In modern philosophy, Kant makes of time an essential category of conscious experience and a defining attribute of subjectivity, insisting that we *not* try to extend time's "reality" beyond experience. (See *Critique of pure reason*, 49ff.) Freud follows on this suggestion by remarking on temporal awareness as a function of the conscious ego; the unconscious, he claims, is timeless. (See, for example, *The ego and the id* [1915], translated by Joan Riviere [NY: W.W. Norton, 1960].)

8. Michel Foucault, "An ethics of pleasure," 380.

9. Benjamin, 1988, 53.

10. I am grateful to Terry Hoople for reminding me of the importance of this point, and for other commentary, which has refined my presentation throughout this chapter.

11. The importance of this receptivity in eroticism is clear; as Pat Califia concisely remarks, "Stoicism is rarely a turn-on" (Pat Califia, *Sensuous magic* [NY: Masquerade Books, 1993], 26).

12. 172; in Mielke, 1996, 34.

13. "Body/Power" in *Power/Knowledge*, 59.

14. see, for example, Dossie Easton, *The bottoming book: how to get terrible things done to you by wonderful people* (San Francisco: Greenery Press, 1995), 15f.—though in general I must commend this book as wonderfully precise.

15. Blanchot, 1973 , 52.

16. "Some [tops] report feeling that they're 'channeling' power from some source outside them" (Easton, 1995, 13).

17. *Supermasochist*, 73.

18. ibid., 87.

19. an idea best expressed, perhaps, by Blanchot, 1973 .

20. Blanchot, 1980, 126.

21. Bataille, 1954, 59.

22. on this play or tension, see Bataille, 1954, 85f.

23. Blanchot, 1973, 54.

24. Lewis and Adler, 1994, 49.

25. "Why I am so wise," section 4, Nietzsche, 1888.

26. ibid.; ellipsis in original.

27. Nietzsche, 1882, section 118.

28. Rubin, 223–24.

29. Deleuze, 1962, 50.

30. ibid., 40.

31. ibid.

32. ibid., 41–42.

33. *Will to power*, section 657.

34. Deleuze, 1962, 42. Deleuze cites Nietzsche, 1886, section 259, and *The will to power*, section 647.

35. Deleuze, 1962, 53–54.

36. "Two lectures," *Power/Knowledge*, 89.

37. Nietzsche, 1882, section 290.

38. Nietzsche, 1886, section 188.

39. Bataille, 1954, 88.

40. Theodor Reik, *Masochism in sex and society*, translated by Margaret H. Beigel and Gertrud M. Kurth (NY: Grove Press, 1962), 333. cited in Silverman, 1992, 196.

41. Grosz, 1995, 198–99.

42. *The bottoming book* tells the story of a woman submissive who swore her utter submission to all her master's desires: "She told me, 'No, I really have no power; I really have no limits. Whatever my master wants is OK with me.' I proposed, 'Suppose your master woke up tomorrow and told you, '"I'm tired of this S/M stuff. From now on, we're only going to have gentle, consensual, egalitarian vanilla sex."' There was a long pause. Finally, sheepishly, she answered, 'You win. I'd be out of here in a minute.' " 20.

43. Resistance scenes, such as kidnapping or rape scenes, entail the play of noncooperation from the bottom. They may be contrasted with most submissive scenes, in which the bottom exerts considerable effort to bring her acts into line with the expressed wishes of the top. A contrast is sometimes drawn between masochists and submissives along these lines, though a strict disjunction seldom holds.

44. see Stychin, 512, on the difficulty of understanding this community standard of trust from the starting point of condemnation.

45. Blanchot, 1980, 49–50.

notes to chapter 8

Jean-Luc Nancy cites the title of this chapter, "love is a series of scars," in his essay "Shattered love" in his collection *The inoperative community*, 91. The source is Elie Wiesel's *The fifth son*: "Love is a series of scars. 'No heart is as whole as a broken heart,' said the celebrated Rabbi Nahman of Bratzlav." Nancy does not provide the page number or further bibliographic information.

1. For some reason, this point is easily missed. Barbara Harrison, in her article previously cited, writes, "If someone catches his penis in his fly zipper and yells, 'Ouch!' is that equivalent to having sex? If you slam a car door on your nipple, is that just another version of making love?" Bob Flanagan in an interview answers this question nicely: "*Context is everything.* Even people who are into s/m are not turned on by getting their hand [still less, one presumes, nipples] slammed in a car door." (*Supermasochist*, 35).

2. Bataille, 1957, 20.

3. "Shattered love," 82.

4. Here I steal a citation I have often seen from Auden: "When shall we learn, what should be clear as day, We cannot choose what we are free to love?"—cited by Halperin as "perfectly Foucauldean in spirit" (Halperin, 1995, 29). It is also, of course, perfectly Nietzschean; see section 188 of Nietzsche, 1886, and section 290 in Nietzsche, 1882.

5. Bataille, 1957, 15.

6. Michel Foucault, "Power affects the body," in *Foucault live*, 212.

7. Jean-Luc Nancy, "Of divine places" (1986), in *The inoperative community*, 130.

8. Bataille, 1957, 144.

9. ibid., 11.

10. Carol Vance, "Towards a politics of sexuality," from Carol Vance, editor, *Pleasure and danger: exploring female sexuality* (Boston: Routledge and Kegan Paul, 1984), 1.

11. Bataille, 1957, 21.

12. Bataille, 1954, 23.

13. Griffin, in *Against sadomasochism*, 189.

14. Susan Farr, "The art of discipline: creating erotic dramas of play and power," in *Coming to power*, 184.

15. see Sally Roesch Wagner, "Pornography and the sexual revolution: the backlash of sadomasochism," in *Against sadomasochism*, 33, citing the pamphlet "What color is your handkerchief?" And note, as before, that the patron of bookmakers and librarians is St. Antony, famously tempted in his eremitic asceticism, while the patron saint of philosophers is Catherine of Alexandria, whose life was ended by torturous stretching on the "Catherine wheel," now adapted as an s/m toy.

16. "Lesbian S&M: the politics of disillusion," Judy Butler, in *Against sadomasochism*, 172. This of course is early in Butler's work, and as will already be obvious there has been considerable advance in her thought since this 1980 article. In fact, her introduction, which slightly postdates the piece itself, already expresses some impatience with the terms of the discussion, and she quickly moves beyond it.

17. Jacques Derrida, "Violence and metaphysics," in *Writing and difference*, translated by Alan Bass (Chicago: University of Chicago Press, 1978), 93.

18. Here I intend "strength" in Nietzsche's sense of a force in favor of life, a love of life, an underlying ability to know how to become well, rather than in the sense of body-builders' muscularity or even what we more commonly call "health."

19. Bataille, 1957, 15.

20. Georges Bataille, *The impossible* (1962), translated by Robert Hurley (San Francisco: City Lights Books, 1991), 36.

21. "Shattered love", 106.

22. ibid., 99.

23. ibid., 97.

24. Bataille, 1957, 242.

25. Bataille, 1954, 42.

26. Blanchot, 1980, 145.

27. "Shattered love," 84.

28. Both attribute this concept to the Cabbalistic mystic Isaac Luria. see "Seventh lecture" in Gershom G. Scholem, *Major trends in Jewish mysticism* (NY: Schocken, 1954).

29. "Between one being and another, there is a gulf, a discontinuity. This gulf exists, for instance, between you, listening to me, and me, speaking to you. . . . If you die, it is not my death. You and I are *discontinuous* beings." Bataille, 1957, 12.

30. ibid., 13.

31. on which, see Nancy's "Of divine places."

32. "Shattered love," 89.

33. "Of divine places," 148–49.

34. ibid., 141.

35. Bataille, 1957, 240.

bibliography

Ahlgren, Gillian T.W. *Teresa of Avila and the politics of sanctity.* Ithaca: Cornell University Press, 1996.

Antoniou, Laura. "Laura, Leather and Life." <http://weber.u. washington. edu~humsex/1/society/latrans.txt>.

————, editor. *Some women.* New York: Rhinoceros Books, 1995.

Aristotle. *Nicomachean Ethics.* translated by Terence Irwin. Indianapolis: Hackett Publishing Co., 1985.

Athanasius. *The life of Antony* (ca. 360 A.D.). translated by Robert C. Gregg. New York: Paulist Press, 1980.

Augustine. *Confessions* (ca. 397 A.D.). translated by Henry Chadwick. New York: Oxford University Press, 1991 .

Barthes, Roland. *The pleasure of the text.* translated by Richard Miller. New York: Hill and Wang, 1975. from: *Le plaisir du texte.* Paris: Éditions du Seuil, 1973.

Bartky, Sandra Lee. *Femininity and domination: studies in the phenomenology of oppression.* New York: Routledge, 1990.

Bataille, Georges. *The accursed share: an essay on general economy.* translated by Robert Hurley. New York: Zone Books, 1991. from: *Le part maudite: précédé de la notion de dépense.* Paris: Éditions de Minuit, 1967.

————*Erotism: death and sensuality.* translated by Mary Dalwood. San Francisco: City Lights Books, 1986. from: *L'Erotisme.* Paris: Éditions de Minuit, 1957.

————*Guilty.* translated by Bruce Boone. Venice, CA: Lapis Press, 1988. from: *Le coupable.* Paris: Éditions Gallimard, 1961.

————*The impossible.* 1962. translated by Robert Hurley. San Francisco: City Lights Books, 1991.

————*Inner experience.* translated by Leslie Ann Boldt. New York: SUNY Press, 1988. from: *L'Expérience intérieure.* Paris: Éditions Gallimard, 1954.

————*Literature and evil.* translated by Alastair Hamilton. New York: Marion Boyars, 1985. from: *La littérature et le mal.* Paris: Éditions Gallimard, 1957b.

————*Theory of religion.* translated by Robert Hurley. New York: Zone Books, 1989. from: *Théorie de la religion.* Paris: Éditions Gallimard, 1973.

————*Visions of excess: selected writings 1927-1939* (posthumous collection). translated by Allen Stoekel, with Carl R. Lovitt and Donald M. Leslie Jr. Minneapolis: University of Minnesota Press, 1985.

Baudrillard, Jean. *Seduction.* translated by Brian Singer. New York: St. Martin's Press, 1990. from: *De la séduction.* Paris: Éditions Galilée, 1979.

de Beauvoir, Simone. *Must we burn de Sade?* translated by Annette Michelson. London: Peter Nevill, 1953.

Bell, Rudolph M. *Holy anorexia.* Chicago: University of Chicago Press, 1985.

Benjamin, Jessica. *The bonds of love: psychoanalysis, feminism, and the problem of domination.* New York: Pantheon Books, 1988.

Bersani, Leo. "Is the rectum a grave?" *October* 43 (Winter 1987).

Blanchot, Maurice. *The space of literature.* translated by Ann Smock. Lincoln: University of Nebraska Press, 1982. from *L'espace littéraire.* Paris: Éditions Gallimard, 1955.

————*The step not beyond.* translated by Lycette Nelson. Albany: SUNY Press, 1992. from: *Le pas au-delà.* Paris: Éditions Gallimard, 1973.

————*The writing of the disaster.* translated by Ann Smock. Lincoln: University of Nebraska Press, 1986. from: *L'écriture du désastre.* Paris: Éditions Gallimard, 1980.

Browning, Frank. *The culture of desire: paradox and perversity in gay lives today.* New York: Crown Publishers, 1993.

Butler, Judith. *Bodies that matter: on the discursive limits of "sex."* New York: Routledge, 1993.

Bynum, Caroline Walker. *Fragmentation and redemption: essays on gender and the human body in medieval religion.* New York: Zone Books, 1991.

————Stevan Harrell and Paula Richman, editors. *Gender and religion: on the complexity of symbols*. Boston: Beacon Press, 1986.

————*The resurrection of the body in western Christianity, 200–1336*. New York: Columbia University Press, 1995.

Califia, Pat, editor. *Doing it for daddy*. Boston: Alyson, 1994.

————*Public sex: the culture of radical sex*. San Francisco: Cleis Press, 1994.

————*Sensuous magic*. New York: Masquerade Books, 1993.

————and Robin Sweeney, editors. *The second coming: a leatherdyke reader*. Los Angeles: Alyson Publications, 1996.

Catherine of Siena, St. *The dialogue*. translated by Suzanne Noffke, O.P. New York: Paulist Press, 1988.

Clark, David Aaron, and Tristan Taormino, editors. *Ritual sex*. New York: Rhinoceros, 1996.

Deleuze, Gilles. *The logic of sense*. translated by Mark Lester. New York: Columbia University Press, 1992. from: *Logique du sens*. Paris: Éditions de Minuit, 1969.

————*Masochism: coldness and cruelty* (1967). translated by Jean McNeil. New York: Zone Books, 1989.

————*Nietzsche and philosophy*. translated by Hugh Tomlinson. New York: Columbia University Press, 1983. from: *Nietzsche et la philosophie*. Paris: Presses Universitaires de France, 1962.

Derrida, Jacques. *Aporias*. translated by Thomas Dutoit. Stanford: Stanford University Press, 1993. from: *Apories: mourir-s'attendre aux limite de la vérité*, in *Le passage des frontières: autour du travail de Jacques Derrida*. Paris: Éditions Galilée, 1993.

————"Violence and Metaphysics," in *Writing and difference* (1967). translated by Alan Bass. Chicago: University of Chicago Press, 1978.

Descartes, René. *Meditations on first philosophy* (1641). translated by Laurence J. Lafleur. Indianapolis: Bobbs-Merrill, 1951.

Diogenes Laertius. *Lives and opinions of eminent philosophers in ten books*. Book X. translated by R.D. Hicks. Loeb Classical Library, New York: G.P. Putnam's sons, 1925.

Dworkin, Andrea. *Intercourse*. New York: Free Press, 1987.

————*Pornography: men possessing women*. New York: Penguin, 1981 (new introduction, 1989).

Easton, Dossie. *The bottoming book: how to get terrible things done to you by wonderful people.* San Francisco: Greenery Press, 1995.

English, Deirde, Amber Hollibaugh, and Gayle Rubin. "Talking sex." *Socialist review* 11 #4 (1981).

Favazza, Armando, and Barbara Favazza. *Bodies under siege.* Baltimore: Johns Hopkins University Press, 1987.

Foucault, Michel. *The care of the self.* translated by Robert Hurley. New York: Vintage Books, 1986. from: *Le souci de soi.* Paris: Éditions Gallimard, 1984.

————*Discipline and punish.* translated by Alan Sheridan, New York: Pantheon Books, 1977. from: *Surveiller et punir: naissance de la prison.* Paris: Éditions Gallimard, 1975.

————*Foucault live: collected interviews, 1961–1984.* edited by Sylvère Lotringer, translated by Lysa Hochroth and John Johnson. New York: Semiotext(e), 1996.

————*The history of sexuality: an introduction.* translated by Robert Hurley. New York: Vintage Books, 1990. from: *La volunté de savoir.* Paris: Éditions Gallimard, 1976.

————*Language, countermemory, practice: selected essays and interviews.* edited and translated by Donald F. Bouchard and Sherry Simon. Ithaca, New York: Cornell University Press, 1977.

————*Power/Knowledge: selected interviews and other writings, 1972–1977.* edited by Colin Gordon, translated by Colin Gordon, Leo Marshall, John Mepham, Kate Soper. New York: Pantheon Books, 1980.

Freud, Sigmund. *Beyond the pleasure principle.* translated by James Strachey. New York: W.W. Norton, 1961. from: *Jenseits des Lustprinzips* (1920), in *Gesammelte Werke*, Bd. XIII. London: Imago Publishing, 1940.

————"A Child Is being beaten." translated by James Strachey. in *Collected papers.* from: "Ein Kind wird geschlagen" (1919), in *Gesammelte Werke*, Bd. XII. London: Imago Publishing, 1948.

————"The dissection of the psychical personality," in *New introductory lectures on psychoanalysis* (1933). translated and edited by James Strachey. New York: W.W. Norton, 1989.

————"The economic problem in masochism." translated by Joan Riviere, in *General psychological theory.* edited by Phillip Reiff. New

York: Macmillan Publishing Co., 1963. from: "Das ökonomische Problem des Masochismus" (1924), in *Studienausgabe* Bd. III, Frankfurt: S. Fischer, 1975.

———"Formulations regarding the two principles in mental functioning." translated by M.N. Searl, in *Freud: general psychological theory.* from: "Formulierungen über zwei Prinzipien des psychischen Geschehens," in *Studienausgabe* Bd. III. Frankfurt: S. Fischer, 1969.

———"Instincts and their vicissitudes." translated by Cecil M. Baines, in *General psychological theory.* from: "Triebe und Triebschicksale," in *Studienausgabe* Bd. II.

———*New introductory lectures on psychoanalysis.* translated by James Strachey. New York: W.W. Norton, 1965. from: *Neue Folge der Vorlesungen zur Einführung in die Psychoanalyse* (1933), in *Gesammelte Werke*, Bd. XV. London: Imago Publishing Co., 1940.

———*The project for a scientific psychology* (1895). translated by James Strachey, in *Standard edition* (undated), volume I. London: Hogarth Press.

———*Three essays on the theory of sexuality.* translated by James Strachey. New York: Basic Books, 1962. from: *Drei Abhandlungen zur Sexual theorie* (1905). Frankfurt: Fischer Taschenbuch, 1961.

Gallop, Jane. *Intersections: a reading of Sade with Bataille, Blanchot, and Klossowski.* Lincoln: University of Nebraska Press, 1981.

———*Thinking through the body.* New York: Columbia University Press, 1988.

Gibson, Pamela Church, and Roma Gibson, editors. *Dirty looks: women, pornography, power.* London: British Film Institute, 1993.

Grosz, Elizabeth. *Space, time and perversion: essays on the politics of bodies.* New York: Routledge, 1995.

Gubar, Susan, and Joan Hoff, editors. *For adult users only: the dilemma of violent pornography.* Bloomington: Indiana University Press, 1989.

Halperin, David. *Saint Foucault: towards a gay hagiography.* New York: Oxford University Press, 1995.

Harpham, Geoffrey Galt. *The ascetic imperative in culture and criticism.* Chicago: University of Chicago Press, 1987.

Harrison, Barbara Grizutti. "Hurting the one you love." *Mademoiselle.* Feb. 1993.

Hart, Lynda. *Between the body and the flesh: performing sadomasochism.* New York: Columbia University Press, 1998.

Hegel, G.W.F. *Phenomenology of mind* (1861). translated by J.B. Baillie. New York: Harper and Row, 1965.

Holland, Michael, editor. *The Blanchot Reader.* Cambridge: Blackwell, 1995.

Hoople, Terry. "Conflicting visions: SM, feminism, and the law. A problem of representation," in *The Canadian journal of law and society* 11 #1 (Spring 1996).

Jo, Bev, Linda Strega, and Ruston, *Dykes loving dykes: dyke separatist politics for lesbians only.* Oakland: self-published, 1990.

Joyce, James. *Ulysses.* New York: Random House, 1946.

Kant, Immanuel. *Critique of pure reason* (1781). translated by Norman Kemp Smith. New York: St. Martin's Press, 1965.

———*Groundwork of the metaphysics of morals* (1785). translated by H.J. Paton. New York: Harper and Row, 1948.

Klossowski, Pierre. *Sade my neighbor.* translated by Alphonso Lingis. Evanston, IL: Northwestern University Press, 1991. from: *Sade mon prochain.* Paris: Éditions du Seuil, 1947.

Knabb, Ken, editor and translator. *Situationist International anthology.* Berkeley: Bureau of Public Secrets, 1989.

Lacan, Jacques. "Kant with Sade." translated James B. Swenson Jr. *October* 51 (Winter 1989).

LeBrun, Annie. *Sade: a sudden abyss* (1986). translated by Camille Nash. San Francisco: City Lights Books, 1990.

Lederer, Laura, editor. *Take back the night: women on pornography.* New York: William Morrow and Company, 1980.

Lewis, Reina, and Karen Adler, "Come to me baby or what's wrong with lesbian S&M" in *Women's studies international forum* 17 #4 (1994).

Linden, Robin Ruth, Darlene R. Pagano, Diana E.H. Russell, and Susan Leigh Star, editors. *Against sadomasochism: a radical feminist analysis.* East Palo Alto, CA: Frog In the Well Press, 1982.

Lovell, Terry, editor. *Feminist cultural studies.* Brookfield: Edward Elgar Publishing Company, 1995.

St. Ignatius Loyola. *The spiritual exercises* (1541). translated by George Ganss, S.J. Chicago: Loyola University Press, 1992.

MacKinnon, Catharine. *Only words*. Cambridge: Harvard University Press, 1993.

Merck, Mandy. *Perversions: deviant readings*. New York: Routledge, 1993.

Mielke, Arthur J. *Christians, feminists, and the culture of pornography*. Lanham, MD: University Press of America, 1995.

Modleski, Tania. *Feminism without women: culture and criticism in a "postfeminist" age*. New York: Routledge, 1991.

Nancy, Jean-Luc. *The inoperative community*. edited by Peter Connor, translated by Peter Connor, Lisa Garbus, Michael Holland, and Simona Sawhney. Minneapolis: University of Minnesota Press, 1991.

Nietzsche, Friedrich. *Beyond good and evil*. translated by Walter Kaufmann, in *Basic writings of Nietzsche*. New York: Modern Library, 1968. from: *Jenseits von Gut und Böse* (1886). Stuttgart: Reclam, 1988.

———*The birth of tragedy*, in *The birth of tragedy and the genealogy of morals*. translated by Francis Golffing. New York: Anchor Books, 1956. from: *Die Geburt der Tragödie* (1871). Stuttgart: Reclam, 1953.

———*Ecce Homo*. translated by Walter Kaufmann. in *Basic writings of Nietzsche*. from: *Ecce Homo* (1888), in *Werke*, Bd. III. Frankfurt: Ullstein Materialien, 1984.

———*The gay science* (1882). translated by Walter Kaufmann. New York: Vintage Books, 1974.

———*Genealogy of morals*. translated by Walter Kaufmann, in *Basic writings of Nietzsche*. from: *Zur Genealogie der Moral* (1887). Stuttgart: Reclam, 1988.

———*Human, all too human*. translated by Marion Faber with Stephen Lehmann. Lincoln: University of Nebraska Press, 1984. from: *Menschliches, allzumenschliches* (1878). Leipzig: Alfred Kröner Verlag, 1925.

———*Twilight of the idols*, in *Twilight of the idols and the Anti-Christ*. translated by R.J. Hollingdale. New York: Penguin Books, 1968. from: *Götzen-Dämmerung (oder: wie man mit dem Hammer philosophiert)* in *Werke: kritische Gesamtausgabe*, Bd. III. Berlin: Walter de Gruyter and Co., 1969.

———*The Will to power*. translated by Walter Kaufmann and R.J. Hollingdale. New York: Random House, 1968. from: *Der Wille zur Macht* (posthumous). Leipzig: Alfred Kröner Verlag, 1928.

Pagels, Elaine. *The Gnostic gospels*. New York: Random House, 1979.

Pascal, Blaise. *Pensées* (ca. 1660). translator unnamed. New York: E.P. Dutton and Co., 1958.

Peers, Larry H., editor. *The Romantic Manifesto: An Anthology*. New York: Peter Lang, 1988.

Re/Search, People Series, Volume One. *Bob Flanagan: Supermasochist*. New York: ReSearch Publications, 1993.

Plato. *Symposium*. translated by Michael Joyce, in *The collected dialogues of Plato*. edited by Edith Hamilton and Huntington Cairns. Bollingen Series 71, Princeton: Princeton University Press, 1989.

Russell, Diana E.H., editor. *Making violence sexy: feminist views on pornography*. New York: Teacher's College Press, 1993.

von Sacher-Masoch, Leopold. "A childhood memory and reflections on the novel." from *Revue bleue*, in *Masochism*. translated by Jean McNeil. New York: Zone Books, 1989.

———*Venus in Furs* in *Masochism*. translated by Jean McNeil. New York: Zone Books, 1989. from: *Venus im Pelz* (1870). Munich: Lichtenberg-Verlag, 1968.

de Sade, D.A.F. *Dialogue entre un prêtre et un moribond*, in *The passionate philosopher: a Marquis de Sade reader*. selected and translated by Margaret Crosland. London: Peter Owen, 1991.

———*Justine*. translated by Helen Weaver. New York: Capricorn Books, 1966. from: *Justine, ou les infortunes de la vertu* (1791), in *Oeuvres complètes du Marquis de Sade*. Tome 2. Paris: Jean-Jacques Pauvert, 1972.

———*The 120 days of Sodom and other writings*. translated by Austryn Wainhouse and Richard Seaver. New York: Grove Press, 1996. from: *Les 120 journées de Sodome* (posthumous). Paris: Jean-Jacques Pauvert, 1972.

Samois Collective, editors. *Coming to power*. Boston: Alyson Publications, revised edition, 1987.

Saxe, Lorena Leigh. "Sadomasochism and exclusion." in *Adventures in lesbian philosophy*. edited by Claudia Card. Bloomington: Indiana University Press, 1994.

Scholem, Gershom G. *Major trends in Jewish mysticism*. New York: Schocken Books, 1964.

Seidman, Steven. *Embattled eros*. New York: Routledge, 1992.

Shaviro, Steven. *The cinematic body*. Minneapolis: University of Minnesota Press, 1993.

Siegel, Carol. *Male masochism: modern versions of the story of love*. Bloomington: Indiana University Press, 1995.

Silverman, Kaja. *Male subjectivity at the margins*. New York: Routledge, 1992.

Snitow, Ann, Christine Stansell, and Sharon Thompson, editors. *Powers of desire: The politics of sexuality*. New York: Monthly Review Press, 1983.

Stychin, Carl F. "Unmanly diversions: the construction of the homosexual body (politic) in English law." *Osgoode Hall law journal* (1995).

Teresa of Avila, St. *The life of St. Teresa of Avila, by herself* (1562). translated by J. M. Cohen. New York: Viking Penguin, 1957.

Tilley, Maureen A., and Susan A. Ross, editors. *Broken and whole: essays on religion and the body*. Lanham, MD: University Press of America, 1993.

Vance, Carol, editor. *Pleasure and danger: exploring female sexuality*. Boston: Routledge and Kegan Paul, 1984.

Vaneigem, Raoul. *The book of pleasures*. translated by John Fullerton. London: Pending Press, 1983. from: *Le livre des plaisirs*. Paris: Encre, 1979.

Williams, Linda. *Hard core: power, pleasure, and the frenzy of the visible*. Berkeley: University of California Press, reprinted 1991 from first edition, 1989.

Footnotes are given to the English translations, except where otherwise noted.

index

Where citations are given to endnotes, numbers in parentheses provide the corresponding pages in the body of the text.

Wiesel, Elie, 192
will, 79–80, 83–84, 106, 108,
    118–20, 125–26, 128–29,
    134–38

Williams, Linda, 60
Williamson, Judith, 11

Zarathustra, 126